Connecting Landlocked Developing Countries to Markets

Connecting Landlocked Developing Countries to Markets

Trade Corridors in the 21st Century

Jean-François Arvis, Robin Carruthers, Graham Smith,
and Christopher Willoughby

THE WORLD BANK
Washington, D.C.

ISBN: 978-0-8213-8416-9
eISBN: 978-0-8213-8417-6
DOI: 10.1596/978-0-8213-8416-9

Library of Congress Cataloging-in-Publication Data
Arvis, Jean-François, 1960-
    Connecting landlocked developing countries to markets : trade corridors in the 21st century / Jean-Francois Arvis, Graham Smith, Robin Carruthers.
        p. cm.
    Includes bibliographical references and index.
    ISBN 978-0-8213-8416-9 — ISBN 978-0-8213-8417-6 (electronic)
    1. Developing countries—Economic conditions. 2. Landlocked states. 3. Developing countries—Commerce. 4. Transportation—Developing countries. 5. Transit, International—Developing countries. 6. Transit by land (International law) I. Smith, Graham, 1945- II. Carruthers, Robin. III. Title.
    HC59.7.A8338 2010
    382—dc22

                                                                                              2010017086

Cover photograph: Graham Smith
Cover design: Naylor Design, Washington, D.C.

Contents

Foreword by Cheick Sidi Diarra   *xiii*
Foreword by Bernard Hoekman and José Luis Irigoyen   *xv*
Acknowledgments   *xvii*
About the Authors   *xix*
Abbreviations   *xxi*

Chapter 1   Landlocked Developing Countries and
             Trade Corridors: An Overview   1
             A Renewed Development Priority   2
             Transit Neighbors and Trade Corridors   4
             A New Conceptual Framework:
                 Transit Systems and Corridor Performance   7
             Structure of This Volume   9
             Notes   11
             References   11

Chapter 2   The LLDC Access Problem and the
             Performance of Trade Corridors   13
             Economic Potential of LLDCs   14
             The Corridor Supply Chain and Its Bottlenecks   17

Unreliability of LLDC Corridors Carries
a High Cost   21
Market Structure and Competition in
Logistics Services   24
Unnecessary Overhead and Informal Payments   27
Investing in Infrastructure: Does It
Actually Promote Trade?   27
Supply Chain Linkages: Exports vs.
Imports, Extra- vs. Intra-regional Trade   30
Notes   31
References   31

Chapter 3   **The Complex Political Economy
of Trade Corridors**   **33**
LLDC Relationship with the Transit Country:
Beyond Dependence   34
Transit Corridors: A History of Public-Private
Partnership with Mutual Benefits   45
How LLDC Traffic Benefits Transit Countries   48
Landlocked Countries Aspire to a Transit Role   50
Transit Systems: From Vicious to Virtuous Cycles   52
Note   55
References   55

Chapter 4   **Moving Goods on Corridors: Transit Regimes**   **57**
Role of the Transit Regime   58
The Basics of Transit   59
Key Concepts and Practices in Transit   62
Regionally Integrated Transit and
Carnet Systems   65
Global Standards and International Legal
Agreements Relevant to Transit   73
Conclusions   77
Notes   77
References   77

Chapter 5   **Improving Transit Regimes and International
Cooperation**   **79**
Implementing Transit Regimes in
Developing Regions   79
Integration of Transit: An Unreached Goal   84

Too Many Legal Instruments?   87
Reengineering the Transit Regime: A Priority
    for LLDC Corridors   88
Pilot Transit Regime Improvement Program:
    The Douala Corridor   92
Technology Helps Manage Transit Trade   94
Conclusions: Progress Toward Global Standards   96
Notes   97
References   98

Chapter 6   **Improving Road Freight Transport**   **99**
Importance of Road Transport in
    Transit Countries   100
Structure of Road Freight Industries   102
Contracting Between Clients and
    Trucking Companies   106
Procedures for Movement of Trucks and
    Drivers Across Borders   107
Quota Systems and Bilateral Transit
    Agreements   109
Facilitating Truck Movement Through
    Transit Countries   114
Recommendations   118
Notes   120
References   120

Chapter 7   **Alternative Transport Modes and the**
            Role of Logistics Intermediaries   **123**
Rail Transport: Underused Potential   125
A Regional Perspective on Railway
    Services to LLDCs   130
Air Freight: A Niche Market for LLDCs   139
An Overview of Inland Waterway Transport   143
Development of Logistics Services   149
Recommendations   156
Notes   158
References   159

Chapter 8   **Managing Trade Corridors**   **161**
Four Corridor Management Models   162
Efficient Corridor Management   165

Monitoring the Performance of Trade
    Corridors   170
Total Logistics Costs on a Transit Corridor   174
Designing the Monitoring System for
    Corridor Performance   175
Corridor Monitoring in Practice:
    Observatories in Africa   178
Conclusions   180
Notes   180
References   181

Chapter 9   **Bringing Together the Solutions**   **183**
Building Trust   185
Making Transportation and Logistics Services
    Work for Trade   185
Redefining or Improving Transit Systems   186
Developing Global Initiatives to Promote
    Common Approaches for Redesigning
    Transit Regimes and Monitoring Trade
    Corridor Performance   188
Note   188

Appendix 1   **Landlocked Developing Countries (LLDCs),**
    Their Transit Neighbors, and Main Trade
    Corridors, by Region   **189**

Appendix 2   **Assessment and Policy Recommendations**
    by Region   **199**
Eastern and Southern Africa   200
Western and Central Africa   204
Latin America   209
Central Asia   213
South Asia   216
Other LLDCS: Armenia, Lao PDR,
    FYR Macedonia, and Moldova   220
Overview of the Policy Recommendations:
    Impact and Ease of Implementation   225

Appendix 3   **Trade Growth and Logistics Performance:**
    LLDCs and Transit Neighbors   **229**
References   235

Appendix 4	Survey Findings on LLDC Logistics Performance	237
	Global Enabling Trade Report 2010	237
	Connecting to Compete: The Logistics Performance Index (LPI) 2010	239
	Doing Business in Landlocked Economies 2009	240
	Comparing the Experience of Countries by Region	240
	The Penalties by Region of Being Landlocked	241
	Notes	245
	References	245
Appendix 5	Measuring Transit Corridor Performance Parameters	247
	Locations at Which Measurements Will be Made	248
	The Products and Their Transport Unit and Transport Route	249
	The Cost and Replicability of Making the Measurements	250
	Note	251
	Reference	251
Appendix 6	Maps of LLDCs and Transit Corridors, by Region	253
	Appendix References	260
Index		261

Boxes

1.1	Almaty Programme of Action (2003) Focus Areas	5
2.1	Spread in Delays and Predictability of Supply Chains	22
2.2	Infrastructure Investment in Africa and Asia: NEPAD and the Asian Highway Network	28
3.1	Connecting Malawi to Markets: A Private Sector Choice	38
3.2	Instruments for Charging Transit Traffic for Road Use	49
4.1	General Requirements With Respect to Seals	62
4.2	Legal Instruments Governing Transit Regimes	74
5.1	India-Nepal Bilateral Transit Agreement	89
5.2	Authorized Economic Operators (AEOs)	90
5.3	Impact of Information Technology: Streamlining Transit Information at Beitbridge	95
6.1	IRU Training Courses	104
6.2	UNECE Resolution R.E. 4	110

6.3   SADC Cost Recovery Mechanism   115
7.1   Railway Border Performance Indicators   128
7.2   Contrasting Railway Concessions in Côte d'Ivoire
        and Senegal   133
7.3   Rail Container Services to Central Asia   137
7.4   Increased Competition Pushes Kenya
        to Higher Unit-Value Exports and Air Freight   142
7.5   Institutional Arrangements for Managing the
        Paraguay–Paraná River Waterway ("Hidrovia")   147
7.6   International Waterway Commissions   148
8.1   National Trade and Transport Facilitation Committees   168
8.2   FastPath Shows Corridor Performance Strengths
        and Weaknesses   173

Figures

1.1   The Transit System and Its Components   8
2.1   An Extended Chain of Operations   18
3.1   Market Shares of Corridors Serving Burkina
        Faso, 1991–2004   39
3.2   Vulnerability of the Supply Chain to
        Rent-seeking Activities   44
4.1   The Transit Regime: International and National Transits
        and Final Clearance   60
4.2   The TIR Operation: Sequence of Procedures   69
4.3   Conceptual Difference of Bond Management
        between TIR and European Common Transit   72
8.1   Typical Output of a UNESCAP Corridor
        Performance Monitoring   172

Maps

A6.1   Africa Region   254
A6.2   Latin America Region   255
A6.3   Europe and Central Asia Region   256
A6.4   South Asia Region   257
A6.5   East Asia Region   258
A6.6   Middle East and North Africa Region   259

Tables

1.1   Landlocked Developing Countries by Region   2
2.1   Poorly Performing Landlocked Countries
        on the Logistics Performance Index, by Region   16

2.2   Supply Chain Sequence and Bottlenecks   19
2.3   International Road Transport Prices, Costs,
        and Profit Margins (from gateway to destination)   25
3.1   Public and Private Agents   40
4.1   General Provisions of International Conventions
        Applicable to Customs Transit   76
5.1   Number of Multilateral Legal Instruments with
        Relevance for Transit Trade in Africa, 2004   87
6.1   Transit Times for Land Transport in Nine
        LLDC Corridors in Asia   100
6.2   Cost and Time Penalties of LLDCs Compared to
        Coastal Neighbors in Africa, Asia, and South America   101
7.1   LLDCs with Rail and Water Transport Connections   124
7.2   Rail Distances of Selected LLDCs to a Port   127
7.3   Economic and Social Comparison of Four
        West African Countries, 2008   132
8.1   Cost, Time, and Reliability of Exports on
        the Vientiane–Laem Chabang Corridor   176
A1.1   Eastern and Southern Africa: LLDCs and
        Transit Neighbors   190
A1.2   Western and Central Africa: LLDCs and
        Transit Neighbors   192
A1.3   South Asia: LLDCs and Transit Neighbors   193
A1.4   Central Asia and the Caucasus: LLDCs and
        Transit Neighbors   194
A1.5   Other Regions: LLDCs and Transit Neighbors   196
A2.1   Impact and Ease of Implementation of the
        Proposed Measures   224
A2.2   Main Recommendations for Consideration and
        Action at Country and Regional Levels: Priorities
        by Region   226
A3.1   Eastern and Southern Africa: LLDCs and
        Transit Neighbors   230
A3.2   Western and Central Africa: LLDCs and
        Transit Neighbors   231
A3.3   Central and South Asia and the Caucasus:
        LLDCs and Transit Neighbors   232
A3.4   Other LLDCs and Their Surrounding Regions   233
A4.1   Trade-Related Survey Scores of LLDCs Compared
        with Other Poor Countries   238
A4.2   Regions with Poorly Performing LLDCs by LPI Score   240

Foreword

This book is an important contribution to the ongoing effort at the United Nations to address the needs of the most vulnerable groups of countries, especially landlocked developing countries. Support from the World Bank is critical to the recipient countries and the international community, not only in funding or technical assistance, but also in timely knowledge of what does and does not work in terms of policy making.

This book is especially relevant to the Almaty Programme of Action for landlocked developing countries and transit countries, which will reach its 10-year milestone in 2013. The book proposes a welcome new perspective on policies that address the performance of trade and transport corridors and that improve the access of landlocked developing countries. Certainly, this book will be a critical reference in steering the program in the years to come.

I especially salute the authors' efforts to develop a rigorous and in-depth analysis of policies and implementation constraints often found in the real world. Some topics, such as the customs transit regime or trucking regulations, may seem arcane to a general reader. However, the authors make a convincing case that those topics are central to the corridor and to the access problem of landlocked developing countries, and there are important gaps only partially addressed until now.

I advise policy makers in landlocked developing countries and in transit countries and other interested parties to pay attention to the observations and recommendation of this volume. It will certainly help us collectively to improve our common understanding, to develop new innovative projects on the ground, and to reach the objectives of the Almaty program.

Cheick Sidi Diarra
United Nations, Under-Secretary-General and High Representative for the Least Developed Countries, Landlocked Developing Countries, and Small Island Developing States

Foreword

The importance of transport corridors for trade and development, including for some of the poorest countries in the world, is widely recognized. A new consensus has also emerged that reducing trade costs and improving access to corridors is not just a matter of building infrastructure. The policies that regulate transport services providers and the movement of goods along corridors are important determinants of the social rate of return on such infrastructure investment.

A recent World Bank book that is a companion to this volume, *The Cost of Being Landlocked*, highlighted the importance of quality of service delivery in determining the logistics costs that confront traders. It stressed that the costs and unreliability of corridor supply chains are, to a large extent, a consequence of administrative procedures that apply to goods in transit and the inadequacy of key ancillary services, notably in trucking.

This volume complements the earlier one with an analysis and discussion of policies that can be used to improve access to markets by landlocked developing countries, with a particular focus on transit regimes and related procedures and cross-border regulation of transport services. Drawing on extensive case study analysis as well as the results of advisory services and World Bank projects in the field over several years, this book provides new insights and evidence as to what does and does not work when it comes to policies that affect the operation of trade corridors.

This book avoids optimistic assumptions regarding the prospects for new high-level agreements and decisions to facilitate transit or the possible benefits from increased use of technology. Instead, the authors argue that much can be done through the implementation of readily available existing tools. The use of these tools is often hampered by not only capacity constraints; but, equally if not more important, a lack of commitment. Political economic factors in both the landlocked countries and their transit neighbors must be recognized and addressed. This book offers examples of possible implementation strategies that, while challenging, should in principle help in overcoming these political economic constraints.

The main message is that to bring about efficient trade corridors governments and stakeholders should focus on properly implementing the fiscal, regulatory, and procedural principles for international transit that encourage quality-driven logistics services. A precedent for this strategy is the development of seamless corridors in Europe over the past six decades. Implementing the needed improvements in developing countries will take time: there are no credible alternative paradigms, no "silver bullets," and no shortcuts.

The various implementation challenges are the primary focus of this book. They include the reengineering of transit regimes, trucking services, multimodal transportation, and corridor management and monitoring. Policy makers and development practitioners will find that this book provides, in addition to a comprehensive treatment of transit and corridors, a series of practical and feasible recommendations that will help identify and address priority areas for policy reform and projects.

Bernard Hoekman

Director

International Trade Department

World Bank

José Luis Irigoyen

Director

Transport, Water, and Information

Technology Department

World Bank

Acknowledgments

The preparation of this volume has been led by Jean-François Arvis, with coauthors Robin Carruthers, Graham Smith, and Christopher Willoughby, under the guidance of Bernard Hoekman (director of the International Trade Department, PRMTR) and Mona Haddad (sector manager, PRMTR). Marc Juhel (sector manager, Transport Unit) and John Panzer (sector manager, AFTPI) suggested the theme of this work and helped to launch it.

The volume summarizes the findings of a program on transit corridors and landlocked countries financed by the Bank Netherlands Partnership Program.

Daniel Saslavsky helped to manage the editorial process of the book. Monica Alina Mustra and Tugba Gurcanlar supported activities under the program.

Critical contributions to background papers, case studies, or expert knowledge to many sections have been provided by John Arnold, Gerard Luyet, Pilar Londoño-Kent, Christophe Cordonnier, Waldemar Czaspi, Paul Kent, Heinrich Bohfinger, Jack Stone, Michel Zarnowiecki, and José Barbero. Several people provided inputs to this volume in the form of review, advice, and reality checks, or they participated in dissemination workshops. Special thanks are given to Jean-François Marteau and Gaël

Raballand who are the coauthors with one of us (Arvis) of the companion volume in the same series, *The Cost of Being Landlocked*. They also provided the opportunity to pilot some of the concepts developed in this book in actual projects in Eastern and Central Africa. Inputs to the review process and to the revisions were provided by a few others, including Eva Molnar (UNECE), José Rubiato (UNCTAD), Gerard McLinden, Charles Kunaka, Toni Matsudaira, and Virginia Tanase.

Many other colleagues in the World Bank and other organizations, partners in countries and other organizations, and individual experts also provided important insights, offering opportunities to air preliminary versions of the content or to pilot some of the ideas in advance. In this group, special mention should be made to the Almaty program team at the UN OHRLLS led by Sandagdorj Erdenebileg and to the TIR team at the IRU.

The authors also express their gratitude to Mary Fisk, editor Valerie Ziobro, and Stephen McGroarty in the Office of the Publisher at the World Bank and to Stacey Chow (Trade Department) for their patience and help in the editing and publishing process.

Above all, the authors would like to refer to the memory of Simon Thomas, who should have been one of the authors of the book. An outstanding infrastructure economist with intellectual clarity, he provided a critical impulse to the initial stages of this work. He helped the task manager and the other authors develop the conceptual framework and focus on the actual issues.

Inquiries about the book should be sent to Jean-François Arvis (jarvis1@worldbank.org).

About the Authors

Jean-François Arvis is a senior transport economist with the International Trade Department at the World Bank, where he is in charge of the knowledge activities in trade logistics. Before joining the World Bank, he worked in various positions (regulation, trade, finance, and development aid) with the French Ministry of Economy and Industry. He is a graduate of the Ecole Normale Supérieure in Paris and Ecole Nationale Supérieure des Mines, and he holds doctorate degrees in physics.

Robin Carruthers was until recently a lead transport economist at the World Bank. Before joining the World Bank, he spent three decades as a partner of a transport consultancy in Australia, Argentina, and the United Kingdom. His main interests have been in regional and national transport strategies; trade facilitation in East Asia; logistics in the Middle East; and transport investment prioritization in Sub-Saharan Africa, the Middle East, and North Africa.

Graham Smith is a 30-year veteran with the World Bank, most of it as a transport economist and strategist and manager of projects in transport and other infrastructure sectors. During his career before and with the World Bank, he has lived and worked in six different developing countries, and, at one time or another, he has worked in all the World Bank's regions. The most recent case was four years in the Beijing Office as lead transport specialist. Before that position, he managed the World Bank's participation in the Trade and Transport Facilitation in Southeast Europe program by covering customs reform and border management in eight countries simultaneously from Albania to Moldova. He is working part-time with PREM Trade on the issue of policy advice to landlocked countries and the transit countries on which they rely. He brings to this book a broad familiarity with transport and logistics systems "on the ground" and a curiosity about how the LPI is likely to be seen by client governments and how they may respond.

Christopher Willoughby is an economist and former director of various departments in the World Bank. British by nationality, he has lived for long periods in Bangladesh, Belarus, France, Portugal, and the United States. He has worked on the management of development in individual countries in all regions. He has a particular interest in economic infrastructure, especially transport, and ways in which the infrastructure sectors can be enabled to contribute more effectively to the reduction of poverty.

Abbreviations

3PL	Third-Party Logistics
ADB	African Development Bank
AEO	authorized economic operator
AFTA	Afghan Trade Transit Agreement
AGOA	African Growth and Opportunity Act
ALADI	Asociación Latinoamericana de Integración (Latin American Integration Association)
ALCO	Abidjan-Lagos Corridor Authority
ALTID	Asian Land Transport Infrastructure Development project
AMU	Arab Maghreb Union
ASEAN	Association of Southeast Asian Nations
ASYCUDA	Automated System for Customs Data
ATIT	International Land Transport Agreement
CAREC	Central Asia Regional Economic Cooperation
CBRTA	Cross Border Road Transport Agency
CCTTFA	Central Corridor Trade and Transport Facilitation Agency
CEMAC	Monetary and Economic Community of Central Africa
CIF	cost, insurance, and freight

CIH	Comite Intergubernamental de la Hidrovia Paraguay–ParanáCIH (Intergovernmental Committee of the Parana-Paraguay Waterway)
CMR	Contract for the international carriage of goods by road
COMESA	Common Market for Eastern and Southern Africa
DTA	Customs Transit Declaration
EAC	East African Community
ECMT	European Conference of Ministers of Transport
ECO	Economic Cooperation Organization
ECOWAS	Economic Community of West African States
EDI	electronic data interchange
EU	European Union
FESARTA	Federation of Eastern and Southern African Road Transport
FIAS	Foreign Investment Advisory Service
FIATA	Fédération Internationale des Associations de Transitaires (International Federation of Freight Forwarders Association)
FOB	free on board (ship)
FOCEM	Fondo de Convergencia Estructural del Mercosur (Structural Convergence Fund)
GATS	General Agreement on Trade in Services
GATT	General Agreement on Tariffs and Trade
GMS	Greater Mekong Subregion
GPS	global positioning system
IADB	Inter-American Development Bank
ICD	inland container (or clearance) depot
ICT	information communications and technology
IDA	International Development Association
IIRSA	Initiative for the Integration of the Regional Infrastructure of South America
IT	information technology
ITCBA	International Trade and Customs Broker Association
IRU	International Road Transport Union
LLDC	landlocked developing country
LPI	Logistics Performance Index
MIC	International Freight Manifest
MERCOSUR	Southern Common Market
NCTS	New Computerized Transit System

NCTTCA	Northern Corridor Transit Transport Coordination Authority
NEPAD	New Partnership for Africa's Development
NTTFC	National Trade and Transport Facilitation Committee
PACITR	Programme d'Actions Communautaires des Infrastructures et du Transport Routier (Community Programme of Action on Road Infrastructure and Transport)
PPP	purchasing power parity
PTCM	Protocol on Transport, Communications, and Meteorology
REC	regional economic community
RECTCC	Transport Coordination Committee of the Regional Economic Communities in Sub-Saharan Africa
RRTTFP	Regional Road Transport and Transit Facilitation Programme
SAARC	South Asian Association for Regional Cooperation
SACU	Southern African Customs Union
SAD	Single Administrative Document
SADC	Southern African Development Community
SANRAL	South African National Roads Agency
SATCC	Southern African Transport and Communications Commission
SEETO	South-East Europe Transport Observatory
SIECA	Central American Secretariat for Economic Integration
SITC	Standard International Trade Classification
SSATP	Sub-Saharan Africa Transport Policy Program
TAR	Trans-Asian Railway
TEU	twenty-foot equivalent unit (= standard international container)
TIM	Transito Internacional Mercancias (international transit of goods)
TIPAC	Transports Internationaux pour les Pays de l'Afrique Centrale
TIR	*Transports Internationaux Routiers* (International Road Transport)
TRACECA	Transport Corridor Europe-Caucasus-Asia
TRIE	Transit Routier Inter-États (Interstate Road Transport)
UEMOA	*Union Economique et Monétaire Ouest Africaine* (West African Economic and Monetary Union)

UIC	Union Internationale des Chemins de Fer (International Union of Railways)
UNCEFACT	United Nations Centre for Trade Facilitation and Electronic Business
UNSAD	United Nations Single Administrative Document
UN	United Nations
UNCTAD	United Nations Conference on Trade and Development
UNDP	United Nations Development Programme
UNECE	United Nations Economic Commission for Europe
UNESCAP	United Nations Economic and Social Commission for Asia and the Pacific
UN-OHRLLS	United Nations Office of the High Representative for the Least Developed Countries, Developing Landlocked Developing States, Countries, and Small Islands
USAID	United States Agency for International Development
VAT	value-added tax
WATH	West Africa Trade Hub
WCO	World Customs Organization
WEF	World Economic Forum
WTO	World Trade Organization

CHAPTER 1

Landlocked Developing Countries and Trade Corridors: An Overview

Landlocked countries are entirely or nearly entirely enclosed by land, meaning they have no shoreline on open seas, as opposed to closed seas or freshwater bodies. Landlocked countries have inherent disadvantages compared to countries with coastlines and deep-sea ports. Trade is more difficult and costly because the landlocked country must access most foreign markets through international transport corridors connecting them to ports in neighboring countries, here called "transit neighbors." While industrialized landlocked countries are all members of the European Union (EU), landlocked developing countries (LLDCs), which face the double challenge of access and development, are among the world's poorest countries.

The United Nations (2009) lists 31 LLDCs[1] (table 1.1), home to about 400 million people, close to 7 percent of the developing world's population. Sub-Saharan Africa has the largest concentration of landlocked countries and population: 15 countries with more than 220 million people, nearly 30 percent of the region's total population. The other large concentration is 12 countries in Europe and Central Asia. The remaining landlocked countries account for around 3 percent of the population in South Asia (five countries) and South America (two countries) and less than 0.5 percent in East Asia (two countries); there are no landlocked countries in North America or Australia.

Table 1.1   Landlocked Developing Countries by Region

Sub-Saharan Africa	Botswana, Burkina Faso, Burundi, Central African Republic, Chad, Ethiopia, Lesotho, Malawi, Mali, Niger, Rwanda, Swaziland, Uganda, Zambia, Zimbabwe
Europe and Central Asia	Armenia; Azerbaijan; Belarus;* Kazakhstan; Kosovo;* Kyrgyz Republic; Macedonia, FYR; Republic of Moldova; Serbia;* Tajikistan; Turkmenistan; Uzbekistan
South Asia	Afghanistan, Bhutan, Nepal
East Asia	Lao People's Democratic Republic, Mongolia
South America	Plurinational State of Bolivia, Paraguay

Source: UN-OHRLLS (UN Office of the High Representative for the Least Developed Countries, Landlocked Developing Countries and Small Island Developing States); World Bank.
*Not included in the UN-OHRLLS list.

In addition to the list of landlocked states, some countries with a coastline have large internal regions that are de facto landlocked, because the only practical access to this part of the territory is through other countries. This is the case in Africa where a large part of southern Sudan and much of the Democratic Republic of Congo are de facto landlocked, an area that accounts for 10 percent of the region's population. The Northeastern States of India, the "Seven Sisters," are quasi-enclaves between Bangladesh, China, and Burma. These distant inland destinations in large countries share some of the same access challenges as fully landlocked countries, notably with regard to infrastructure.

Much of the analysis in this book was conducted from the perspective of how to make international trade corridors in general perform more effectively. Therefore, the lessons learned and the reach of the recommendations are intended to apply beyond the case of LLDCs. For example, they are also relevant for land trade corridors between coastal countries, especially, as is frequently the case, when goods are cleared by customs not at borders but in inland destinations. Such corridors are very active in Eastern Europe and the Middle East and significant in North Africa and the Western hemisphere, but more are marginal in Asia and Sub-Saharan Africa.

A Renewed Development Priority

The focus on the special access challenges LLDCs face is a relatively recent trend in development policy. From the 1960s through 1980s, most LLDCs in Africa received economic aid and advice as part of the international community's attention to least-developed countries (LDCs) in

Africa and throughout the world. However, LLDCs were given no special consideration as a group.

Since the 1960s, the international community has increased its efforts to improve international transport links for landlocked countries. These efforts have focused primarily on building or upgrading physical infrastructure. For example, urgent assistance was provided to help develop trade route alternatives when political problems in a transit country threatened to interrupt operations of key routes to the LLDC, such as routes to the sea from Zambia in the 1970s and Malawi in the 1980s. Limited efforts targeted the building of institutions to manage corridors effectively to enable Africa and other developing regions to improve their markets for international road transport and to set up efficient transit systems to allow goods to move to and from landlocked countries through their coastal neighbors' territories.

In the 1990s, 9 of the 15 former Soviet republics were added to the list of landlocked countries when they gained independence, as were three former Yugoslav republics (and a fourth, Bosnia, which is very nearly landlocked). They account for some 80 million people, or more than 15 percent of the total population of Eastern Europe and Central Asia. As they struggled in the difficult transition period of the 1990s to set up international borders and border agencies, and their income levels collapsed to less than half of what they had been in the Soviet era, these countries received financial aid and advice as part of the international community's efforts to stabilize their economies.

The full recognition since the 1990s of the links between economic development and trade also underlines the situation of countries with limited trading opportunities and access challenges. The General Agreement on Tariffs and Trade (GATT) was transformed into the World Trade Organization (WTO) in 1995, and increasing numbers of countries signed on. Also during the 1990s, the information technology revolution and the development of the "Washington Consensus" on economic growth greatly expanded world trade volumes and attracted many new players seeking to improve their competitiveness. The current Doha Round of WTO negotiations, launched in 2001, seeks to be a "development round" intended to extend trade benefits to countries not caught up in the initial "globalization" boom" (Friedman 2005), such as the LLDCs.

The WTO's early focus was on lowering tariffs, mainly for imports. As progress was made on that front, the international community became more aware of the "softer" problems that are now listed under "trade facilitation," and began to channel international efforts into identifying and finding solutions for the more acute problems. Of particular importance is the principle of "freedom of transit," spelled out in Article V of the GATT, and its operationalization.

The 1990s saw rising concern in the development community about the special difficulties faced by landlocked countries in a world where economic development was becoming increasingly dependent on trade. LLDCs are typically isolated from major markets and have small economies, weak institutions, and, in many cases, a recent history of conflict. As a result, the Millennium Development Goals adopted by all government heads at the UN in 2000 include an explicit commitment "to address the special needs of landlocked developing countries," and initiatives were launched to make world trading systems more inclusive.

One of the first initiatives was the first global conference on the problems of LLDCs, which the UN sponsored in Almaty, Kazakhstan, in 2003. It brought together the international community at the ministerial level to focus on overcoming the difficulties faced by LLDCs and their transit neighbors in ensuring reliable and efficient transport. The resulting Almaty Programme of Action (box 1.1) stressed the need for major reforms over the next decade to overcome inefficiencies as well as investment to reduce operating costs and delays. The mid-term review of the program undertaken in 2008 reported significant and faster progress with some positive results already visible, but it also called for acceleration to achieve solid improvements by 2013, the tenth anniversary of the Almaty conference.

Transit Neighbors and Trade Corridors

Most landlocked countries depend on one or two overland routes through "transit neighbors," neighboring countries that have agreed to provide access to carry their international trade to and from the sea. The relationship raises many potentially divisive issues: infrastructure provision, maintenance, and compensation, as well as vehicle and driver entry rights, licensing, and insurance. Customs of both parties often fear that the merchandise will be disposed of en route without paying customs duties. Additional issues relate to bilateral trade and transit of passengers between the LLDC and its transit neighbors.

The evidence shows that the LLDCs have indeed generally faced greater difficulties than coastal countries in expanding international trade. Those few landlocked countries rich in natural resources that have successfully extracted those resources are the exceptions to this

Box 1.1

Almaty Programme of Action (2003) Focus Areas

The Almaty Conference (UN 2003) highlighted five priority areas for landlocked countries as follows:

- **Transit policy and regulatory frameworks:** Both landlocked and transit countries should review their transport regulatory frameworks and establish regional transport corridors.
- **Infrastructure development:** Landlocked countries need to develop multimodal networks (rail, road, air, and pipeline infrastructure projects).
- **Trade and transport facilitation:** Landlocked countries need to implement the international conventions and instruments that facilitate transit trade (including the WTO).
- **Development assistance:** The international community should assist landlocked countries by: (1) providing technical support, (2) encouraging foreign direct investment, and (3) increasing official development assistance.
- **Implementation and review:** The participating agencies[a] should monitor the implementation of transit instruments and conduct a comprehensive review of their implementation in due course.

Source: Almaty Programme of Action 2003.
a. UN Office of the High Representative for the Least Developed Countries, Landlocked Developing Countries and Small Island Developing States (UN-OHRLLS); UN regional economic commisions; World Bank; WTO; and regional development banks.

generalization. A UN review of the Almaty Programme of Action in 2008 (UN 2008) showed some progress in pinpointing where "landlockedness" hurts and in measuring its effects. In recent years, some LLDCs have improved their logistical performance, reducing trading delays and costs. These joint efforts by the LLDCs, transit countries, and regional and international bodies began to close the gap somewhat (UN 2008), but these measures need to be taken much further if LLDCs are to overcome their inherent disadvantages.

So far, much emphasis has been placed on infrastructure, legal instruments, and, more recently, technology. Traditionally, the LLDC access problem has been understood in terms of physical infrastructure and dependence upon the transit country (Arvis, Raballand, and Marteau 2010). Hence, the international agenda has focused on roads and railroads and securing the principle of "freedom of transit" in bilateral and regional transit-related agreements.

Infrastructure has had its ups and downs in the agenda of the international aid community. Since about 2000, infrastructure has regained recognition as a critical requirement for growth, and funding for it has recovered. The World Bank and regional development banks have worked together to address weak links and the rehabilitation of entire corridors, such as was done recently with the Northern Corridor in East Africa or the Douala corridor in Central Africa. Regional initiatives such as the NEPAD (New Partnership for Africa's Development) have helped countries agree on priority corridors and investment allocations. Thanks to large investments in transit infrastructure and improved maintenance policies over the past decade, landlocked countries no longer suffer from those problems more than the transit countries. As of 2010, road conditions on virtually all active corridors guarantee continuity of traffic.

International law and treaties addressing the movement of goods and vehicles are an essential part of the corridor framework. And since comprehensive legal toolkits have been made available to LLDCs, any elusive performance on corridors cannot be tracked to lack of legal instruments and (Grosdidier de Matons 2004). If anything, there have been too many "legal instruments"; because implementation is dependent on local institutions, business practices, or governance, much of the content of the new rules has not been implemented. In many instances, it is lack of capacity in key institutions (customs or transport agencies), poor service quality, or monopolistic arrangements that have essentially neutralized the potential impact of legal changes.

To address the implementation gap, since 2000, international financial institutions increasingly have highlighted the importance of tackling the "soft" side of trade facilitation on corridors and have improved support of corridor-related institutions, starting with substantial involvement in customs reform. The first such project was the Trade and Transport Facilitation in Southeast Europe Program, under which the World Bank, European Union, and other donors supported customs modernization and related reforms in eight Balkan countries between 2000 and 2004. This involvement showed the importance of mobilizing sustained support for such reforms from the trading community (private sector), as well as the importance of cross-border cooperation among governmental agencies (for example, customs at paired border checkpoints).

A New Conceptual Framework: Transit Systems and Corridor Performance

The present study thus focuses on these trade corridors and all their complexities. The World Bank's global perspective made it possible for the authors to learn about LLDCs' access problems and their solutions in one region and to derive potential solutions for other regions, from Mongolia to Bolivia and from Malawi to Armenia.

This study looks at improving LLDCs' access to trade by improving corridor efficiency and by ensuring that all LLDCs connect effectively to international markets through affordable and reliable supply chains. Its narrow focus is on the corridors, not on analyzing the broader development challenges of landlocked countries or their political implications, nor related supply-side policies such as diversification.[2] However, it does cover some issues in regional integration of LLDCs in discussion of customs, transit, and transport services policies.

The conceptual framework for the present analysis is provided in the companion to this study, *The Cost of Being Landlocked* (Arvis, Raballand, and Marteau 2010), which analyzes the sources and structure of access costs based on the microanalysis of the corridor supply chain. The primary sources of these costs are found by examining the inner workings of the corridor and its institutions, notably those involved in moving goods and regulating vehicles, as well as by looking at mechanisms and incentives for cooperation between participants in the corridor supply chain: traders, transport companies, and customs and control agencies.

The central objective of this volume is to clarify the components of the transit system for trade corridors and to determine why the system works or doesn't. "Transit system" refers here to the infrastructure, legal framework, institutions, and procedures serving trade corridors, seen as a whole. A transit system has the following components that will be reviewed in subsequent chapters:

1. Hard and soft infrastructure of the transit system (see figure 1.1):
   - Political commitment to allow transit trade, formalized in treaties that can be bilateral, regional, or multilateral.
   - Physical infrastructure, including border checkpoint facilities.
   - Market for services available in the region, including the trucking industry, customs brokers, and freight forwarders.

Figure 1.1   The Transit System and Its Components

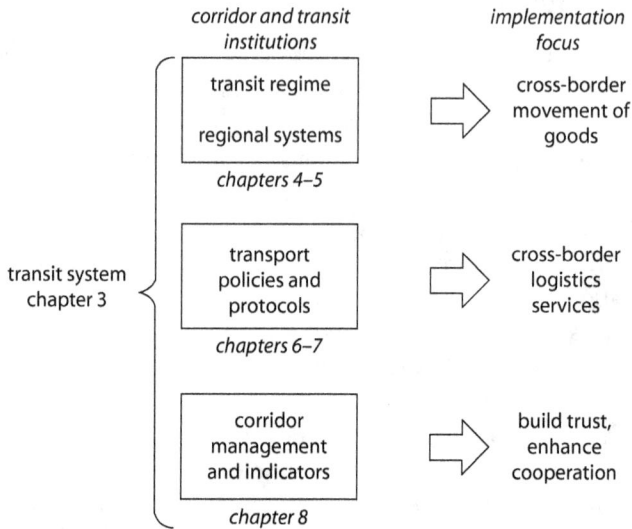

	corridor and transit institutions	implementation focus
	transit regime	cross-border movement of goods
	regional systems	
	chapters 4–5	
transit system chapter 3	transport policies and protocols	cross-border logistics services
	chapters 6–7	
	corridor management and indicators	build trust, enhance cooperation
	chapter 8	

Source: Authors.

2. Institutions that enable the transit system to move goods and vehicles on the corridor:
   • Transit regime, implemented mostly by customs agencies, comprising the operating procedures that govern the movement of goods.
   • Transport policies and protocols that govern the movement of vehicles. They are implemented in countries and across borders to regulate logistics services, to recover infrastructure costs, and to improve competition within and between modes of transportation. Also included are complementary mechanisms to facilitate the movement of vehicles and people, including vehicle regulations, visas for drivers, insurance, and law enforcement.
   • Initiatives to facilitate cooperation and to build trust between transit and landlocked countries and between public and private participants, including the set up of joint corridor management institutions or the survey of corridor performance indicators common solutions.

The framework in this study of the transit system is based on four major assumptions.

• At the heart of a functioning transit system is a public-private partnership between competent private logistics operators and the authorities of the country of transit. It is, therefore, essential to ensure quality and compliance through policies that enhance competition and the development of service markets.

- The principles of design and implementation of working transit procedures that facilitate trade and safeguard the interest of the country of transit are essentially universal and low-tech, the fruit of millennia of evolution.
- While managing transit is part of each country's sovereignty, huge gains may be realized from integrating transit systems within a region. Very efficient systems developed in Europe after World War II are the de facto benchmarks for transit regimes, while ad hoc mechanisms have essentially failed.
- Trust building and cooperative mechanisms have proven very important to overcome reluctance to change, especially in transit countries.

This report summarizes the authors' review of existing transit systems and corridors and the lessons from improvement projects they have been involved in. It identifies the critical areas for action and cooperation and recommends a policy and aid agenda for the international community, with an eye to the Almaty Programme of Action target of achieving visible improvements by 2013.

Structure of This Volume

This book is organized as follows (figure 1.1). Chapter 2 explains the importance for LLDCs of obtaining affordable and dependable access through corridors that perform well. It reviews the commodities typically exported by LLDCs and notes their vulnerability to trade costs in addition to global trends, such as the commodity price boom of the past decade and the financial crisis that followed in 2008–09. It presents recent microeconomic evidence on the nature and structure of trade corridor logistics costs, including delays, and how these costs relate primarily to institutional causes, such as procedural arrangements or markets for services, rather than to the physical infrastructure.

Chapter 3 explains the political economy of the international trade corridor by examining the relationship between the LLDC and the transit country or countries on which it depends and by focusing on the incentives and benefits for transit countries to facilitate their LLDC neighbor's trade. It also emphasizes the role of public-private cooperation in delivering freight services within corridors and the need to align incentives to improve service delivery for the LLDC. This chapter also identifies the institutions that construct the transit system within a corridor.

Chapter 4 looks at what makes the transit regime work—the arrangements and institutions, notably customs, that govern the movement of goods within corridors—which forms the core of this study. This chapter sets out the universal principles that underpin a transit system. The working details of the transit regime are described in chapter 5, with a focus on regionally integrated solutions and examples of current experience in different regions.

One of this study's main policy recommendations is to reform the regulation of the road transport industry for freight (trucking) to encourage the development of high-quality service among firms operating across borders. Only through such quality improvement is the paradigm of mutual trust between transporters and border control agencies likely to be achieved. How this can be done is explored in chapter 6.

Although road transport will remain dominant in the flow of goods along most transit corridors, railways, air freight, and inland waterways offer unrealized potential in certain markets. Chapter 7 examines the conditions under which these forms of transport can best play this role and the policy implications of such alternatives for LLDCs.

Chapter 8 examines the concept of a transit corridor, defining "good practice" in its management and suggesting consistent performance measures, such that performance can be compared across corridors.

Chapter 9 presents the main policy recommendations that emerge from the study, most of which are addressed to the governments and private stakeholders involved in trade along transit corridors. But suggestions are also offered on how the international community can reorient its support to best effect.

The appendixes contain supporting analysis of individual trade corridors, institutional arrangements region by region, and descriptions of regional transit systems and regimes.

Implementation of the conceptual framework recommended in this report will make LLDCs more active and successful participants in world trade. It does not require major investment or resources but primarily a change of mindset that departs from the vision of a state-led access program with emphasis on infrastructure investment. Rather, the new vision is that of seamless transit systems involving mutually beneficial partnerships between LLDCs and transit countries and the promotion of private logistics services. This objective can be achieved in a relatively short time with a catalytical contribution of international agencies, not only in terms of financial support and technical assistance, but also through harmonization of practices and procedures related to transit and trade corridors.

Notes

1. Definitions vary. The UN Office of the High Representative for the Least Developed Countries, Landlocked Developing Countries, and and Small Island Developing States (UN-OHRLLS) lists 31 countries. However, non-EU landlocked countries or territories (Belarus, Kosovo, and Serbia) are considered as developing in the World Bank income-based classification system.
2. The broader agenda for LLDCs is covered in such influential publications as Faye et al. (2004) and Chowdhury (2005).

References

Arvis, Jean-François, Gaël Raballand, and Jean-François Marteau. 2010. *The Cost of Being Landlocked: Logistics Costs and Supply Chain Reliability.* WB Directions in Development. Washington, DC: World Bank.

Chowdhury, Anwarul K. 2005. "Statement for the Least Developed Countries, Landlocked Developing Countries, and Small Island Developing States." Sixth Annual Ministerial Meeting of Landlocked Developing Countries, United Nations, NY. September.

Faye, Michael A., John W. McArthur, Jeffrey D. Sachs, and Thomas Snow. 2004. "The Challenges Facing Landlocked Developing Countries." *Journal of Human Development* 5 (1): 31–68.

Friedman, Thomas L. 2005. *The World Is Flat: A Brief History of the 21st Century.* New York: Farrar, Straus, and Giroux.

Grosdidier de Matons, Jean. 2004. "A Review of International Legal Instruments." Sub-Saharan Africa Transport Policy Program Working Paper 73, World Bank, Washington, DC.

UN (United Nations). 2003. "Almaty Programme of Action: Addressing the Special Needs of Landlocked Developing Countries within a New Global Framework for Transit Transport Cooperation for Landlocked and Transit Developing Countries. UN General Assembly Resolution 58/201. December 23.

———. 2008. "Implementation of the Almaty Programme of Action: Addressing the Special Needs of Landlocked Developing Countries within a New Global Framework for Transit Transport Cooperation for Landlocked and Transit Developing Countries." Report of the Secretary General, UN General Assembly, July.

———. 2009. *World Population Prospects: The 2008 Revision.* New York, United Nations, Department of Economic and Social Affairs, Population Division.

CHAPTER 2

The LLDC Access Problem and the Performance of Trade Corridors

The constraints landlocked developing countries (LLDCs) face in their access to seaports puts them at a greater disadvantage than other country groups, even compared to least developed countries (LDCs). The severity of this disadvantage in terms of lesser trade, lower development level, and smaller economic growth has been well documented (Chowdury 2005; Faye et al. 2004).[1] Until recently, little effort has been devoted to investigating LLDCs' access problem, to analyzing how the function of transit corridors affect trade at the microeconomic level, or to determining what policies might improve the performance of corridors. For some time, the access problem has been thought of in terms of additional transportation costs, for instance, as measured by macroestimates such as the CIF/FOB (Cost, Insurance, and Freight/Free on Board) ratios comparing LLDCs to average coastal countries.

However, research documented in Arvis et al. (2010) has shown that macroestimates are not reliable and that it is essential instead to look at service delivery to the trader, exporter, or importer to measure total logistics costs of trade on corridors; in other words, transportation costs alone do not take into account other important outcomes in corridor performance, such as delays, reliability, or service quality. Thus, this chapter will analyze the corridor and transit supply chains to understand the performance bottlenecks, their causes, and how they can be corrected. Solutions will then be covered in later chapters.

Economic Potential of LLDCs

What do the 31 LLDCs have to offer the world? Their exports are generally limited to a few commodities, typically unprocessed foodstuffs, timber, and wood products. Few LLDCs have taken advantage of preferential market opportunities for LDCs in the European and North American markets where they might have developed even low value-added manufactures such as textiles and apparel. However, some LLDCs do have oil and gas resources or substantial mineral reserves. An LLDC having such sought-after natural resources is important in any typology, as is determining who their trading partners are.

Landlocked countries of Central Asia and southeastern Europe trade mainly within their regions, whereas those in Africa have traditionally traded cross-continentally with Europe and North America rather than within their subregions. Hence, African LLDCs are especially dependent upon the full extent of their trade corridors up to the port. The surge in South–South trade and the increasing role of large emerging economies (Brazil, China, and India) are creating new markets, especially for primary products. These changing trade patterns make alleviating the access constraint more pressing than before.

Measuring LLDC Economic Disadvantages
Documentation of LLDCs' economic disadvantages compared to those of coastal neighbor countries comes from various sources:

- Econometric research focusing on contrasts typically found between landlocked and coastal countries
- Recent worldwide surveys of countries' trade and logistic performance and related broader research
- Growth and trade experience of LLDCs in each region over the past 10–15 years compared to that of coastal neighbors.

Econometric studies comparing the growth experience of large numbers of countries over several decades at the end of the 20th century show that being landlocked sharply depresses economic growth. Analysis of data for 92 low- and middle-income countries over the period 1980–96 shows that the landlocked economies grew more slowly than those of coastal countries, by about 1.5 percentage points per year (MacKellar, Wörgötter, and Wörz 2000).

More recent research (Collier 2007) covering a few more countries from 1960 to 2000 makes a distinction between resource-rich LLDCs and others. It shows that resource-scarce LLDCs outside Africa average 1.5–2.0 percentage points per year slower per capita income growth than coastal countries. The LLDCs of Sub-Saharan Africa, which are also resource-scarce (that is, all 15 except Botswana, Zambia, and Zimbabwe) typically experienced twice as much negative growth differential, indicating no sustained growth over the entire 40-year period.

Recent research has also deepened the understanding of the significance of transport in contributing to this poor economic performance. Data on developing countries' international trade flows and transport costs show that being landlocked raises the transport costs of a country's foreign trade by around 50 percent compared to average coastal economies and reduces trade volume by as much as 60 percent (Limão and Venables 2001).

The slow trade growth of most LLDCs, especially the poorest, remains a serious problem. Even though, according to the data, LLDCs' large growth-rate lag in the final decades of the past century began to be reversed after 2000, the new pattern seems mainly to reflect the boom in minerals and energy demand. This was the case until mid-2008 when the financial crisis caused a sharp decline in commodity and raw material prices, which had a particularly great impact on some resource-rich LLDCs.

LLDCs are particularly vulnerable to global economic shocks, because their economies are small and indebted and because their formal institutions are weak. The rapid inflation in commodity prices up to the 2008 financial crisis was one such shock: the soaring price of oil hurt most LLDCs (few have oil or gas resources), while high food prices hurt those not agriculturally self-sufficient. The subsequent global financial crisis caused the terms of trade to deteriorate and donors to cut back on aid. Between the first semesters of 2008 and 2009, the value of LLDC trade fell by almost 50 percent (ITC 2010), against 46 percent for the LDCs. As the global economy recovers, commodity prices are expected to climb again: indeed, the overall LLDC trade value recovered in the first half of 2010 almost to the level of 2008. However, most LLDCs lack the resilience to make a full recovery, as they have no reserves to draw on to smooth out these shocks and maintain competitiveness. For instance, LLDCs are still losing export potential in the textile and garment trade even after the crisis: a loss of 10 percent in 2010 compared to the already low level of 2009. Lowering access costs would help make them a little less vulnerable to fluctuations in international prices.

LLDC Corridor Logistics Performance

Worldwide surveys, such as the World Economic Forum's *The Global Enabling Trade Report 2008* (Lawrence et al. 2008) and World Bank's (2009b) *Doing Business in Landlocked Economies 2009*, document that trade facilitation at the border and transport penalties borne by LLDCs' international trade are indeed high and problematic. More detailed insights are provided by the Logistics Performance Index (LPI) (Arvis et al. 2010), especially for the key case of Africa. Table 2.1 provides some of the background data that goes into the LPI calculations for three regions and shows a comparison of landlocked and coastal countries for two of them.

These data show that the transport infrastructure of LLDCs in Sub-Saharan Africa has a 7 percent worse LPI score than coastal countries, a

Table 2.1   Poorly Performing Landlocked Countries on the Logistics Performance Index, by Region

	Sub-Saharan Africa		Central Asia	South Asia	
Background data	*Landlocked*	*Coastal*	*Landlocked*	*Landlocked*	*Coastal*
Overall LPI	2.22	2.43	2.25	1.84	2.64
Selected LPI components*					
Logistics competence	2.21	2.45	2.18	1.84	2.69
Infrastructure quality	1.97	2.11	1.98	1.61	2.41
Customs and trade processes	2.10	2.30	2.04	1.69	2.34
LPI input data					
Customs clearance (days)	3.2	4.7	n.a.	2.6	2.2
Physical inspection (%) (higher is worse)	62	42	n.a.	56	27
Possibility of review (%) (higher is better)	52	19	n.a.	33	30
Lead time to (days)					
Export (median) shipper to port	11.8	6.2	n.a.	6.5	2.5
Import (median) port to consignee	18.4	9.3	n.a.	14.7	3.3
Import (best 10 %) Port to consignee	9.1	5.0	n.a.	11.0	2.5

Source: Arvis et al. 2010.
Note: n.a. = not applicable.
* LPI ratings are on a 5-point scale, with 1 being "worst" and 5 "best."

significant deficit, but not the worst among the LPI measures. The competence of services or trade processes indicates a larger penalty: on average about 10 percent worse than coastal countries. This reflects the same hierarchy of constraints that has appeared in case studies and projects.

The data for time to export or import in Africa suggest the same conclusions as far as penalties:

- Being landlocked adds four days to exports or the fastest imports, which reflects the time it takes to cover the extra distance given the current infrastructure, plus clearance at destination.
- However, the average imports take much longer in transit—about nine days more than for their coastal neighbors. Imports are widely subject to more demanding transit controls than exports, so it is reasonable to blame the transit system for this difference.
- Customs clearance itself does not explain the poor performance of LLDCs because the data show it does not take more time in landlocked countries, which points instead to the transit procedure that takes place before customs clearance.

The average import time (time from seller's point of origin to the buyer's warehouse) for Africa varies widely. The median import time for some LLDCs in both Central and Eastern Africa can be more than four weeks, but it is somewhat better in Western and Southern Africa.

For LLDCs in South Asia (with average values heavily affected by the very low scores of Afghanistan), quality of transport infrastructure, which is 50 percent worse for landlocked than coastal countries, is a serious constraint. But, again, it is not a significantly greater problem than the border and services components of the LPI, which on average are about 42 percent worse for LLDCs. Transit time is also disproportionately high for LLDCs.

The Corridor Supply Chain and Its Bottlenecks

The trade and transport costs borne by LLDCs now depend more on operations than on infrastructure capacity. The main factor is the fragmentation of the supply chain. Few traders in LLDCs have access to the door-to-door logistics infrastructure that has developed in industrialized countries over the past two decades. Instead, they rely on an extended sequence of distinct operations, with many procedures, agencies, and services, all prone to rent-seeking and overregulation. LLDCs face not only multiple clearances, but also transloading from one vehicle or mode of freight to another. The main steps in this extended supply chain (figure 2.1) include

Figure 2.1   An Extended Chain of Operations

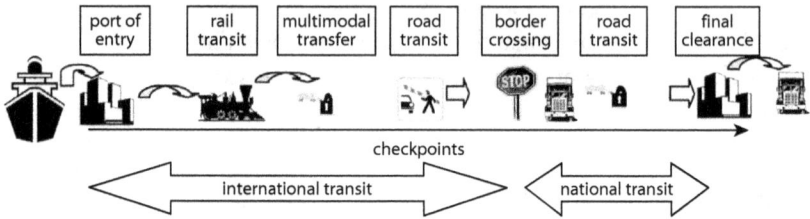

Source: Arvis et al. 2010.

(on the import side; the chain is reversed for exports) port handling, initiation of transit, loading and multimodal operation, control en route, border procedures, and customs clearance at the destination. These activities take place mostly in the transit countries (table 2.2).

Therefore, the logistics costs borne by traders in LLDCs comprise more than just transport fees. Traders must also support logistics costs resulting from (1) procedural fees, including those for compulsory, but not always useful, activities such as compulsory warehousing or inspection; (2) facilitating payment en route, but also typically to get things done to initiate transit; and (3) agent fees, which depend on competition but also the complexity of the situations the agent has to deal with. Even more important, traders must support the consequences of delays in the form or interruption of services and unreliability of the delivery lead time.

The following examples provide insights into how intricate the movement of goods can be for LLDCs in African corridors. In fact, transit systems in Africa are still far from working effectively, resulting in heavy cost and time penalties to LLDC trade as these examples show.

Example 1

A load in transit to Blantyre in Malawi may come from Durban, South Africa, about 2,500 km away. It will be transported by a Malawian or South African carrier, both of which offer good service. It will benefit too from the efficient handling operation in the port of Durban. However, before being cleared at destination in Blantyre, it will have to go through the following lengthy sequence of procedures with many participants:

1. Transit is initiated in South Africa in Durban by the freight forwarder.
2. At each of three borders (South Africa–Zimbabwe, Zimbabwe–Mozambique, Mozambique–Malawi), the cargo and trucks undergo the following sequence between country A and country B:
   - A broker gets the truck information.

Table 2.2   Supply Chain Sequence and Bottlenecks

Step	Participants	Typical issues	Covered in
Unloading; declaration and initiation of transit	Port authority Terminal operator Forwarder* Customs	Excessive time to clear transit, sometimes longer than for local clearance; cumbersome transit declaration	Chapters 4 and 8
Loading on truck	Forwarder Trucking company Handling company	Overregulation of trucking industry Inadequate market structure Formal or informal queuing system	Chapter 6
Loading on train/ Multimodal facility	Terminal operator Railway company	Lack of coordination between port and rail operators Inefficient train operations and long lead time	Chapter 7
Control en route	Road agencies (e.g., weighbridge) Customs	Convoys Multiplication of checkpoints, formal or not, and payments Weak link or congestion on the corridor	Chapters 4, 6, and 8
Border crossing	Forwarder's agent or broker Customs Other border agencies Road agencies (weighbridge and tolls)	Duplication of controls on each side of the border Waiting time Inconsistency of procedures Fragmentation of brokerage services across borders	Chapters 4, 5, and 8
Transit in destination country and final clearance	Forwarder Customs	No continuity of procedures or portability of documents Improper use of IT for transit Lack of capacity (IT risk management) for proper clearance at destination Inefficient discharge of transit increases the cost of guarantee	Chapters 4 and 5

Source: Authors.

Note: IT = information technology.

* The freight forwarder acts as an agent for the owner of the goods and deals with control agencies, such as customs (exercising the role of broker), operators of facilities, and also transport services. The forwarder is an integrator of services, who may provide brokerage services himself but also may subcontract in part or whole the other logistics services in the chain of transit, such as transportation or warehousing.

- Submission by broker to customs in country A.
- Discharge of transit in country A.
- Crossing to customs office in country B.
- Another broker in country B gets the information from the truck.
- Submission by second broker of transit declaration to customs in country B.
- Truck cleared by customs in country B.
- Truck weighed by road authority, transit toll paid if the truck is not registered in country B.

Thus, the same transit declaration is input seven times because of the intervention of many agents (World Bank 2009a).

Example 2
Although there is only one border to cross, the procedure is even more complex to move a load in transit from the port in Douala in Cameroon to N'Djamena in Chad:

1. Transit is initiated in Douala.
2. At the border, the cargo and trucks undergo the following sequence:
   - Container is unloaded in the terminal.
   - The freight forwarder lodges a transit declaration with proof of guarantee.
   - Customs clears the container for transit.
   - A private railway company transfers the container to a dry port (an inland cargo depot) in Ngaoundéré in central Cameroon, 800 km away.
   - The freight forwarder's agent applies for a truck at the freight bureau and submits a freight transit declaration (official waybill).
   - The freight bureau assigns a truck to carry the load and validates the declaration (truckers queue for days at a parking lot near the dry port).
   - Local customs bureau clears the transit declaration (from Douala).
   - After loading the cargo and exiting the dry port, the truck is weighed and the documents stamped at several stops en route by both the customs agents and the freight bureau. (Trucks are supposed to stop at night at designated facilities en route.)
   - Cameroon customs at the border (Kousseri), with participation of the freight forwarder's agent, provides authorization to cross the border, a bridge over a river.

- Several checkpoints at the Chad end of the bridge include security, freight bureau, and customs.
- Admission into the clearance facility in Chad is the end of transit and beginning of clearance procedure in Chad.

This procedure is currently being simplified under the World Bank Central Africa Transport and Transit Facilitation project (World Bank 2007). This example of reengineering of a transit regime will be covered in more detail in chapter 5.

Unreliability of LLDC Corridors Carries a High Cost

The main transit delays usually occur at the origin or destination in initiating or clearing transit cargo. These delays are primarily in ports because traders must submit and clear the transit declaration with customs, and, if transport is still regulated, to get the official waybill and get a truck assigned for the load. The paradox is that in most countries, goods in transit spend the same amount of time or more at the port than goods cleared locally, even though the transit procedures are, in principle, much simpler, especially since inspection or payment of duties are not required. Delays at the border crossings and, to a lesser extent, controls—customs and other routine checks (for weight overloading or customs' seals control, or security such as antinarcotics or health, and so on)—en route can also contribute to unreliability of delivery times.

For traders, the low reliability of the transit supply chain is more worrisome than is the average transit time. The many steps, the fragmentation of control, and the low quality of services make the supply chain unpredictable, which shows up in transit times (see figure 2.1). The system lacks redundancy: if one link fails, few alternatives are readily available. These risks give rise to additional inventories, emergency shipments, suspended operations, and lost markets. Unreliability, in essence a stochastic problem, can take several forms, as follows:

- Unpredictability of the overall lead time of the transit supply chain and some of its components in the form of spread of the distribution of time (box 2.1). This is the most apparent phenomenon and has been shown to have a significant impact on logistics costs (Arvis et al. 2010).
- Probability of interruption of service. This may come from disruption of infrastructure, such as a train derailment or a bridge failure. The probability of strikes in ports is also taken in account where corridors compete

Box 2.1

Spread in Delays and Predictability of Supply Chains

Half the containers going to Uganda and Rwanda from the port of Mombasa, Kenya, are cleared for transit within nine days, but 1 in 20 takes more than a month.

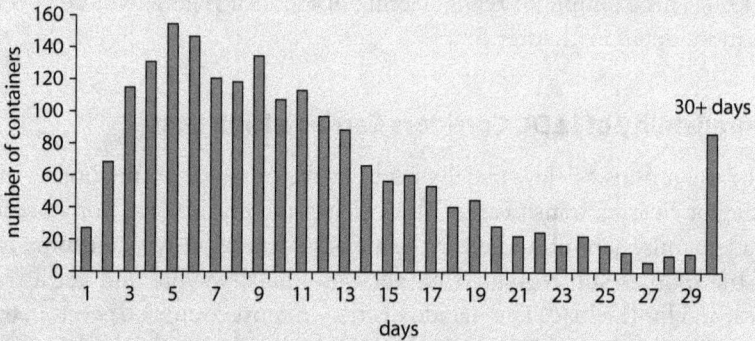

Probability distribution of delays at Mombasa port*, Kenya

Source: Arvis et al. 2010.
* number of transit containers for one operator in the second half of 2004.

Clearance of transit cargo from South Africa into Zambia at the Chirundu border post between Zimbabwe and Zambia is another example of how the fragmentation of the process (two agents, two customs clearances, one weighbridge [truck scale], and several movements of trucks) can lead to dispersion of the transit time (see figure below). In that case, the unreliability is increased and delays are spread because delays propagate by half a day when one step cannot be completed within daytime office hours.

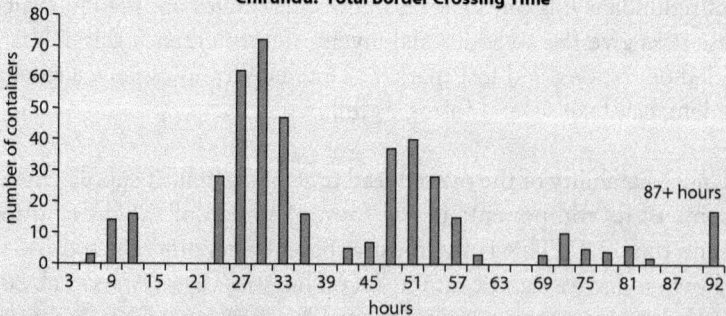

Chirundu: Total Border Crossing Time

Source: Authors.

with each other. It may also be the consequence of seemingly discon-
nected policies or activities.

In Bolivia in 2007, for example, the authors found in a trade facilitation audit that traders were concerned by the potential interruption of
truck traffic to the port of Arica in Chile because of recurrent diesel fuel
shortages. These shortages resulted from a fuel subsidy policy, established
to ease internal access costs, that made it profitable for truckers to exploit
the price differential to smuggle oil out of the country, at times beyond
import capacities.

The risk of unreliability is especially great for intercontinental shipments. For imports, the problem usually starts at the port of entry in
the transit country, where some containers may be released within a
week, while others may be held up for more than a month. The frequent 5 percent or higher chance that customs can hold up any
importer's container for a month can increase logistics costs significantly more than normal releases of about nine days. The trader has to
take into account in his production process the not so small possibility
of long delays. Unreliable delivery times are costly for the importer, for
example, in having to permanently carry a larger inventory to cover
against the risk of delayed delivery. It also means the possibility of
switching, especially for exports, to more expensive means of transportation, such as rush air transport or using a longer corridor to reach
a port with a more frequent shipping schedule.

For goods that are intermediate products in a supply chain, markets
highly value on-time delivery. The risks of high unreliability costs to the
trader or manufacturer in a landlocked country are likely to greatly discourage investment, expansion of the scale of an enterprise, or start of
new export initiatives in those countries. Manufacturing in LLDCs faces
a double penalty compared to traditional commodity exports or production next to a port because both shipping exports and bringing in the
inputs, equipment, and parts, typically sourced internationally as the local
market is too small, are dependent on the transit corridor.

Although not as critical as the impact on production and trading
activities, this lack of reliability also brings up some of the components
of the cost of transportation that can hinder modern logistics practices.
One common example in LLDCs, such as Mongolia and Bolivia, is the
addition of penalty surcharges, called demurrage, on containers to encourage the rapid return of containers moving inland. Container leasing contracts commonly fix the maximum number of days the container's

owner—most commonly a shipping line—is willing to see its boxes stay inland before they must be returned to the port and reloaded, after which the escalating demurrage charge is levied. However, on some corridors, the shipping lines do not trust that the container can reliably be returned within a predictable time period, so the shipper may have to purchase the container as a one-way routing instead of paying smaller demurrage fees that could amount to a few percent of the value of the box.

Market Structure and Competition in Logistics Services

A second source of higher transport cost is the organization and market structure of services, particularly trucking (Teravaninthorn and Raballand 2008). Transporters on trade corridors operate under systems that limit productivity, discourage competition, and often perpetuate poor-quality services and excess capacity. All of these issues may bump prices to as much as twice what they should be, as shown in the following examples:

- On the Douala–Ndjamena Corridor, intervention by the freight bureaus doubled road freight rates.
- On the Vientiane–Bangkok Corridor, ending a monopoly and opening Lao transit trade to all Thai truckers reduced logistics costs by 30 percent.
- In Southern Africa, the quality and organization of long-distance transportation are similar to those in Europe, with comparable operating costs (US$.08 per ton-km in summer 2008). But on international routes, freight rates can be pushed up 10–30 percent because of queues at the border or market restrictions that reduce productivity and prevent optimization of backhaul loads.

Protectionist legislation and overregulation of freight are especially prevalent in Africa. Extensive recent research on road freight costs in Africa (Teravaninthorn and Raballand 2008), based on surveys of truckers using selected corridors in each of four subregions (West, Central, East, and Southern Africa), concluded that costs to the transport provider in Africa were not very different from levels in other countries, but prices charged on some corridors were, such as in Central Africa and on some routes in West Africa. The basic cause was heavy market regulation, which had come to be used mainly for protecting existing providers and discouraging competition in service to the user. The result was a combination of both poorer service quality and higher prices as compared to services in other countries or even in other parts of Africa, notably Southern Africa.

Statistics assembled in a World Bank study (Teravaninthorn and Raballand 2008) documented these high tariffs, which were well above the vehicle operating costs of efficient operators (table 2.3). These data were obtained from trucking surveys that combined large and small firms. However, the prices in Central and West Africa show exceptionally large profit margins. Even if respondents systematically understated their overheads—which is possible—the margins are still very large. They also showed unusually large variation from one respondent to another.

Table 2.3   International Road Transport Prices, Costs, and Profit Margins (from gateway to destination)[a]

Corridor	Route Gateway–Destination	Price[b] ($/km)	Variable cost ($/km)	Fixed cost ($/km)
West Africa (Ghana and Burkina Faso)	Tema/Accra–Ouagadougou, Burkina Faso	3.53	1.54	0.66
	Tema/Accra–Bamako, Mali	3.93	1.67	0.62
Central Africa (Cameroon and Chad)	Douala–N'Djaména, Chad	3.19	1.31	0.57
	Douala–Bangui, Central African Republic	3.78	1.21	1.08
	Ngaounderé–N'Djaména, Chad	5.37	1.83	0.73
	Ngaoundéré–Moundou, Chad	9.71	2.49	1.55
East Africa (Kenya and Uganda)	Mombasa–Kampala, Uganda	2.22	0.98	0.35
	Mombasa–Nairobi, Kenya	2.26	0.83	0.53
Southern Africa (Zambia)	Lusaka–Johannesburg, South Africa	2.32	1.54	0.34
	Lusaka–Dar es Salaam, Tanzania	2.55	1.34	0.44

Source: Teravaninthorn and Raballand 2008.
a. Prices are US$ per vehicle-km because, on a given corridor, most firms have the same truck capacity and similar loading practices. Moreover, because of uncertainties about the reporting of overloading, prices per km are probably more reliable than prices per ton-km. Prices and costs are for a typical 30-ton truckload.
b. In Africa some ministries of transport set indicative prices, but they are not widely applied. Prices set by freight allocation bureaus in Central Africa may be more respected.

How can these high prices be explained? It has been common practice in French-speaking West Africa to regulate the right to operate international road transport services on the basis of a mandatory queuing system (*tour de role*), managed by state-owned national freight bureaus. They offer shipments to waiting truckers on a first-come, first-served basis. This has the effect of barring direct contracting between shippers and truckers. It runs counter to international best practice, in which confidential contracts directly between cargo owners and truckers have become a key to improved performance and superior quality of service.

These systems apply exclusively to transit corridors in application of the quotas allocated between the LLDC and the transit country. Generally, the trucking industry of the transit country is judged stronger, so the quota protects the carriers of the LLDC. In some cases, these quotas grant the truckers the exclusive right to pick up cargo in their home country, implying 100 percent empty returns, a cost that someone has to pay for. Thus, the importers are penalized by also paying for the empty return of the truck to the transit country, whereas full backhauls decrease the cost to the importer, because the return cost can be charged to the exporter. Queuing systems also occur informally in some countries for domestic as well as freight traffic, notably in the Middle East, South Asia, and Africa, where traditionally independent drivers queue to get loads at the main origin point for freights.

These arrangements have two adverse effects on corridor performance. First, they reduce truck use, thereby increasing unit costs per ton-km of carriage. The cost of transportation per kilometer increases as its fixed component is higher because the truck travels shorter distances than the international norm of 150,000 km per year. This phenomenon is evident in table 2.3, which shows that costs of transportation are very high in central Africa, where mandatory loading and queuing is strictly imposed. Detailed explanations and models are provided in Arvis et al. (2010) and Teravaninthorn and Raballand (2008). Furthermore, by restricting competition, queuing systems not only protect monopolistic pricing but also inhibit the development of the kinds of higher quality services required by modern supply chains, because there is no incentive to invest in better equipment or commercial services.

The main transport markets in Africa are in the coastal countries, with their larger scale of economic activity. The framework for operation of the transportation sector, including the nature and level of regulation, has been set largely by these countries. The tendency to form cartels and price gouge nonetheless seems greater on shipments to and from landlocked neighbors than on domestic freight movement. It appears that the premium characteristic of long international movement, the complications of border crossings, even the arrangements to try to ensure a reasonable sharing of the work between truckers from both countries have all been taken advantage of to permit the addition of special overhead charges or profit additions that can cause prices to the shipper to be between 150 and 200 percent of the identified costs to the transport provider.

Unnecessary Overhead and Informal Payments

Finally, compared to domestic freight service, transit is subject to "overhead" for unnecessary services, charges, and bribes, in both the public and private sectors. These payments can add 50 percent or more to transport costs between a port and a landlocked country. On the Lomé–Ouagadougou Corridor, for example, shippers pay an additional 70 percent on top of freight costs, only 15 percent of which is justified by actual forwarding services; the rest is paid in either bribes (28 percent) or legal but superfluous procedures or services (Arvis et al. 2010). A World Bank survey in Kazakhstan estimated such payments at roadside checkpoints at US$800–US$900 per truck per transit trip (Arvis et al. 2010).

In short, neither the distance covered nor the unit cost of available transport services is necessarily much higher in landlocked developing countries than in the wealthiest countries. Instead, shippers suffer extra costs due to three factors: unreliability of deliveries, monopolistic trucking services, and unnecessary overhead charges and informal payments.

Investing in Infrastructure: Does It Actually Promote Trade?

As noted, the high costs and low competitiveness of landlocked countries have traditionally been blamed on the low availability and quality of transport infrastructure, especially road and rail. The need to build and maintain adequate infrastructure in both transit and destination countries has been widely acknowledged and is a major goal in the Almaty Programme of Action (see chapter 1, box 1.1).

Regional initiatives have actively targeted road or multimodal corridor development, for instance under the New Partnership for Africa's Development (NEPAD) in Africa or the Asian highway (box 2.2). These initiatives have helped the countries agree on long-term development but also on priorities for addressing missing or weak links in the infrastructure.

Box 2.2

Infrastructure Investment in Africa and Asia: NEPAD and the Asian Highway Network

NEPAD is an economic development program of the African Union, adopted by African leaders in 2001, with the primary objectives of poverty eradication, promotion of sustainable growth and development, and empowerment of women through building genuine partnerships at country, regional, and global levels. Through its Planning and Coordinating Agency, NEPAD facilitates and coordinates the implementation of regional and continental priority programs and projects, as well as partnerships, resource mobilization, and research and knowledge management. The First Short Term Action Plan under NEPAD consisted of several projects prioritized by the Common Market for Eastern and Southern Africa (COMESA), the East African Community (EAC), the Economic Community of West African States (ECOWAS), the Southern African Development Community (SADC), and the Arab Maghreb Union (AMU), among other African organizations. This plan included road financing in the Northern and Central Corridors and West Africa; expansion of port infrastructure in Mombasa, Kenya, and Nacala, Mozambique; introduction of joint border posts and overload controls for road freight; inland water navigation facilitation; and capacity-building of stakeholder organizations for transport.

The NEPAD Action Plan for the next four years includes different efforts in the Mombasa–Nairobi–Addis Ababa Corridor Development Project; Maghreb Highway Project (missing links in the Mauritanian network and Tripoli–Casablanca to complete the Cairo–Dakar Highway Corridor); rehabilitation and construction of railway links under the AfricaRail project (rehabilitate and construct 2,000 km of new railway to link the railway systems of Benin, Burkina Faso, Côte d'Ivoire, Niger, and Togo, including a train service linking the ports of Lomé and Cotonou); a Trade Facilitation Program for the North–South Corridor; and feasibility studies for the Isaka–Kigali–Bujumbura Railway and for the missing links in the Dakar–N'djamena–Djibouti Highway Corridor (Trans-Sahelian Highway).

The Asian Highway network, also known as the Great Asian Highway, is a cooperative project among countries in Asia and Europe and the United Nations Economic and Social Commission for Asia and the Pacific (ESCAP) to improve the highway systems in Asia. It is one of the three pillars of the Asian Land Transport Infrastructure Development (ALTID) project, endorsed by the ESCAP commission at its 48th session in 1992, comprising the Asian Highway, Trans-Asian Railway,

(continued)

Box 2.2 *(continued)*

(TAR), and facilitation of land transport projects. The Asian Highway is a network of 141,000 km of standardized roadways crisscrossing 32 Asian countries with link-ages to Europe, which was initiated in 1959 with the aim of promoting the development of international road transport in the region. The first phase of the project (1960–70) saw considerable progress; however, progress slowed when financial assistance was suspended in 1975. In the 1980s and 1990s, regional political and economic changes spurred new momentum for the Asian Highway Project.

Source: Authors based on NEPAD (http://www.nepad.org) and UNESCAP (http://www.unescap.org).

Regional integration of trade and increases in trade volume are typically the key goals of those plans, as well as of individual road corridor projects. Although there is consensus among development practitioners on the importance of transport infrastructure, they disagree on two areas: sustainability and actual impact of investment on trade expansion.

The sustainability of infrastructure maintenance policies in a context of limited fiscal resources in LDCs is a serious problem. This is especially true in the LLDCs of Africa (World Bank 2009a) because their low volume of traffic does not allow for recovery of the costs of maintenance, especially in the interior that handles the least amount of traffic. With the exception of the traffic generated from South Africa, African transit corridors may carry fewer than 500, and often under 100, trucks per day in each direction. A recent study in Malawi concluded that even a relatively well-managed road fund could cover only routine maintenance needs because of structurally low traffic and that donor money should be reallocated from new projects to funding some of the maintenance needs (World Bank 2009c).[2]

Economists consider the impact of infrastructure investment on trade as even more controversial. On one hand, trade economists have concluded that road investment has a huge impact and have advocated the creation of new links, based on extensive gravity modeling (Buys, Deichmann, and Wheeler 2006; Portugal-Perez and Wilson 2010) and road quality and density indicators. On the other hand, analysis of the constraints as part of a World Bank Trade and Transport Facilitation Assessment, or microlevel modeling of logistics costs on corridors (Arvis et al. 2010), point to the opposite conclusion: that while infrastructure is still important, soft bottlenecks are the primary problem. The quality of infrastructure does not have a significant impact on delays or predictability. The cost of transportation reflects, first, market organization (as shown in table 2.3) and overhead. Road quality affects the cost of transportation by increasing the need for maintenance and fuel consumption, which would be a small percentage of total logistics costs.

However, infrastructure also has nonlinear effects on logistics costs. For example, investment in basic infrastructure is essential, at least to a certain threshhold, so that there is no interruption of service (for example, under bad weather conditions) or congestion (usually at port gateways or bridges). Thanks to the donor contributions since 2000, continuity of infrastructure is virtually guaranteed today on all road corridors. As of 2010, all capital cities in LLDCs were effectively accessible from their gateway port or their main trading partner within four days.[3]

A plausible reconciliation of the trade analysis and the microeconomic understanding is to include under infrastructure not only the physical infrastructure but also the service actually delivered through that infrastructure. Therefore, most of the trade gain would indeed come from addressing the soft constraint to service delivery outlined earlier. The operational conclusion is that investment in infrastructure should prioritize upgrading and rehabilitation of existing links and should be tied to assistance in order to address improvement in the transit system and its institutions, as outlined in this study.

Supply Chain Linkages: Exports vs. Imports, Extra- vs. Intra-regional Trade

Which deserve more attention—exports or imports? The general answer is imports. Most LLDCs find it difficult to balance their trade: imports exceed exports in aggregate value, as well as in volume. Most exports from LLDCs are raw materials, while imports include many manufactured goods and processed foods, so imports have higher value per ton. As dutiable goods, imports undergo the most control and suffer greater cost and time penalties in transit than exports.

As table 2.1 shows, in Sub-Saharan Africa the median time for moving an imported shipment from the transit port to the destination in an LLDC is almost seven days longer than for an export shipment to make the reverse trip. In South Asia, the difference is eight days. Hence, most trade facilitation measures in ports or on trade corridors essentially target facilitation of importing.

However, from the perspective of improvement of service delivery, the distinction of import or export is irrelevant. Exports and imports in practice use the same service providers (forwarders and truckers); exports are often the backhaul of imports, given directional imbalance (that is, the differences between type, volume, and origin and destination of goods entering and leaving the country). Therefore, improvements in cost or quality of service increase competition, benefitting both directions of trade. The same is true for enhancement of implementation capacities in customs and other agencies. Furthermore, in more diversified economies, manufacture exports, such as textile exports under the African Growth and Opportunity Act program, depend on import logistics for their own competitiveness.

For the same reasons, measures tackling corridor performance benefit not only transit to distant markets but also regional trade. Shorter waits at the borders and improved quality of services may unlock regional trading opportunities for landlocked countries. For instance, Sahelien countries could export agricultural products from their climate zone to their coastal neighbors on the Gulf of Guinea, provided they are not damaged by excessive controls or long wait time under the scorching sun. A World Bank project is underway to determine how to facilitate exports to Côte d'Ivoire or Ghana from Niger of garden products such as onions, which currently are exclusively imported from Europe.

Notes

1. See appendix 4 for indicators comparing LLDCs to other relevant country groups on a series of macro and trade outcomes.
2. A back-of-the-envelope calculation illustrates this point. Under the best circumstances, maintenance of 1 km of road may cost US$30,000–US$60,000 per year, or US$100–US$200 per day, while reference recovery fees are in the range of 5 to 20 cents per km per truck.
3. The only capital city of an LLDC still lacking all-weather access is Bangui, Central African Republic, but a paved road from it to Douala, Cameroon, is being built.

References

Arvis, J.-F., M. A. Mustra, L. Ojala, B. Shepherd, and D. Saslavsky. 2010. *Connecting to Compete 2010: Trade Logistics in the Global Economy: The Logistics Performance Index and Its Indicators.* Washington, DC: World Bank.

Buys, Piet, Uwe Deichmann, and David Wheeler. 2006. "Road Network Upgrading and Overland Trade Expansion in Sub-Saharan Africa." World Bank Policy Research Working Paper 4097, World Bank, Washington, DC.

Chowdhury, Anwarul K. 2005. "Statement for the Least Developed Countries, Landlocked Developing Countries, and Small Island Developing States." Sixth Annual Ministerial Meeting of Landlocked Developing Countries, United Nations, New York.

Collier, Paul. 2007. "Africa's Economic Growth: Opportunities and Constraints." *African Development Review* 19 (1): 6–25.

Faye, Michael A., John W. McArthur, Jeffrey D. Sachs, and Thomas Snow. 2004. "The Challenges Facing Landlocked Developing Countries." *Journal of Human Development* 5 (1): 31–68.

ITC (International Trade Center). 2010. "Trade Performance of the LLDCs during Crisis and Recovery." Presentation at the UN Office of the High Representative for the Least Developed Countries, Landlocked Developing Countries, and Small Island Developing States, New York. November.

Lawrence, Robert Z., Jennifer Blanke, Margareta Drzeniek Hanouz, and John Moavenzadeh. 2008. *The Global Enabling Trade Report 2008*. Geneva: World Economic Forum.

Limão, Nuno, and Anthony J. Venables. 2001. "Infrastructure, Geographical Disadvantage, Transport Costs, and Trade." *The World Bank Economic Review* 15 (3): 451–79.

MacKellar, Landis, Andreas Würgötter, and Julia Wörz. 2000. "Economic Development Problems of Landlocked Countries." IHS Transition Economic Series 14, Institut für Höhere Studien, Wien, Austria.

Portugal-Perez, Auberto, and John S. Wilson. 2010. "Export Performance and Trade Facilitation Reform: Hard and Soft Infrastructure." Policy Research Working Paper 5266, World Bank, Washington, DC.

Teravaninthorn, Supee, and Gaël Raballand. 2008. "Transport Prices and Costs in Africa: A Review of the International Corridors." World Bank Directions in Development, Washington, DC.

World Bank. 2007. CEMAC Transport and Transit Facilitation Project. Project Information Document, CEMAC, Washington, DC.

———. 2009a. *Africa's Infrastructure: A Time for Transformation*. Washington, DC: World Bank.

———. 2009b. *Doing Business in Landlocked Economies, 2009*. Washington, DC: World Bank.

———. 2009c. "Malawi Country Economic Memorandum." World Bank, Washington, DC.

———. 2010. *Logistics Performance Index 2010: Connecting to Compete 2010: Trade Logistics in the Global Economy*. Washington, DC: World Bank.

CHAPTER 3

The Complex Political Economy of Trade Corridors

A remarkable picture emerges from the previous chapter of the complexity of operations on a trade corridor. Many different agents, public and private, in several countries interact and conduct many types of transactions to implement contracts, controls, and procedures or to deliver services. Examples in the last chapter also show that these complex interactions can have results that adversely affect transit system performance, for example, from rent-seeking behavior or from conflicting incentives between groups of agents.

This chapter analyzes the political economy of trade and transportation corridors and identifies the actors and policies that facilitate trade and transportation on corridors in landlocked developing countries (LLDCs). The key policies include transit regime (examined in chapters 4 and 5) and transportation policies (chapter 6).

The emphasis in this chapter on the behaviors and incentives of agents on the corridor goes beyond the traditional vision of state-led corridor development and the dependence of LLDCs on their transit neighbors. The state-to-state relationship and the contribution of treaties and international law to reduce dependence and to promote freedom of transit are indeed important. However, any voluntary decisions by states or groups of states in and of themselves have little influence on corridor performance.

Reducing access costs and improving corridor performance and connectivity of LLDCs ultimately mean reducing the costs and unreliability of logistics services available to traders at the ends of the corridors. The historical development of transit trade and current practices suggest that forging mutually beneficial arrangements and partnerships between agents—including those in the country of transit—is the primary force behind corridor efficiency. The logistics of transit corridors are made possible by partnerships between private operators and public control or regulation, with a shift from the current state of public control-driven mentality to a trust-but-verify approach.

Hence, reforms and policy intervention by governments, regional organizations, and aid agencies should aim at improving the political economy framework of corridors to improve their connectivity and service delivery. It is more about implementing a series of universal principles to set the right incentives than about introducing new international treaties or state-driven corridor development. Regulations on transportation or procedures and controls embedded in the transit regime may develop or hamper incentives for cooperation and compliance by the operators and traders on the corridor.

This chapter also looks at some of the implementation issues in question. Governance, notably with involvement of public agencies, and entrenched rent-seeking behaviors may mean that certain groups may in effect "capture" the corridor for their own profit and at the expense of the traders, as in the case of trucking cartels, such as those in Francophone Africa. Overcoming these barriers, stimulating incentives for changes in business practices, or building trust between private operators and public regulators or controllers remain the most difficult and enduring challenges for which solutions must be developed on a case-by-case basis.

LLDC Relationship with the Transit Country: Beyond Dependence

Improving access for LLDCs has been analyzed primarily in terms of their dependence on the transit state. Fahrer and Glassner (2003, chapter 29) sum up this approach: "[T]he single, inescapable, defining characteristic of a land-locked State is that at least one international boundary lies between it and the sea.... Therefore, all attempts to mitigate the obvious handicaps of landlockedness must involve negotiations with at least one transit State."

Further, Gallup, Sachs, and Mellinger (1999) see two reasons why landlocked countries may be disadvantaged:

• Coastal countries may have military or economic incentives to impose costs on landlocked countries.
• Infrastructure development across national borders is more difficult to arrange than are similar investments within a country.

Therefore, policies intended to improve the access of LLDCs to markets have concentrated on areas to be decided in the context of a bilateral relationship between states (or plurilateral if more than two countries are on the corridor). The two primary actions have been, first, to adopt transit principles recognized by international law and, second, to develop regional transport infrastructure.

Indeed, the primary way an LLDC can have any leverage concerning another nation's policy decisions and enforcement is by entering into a formal relationship with that country. Attaining such leverage can be all the more difficult because the transit country is usually bigger and richer, with stronger institutions and a more diversified economy, especially compared to the least developed LLDCs. Often the LLDC's trade volume is tiny compared to that of the transit country (for example, Nepal to India, Lao People's Democratic Republic to Thailand, Mongolia to China, and Bolivia to Chile or Brazil).

Dependence makes the LLDC vulnerable to unfriendly attitudes or serious political or social disturbances in the transit country. Where there are historic hostilities between LLDCs and their transit neighbors, or at least mistrust and an unequal relationship, it may be unrealistic to expect LLDCs and their transit neighbors to cooperate readily. Yet a transit state engaging in active policies to suppress or impede transit is indeed rare, because such action would be contrary to the obligations of international agreements, such as the General Agreement on Tariffs and Trade (GATT) Article V on freedom of transit. As an example, since 2000, tense relationships between LLDCs and their transit states in the former Soviet Union have impacted transit and cross-border trade significantly. Fortunately, this is an exception; in Africa and other parts of the world, bilateral politics have less effect on trade corridor performance than do operational inefficiencies or localized supply chain disruptions.

Indeed, serious disturbances in the transit state make the LLDCs especially vulnerable. For example, when post-election unrest in Kenya in

2008 effectively cut off Uganda and Rwanda from their primary gateway in Mombasa, they then had to improvise by rerouting their trade through Tanzania's port of Dar es Salam. Civil wars in transit counties can even create more permanent shifts in corridors. When the 15-year-long civil war in Mozambique cut Malawi off from its historical, closest sea access through the ports of Beira and Nacala, trade had to take longer routes to Tanzania and South Africa. The 2002–07 political crisis in Côte d'Ivoire affected Burkina Faso and Mali by reducing the role of the port of Abidjan as the main regional gateway.

And LLDCs' own vulnerability to internal conflicts adds to this dependence: almost half the LLDCs have had recent conflicts or at least serious civil disturbances that affect their own stability and governance. Post-conflict LLDCs lack basic institutional capacity, including corridor-related agencies; therefore, solutions must be simple and robust. Finally, climate change is likely to magnify this vulnerability, both directly as a result of extreme weather in their own territory and indirectly as a knock-on effect from trading partners and transit countries that are affected (World Bank 2010).

Multiple Corridors May Give LLDCs Leverage

The challenge is to manage these political, economic, and environmental shocks and risks, which are already substantial and likely to intensify. It requires raising awareness; monitoring and strengthening institutions and partnerships; preparing contingency plans; and evaluating alternatives, with attention to supply chain reliability, management of the transit system, and fall-back options in the event that one or another trade corridor is disrupted. Diversifying their options should give LLDCs the opportunity not only to reduce their dependence on new political and social development in the transit country, but also to gain some degree of bargaining power to improve their overall access by stimulating competition between transit neighbors.

Policy makers in LLDCs have incentives to diversify their options of transit routes and transport modes. From their perspective, access is a public good that the LLDC government should develop. Thus, the government must devise contingency plans for continuity of access, particularly if a country's transit flow is concentrated in one corridor. Long aware of this issue, LLDC governments, with a few exceptions,[1] have developed more than one useful, dependable corridor (see appendix 1 for LLDC corridors by country).

Although such diversification might reduce LLDCs' vulnerability and improve connectivity (access to several ports) and, thus, reduce trade costs, it is not clear that an LLDC government can or should expand this strategy. Developing new corridors, and trying to stimulate active competition between corridors in different transit countries, while a good idea, may not be a practical or sustainable one. The main reason is that by nature the dynamics of corridor competition cannot be much influenced by proactive government policies in the destination country. This is because the LLDC typically has marginal bargaining power in relation to its transit neighbors, for instance, to push for additional investments in regional links. Trade volumes of most LLDCs are relatively modest (a few million tons at most), so they would be below the threshold of profitability of commercially run infrastructures such as railroads (see chapter 7). Investing actively in several corridors may result in diseconomies of scale in infrastructure and logistics services.

An even more significant reason is that the choice of routes and corridors is the role of the private sector, not the government. The choice of route is determined by the reliability of the corridor and connectivity of the ports, as much as by transportation cost. This is especially true for exporters, which, except for low-value commodities, by far prefer a route with better connections to markets. Exporters of time-sensitive products (textiles or perishable products) will try to reach the port that consolidates the most regional trade and has the most frequent connections, such as Abidjan in West Africa or Durban in southern Africa. Tea exporters from Rwanda or Malawi, for example, will pay a premium to sell on Mombasa's auction floor because the large volume attracts more buyers (see box 3.1).

Finally, even if active diversification of corridors could be achieved, it may not have the level of benefits that policies designed to improve individual corridor performance might have. Trade depends on corridor performance, which itself depends on many institutional factors that determine the quality of service delivery on the corridors, such as the transit regime or markets for logistics services. Competition within a corridor is more critical to reducing trade costs than competition between corridors.

West Africa has the most effective competition between corridors. The three LLDCs in the interior (Burkina Faso, Mali, and Niger) can trade internationally through any of the four countries on the Gulf of Guinea (Benin, Côte d'Ivoire, Ghana, and Togo). There is competition between corridors, given the proximity of the ports and routes and the fact that the volume of trade going to the LLDCs in the interior is significant compared to the overall trade of the coastal countries, especially for Togo and Benin. Market share of the various corridors has been shifting in the

Box 3.1

Connecting Malawi to Markets: A Private Sector Choice

Exporters tend to optimize their supply chains according to their own arbitrage between cost and reliability. Malawi, a small landlocked economy, provides a cogent example. Malawi exports tobacco, sugar, tea, cotton, and garments. Its four corridors to the sea have advantages and disadvantages that attract different traders, depending on their commitments, products, and destinations, as well as on the transport cost (see table). While trading through Durban, South Africa, is the more reliable route, it is also the longest and most expensive. The government prioritizes investment for the railway to Nacala. It is the cheapest route to the sea but also the least consistent. Only sugar uses this route (as of 2010), since it is a lower value, nontime-sensitive product that has buffer storage at the port.

Malawi's Four Trading Corridors

Comparison factors	Beira, Mozambique	Nacala, Mozambique	Durban, South Africa	Dar es Salaam, Tanzania
Main transport mode	road	railway	road	road
Infrastructure condition	good/fair	poor	good	good/fair
Port reliability	medium	low	high	medium
Delay in the port	2 weeks	3 weeks or more	1 day	4 weeks
Transit time by road or train	2–3 days	unpredictable	1 week	
Main product for export	tobacco	sugar	nontraditional commodities (e.g., garments), tea, tobacco	limited
Distance	900 km	1,000 km	2,300 km	2,000 km

Source: World Bank 2009.

2000s, largely determined by stability issues in Côte d'Ivoire and the operational performance of different ports. Transit corridor competition in West Africa is illustrated by the market share commanded by each of Burkina Faso's four corridors (figure 3.1).

Figure 3.1   Market Shares of Corridors Serving Burkina Faso, 1991–2004

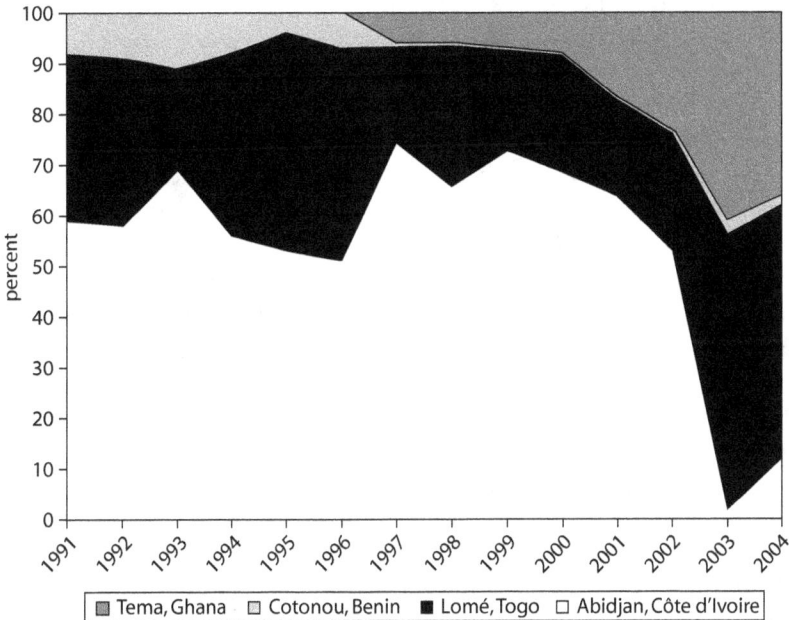

Legend: ▨ Tema, Ghana   ☐ Cotonou, Benin   ■ Lomé, Togo   ☐ Abidjan, Côte d'Ivoire

Source: World Bank 2007.

A Complex Political Economy: Private Sector and Service Delivery

Reducing the dependence of LLDCs obviously requires cooperation between neighbors and the development of partnerships among countries. However, this hardly new notion cannot be reduced to bilateral dialogue or bargaining power between two states; it happens in the context of the activities undertaken by the many actors in transit and destination countries. These public or private actors have different functions and respond to different incentives.

From the perspective of service delivery to the traders and the performance of corridor logistics, the bottlenecks summarized in chapter 2 indeed include activities that take place primarily in the country of transit, such as the following:

- Port activities, handling, customs control, other control, removal
- Trucking and logistics services market
- Customs brokerage at initiation or final clearance at border posts
- Implementation of customs regime and control to goods in transit

- Border controls
- Control en route.

The performance of these components of the corridor supply chain in terms of cost delays or reliability depends on the interaction between regulators and private agents. The multiplicity of factors of performance at each stage reflects the relative complexity of the corridor political economy. Public or private agents (table 3.1) have different functions, hence different incentives. Corridor performance is influenced by their practices and behaviors. Furthermore, private activities (trucking, forwarding, brokerage) are also regulated domestically or in implementation of treaties (for example, transit regimes). Hence, lack of capacity of public and private agents to actually implement their commercial, operational, or regulatory roles is a major performance bottleneck. From this perspective, the next two sections review the respective functions and incentives of the public agencies and private operators.

Public Sector Functions in the Transit Regime

The two cross-border institutional activities specific to the trade and transport corridor are the implementation of a transit regime for goods and the provision of policies and bilateral protocols applicable to cross-border logistics services, especially international trucking. Implementation is by government agencies in each country on the corridor. There are two primary government functions with regard to the corridor: controlling the flow of goods and facilitating the movement of vehicles to carry them.

Table 3.1   Public and Private Agents

Type of agent	Transit country	Destination country
Public	Customs	Customs
	Port authority	Other border control agencies
	Transport and road infrastructure	Transport and road infrastructure
Private (or operating on commercial basis)	Multimodal facility operator (port, railway)	Freight forwarder
	Freight forwarder	Broker
	Broker	Bank, insurance
	Bank, insurance	Trucker
	Trucker	Importer
	Exporter	Exporter

Source: Authors.

Customs has the primary responsibility for regulating the flow of goods and preserving fiscal interests. For goods transiting to another country, customs' purpose is to implement freedom of transit, while ensuring that the goods in transit are not being leaked into the transit country to evade duties for imports into that country.

Customs agencies at origins or destinations process the exports and imports and collect duties and taxes in similar ways in landlocked or coastal countries. Other border agencies, such as standards, health, veterinary, and agriculture, are also likely to participate in this clearance process, but not in transit. Customs also has the responsibility of regulating certain professions, such as brokers.

Transport agencies in both countries have the responsibility of organizing the service market with economic regulation of trucking companies and technical regulation of trucks (including axle loads). Cross-border transport agencies will be jointly responsible for implementing transport treaties and for activities such as permitting and licensing for international trucking on the corridor.

Infrastructure institutions governing road funding and maintenance, such as road fund agencies, focus primarily on cost recovery for the corridor infrastructure to ensure maintenance and continuity of service. These agencies may also be in charge of enforcement of load regulations, such as at weigh stations.

Hence, movement of goods and vehicles depends on quite a few procedures, controls, and authorizations, with substantial money at stake. Unfortunately, as Arvis et al. (2010) note, corridor performance is very vulnerable to corruption and rent-seeking activities, especially in the weak governance environment found in many corridors in the least developed regions. These governance deficits not only affect the performance of the corridor (chapters 4–6) but also encourage groups of agents that will be hostile to reforms addressing those shortcomings.

Private Services and Commercial Activities Support Trade

Movement of goods on corridors also depends on a wide array of support services. The operators of multimodal facilities, such as ports and railways, provide key services to the traders. Their incentive is to maximize turnover to recover their investment, at least if they are private or commercially managed. Except in the few ports that are very dependent on transit, such as Djibouti, Lomé, and Mombasa, there is little incentive to discriminate in favor of transit trade (for example, specific off-dock facilities) over the movement of goods for consumption in the transit country. Depending on the breakdown of imported and exported commodities, port or rail operators may be biased in favor of volume at the expense of small loads going to the LLDC. This is especially true for railways, which tend to favor slow, bulk business at the expense of unitized (container) cargo.

Importers have country-specific markets, which fall into two categories:

- Traditional trading networks, which tend to dominate the imports of food and consumer goods in developing countries, are small or large local family-owned wholesalers and retailers. Typically they are driven by price more than quality and look for savings in terms of transportation costs; they may also be less inclined to comply with regulations, pay duties, or enforce good business practices.
- Importers that are part of a global value chain are regional or international companies involved in production (for the regional market or exports to overseas) or distribution (for example, chains of supermarkets such as Shoprite supermarkets in southern and eastern Africa). This group is bound by corporate compliance standards and is more sensitive to quality of production and services.

The latter groups also have incentives to optimize sourcing and production at the subregional level, hence a strong interest in corridor facilitation. In 2009, one group of leading multinational manufacturers of consumer goods entered into a joint project with the World Bank to improve corridors in West Africa. Today, delays mean that goods should be imported instead of being produced in several complementary plants based in the regions and serving several countries.

Exporters are the group with the most interest in corridor performance, especially when they deal with value-added and time-sensitive commodities. Most LLDCs export bulk commodities that are not time-sensitive—for which price of transportation may capture a significant part of the margin, especially of the free on board price—compared to a would-be competitor in the transit countries. However, the few exporters of manufactured or time-sensitive goods are the ones most constrained by logistics performance and are willing to pay a premium for quality and reliability (see table 3.1).

Traders in transit countries in theory might not be adverse to the development of competing trade from their landlocked neighbors. In fact, there is no evidence of significant hostility of the private sector in transit countries to LLDC trade deveopment. To the contrary, transit countries' exporters are among the main beneficiaries of corridor facilitation. Investors from economically stronger and more advanced transit countries may see opportunities for business development in transit countries and could be a constituency for transit facilitation. For example, Thai investors are the main exporters from Lao PDR. Mango exports in Mali and Burkina Faso were started by an alliance of investors from Côte d'Ivoire. Agricultural products from different climate zones in LLDCs may complement the transit country's products. Even when there is overlap in the products exported by LLDCs and transit countries, traders may see advantages in having higher volumes from the same region and may increase the visibility of the "brand name" of the region, as was the case for coffee or tea from East Africa (produced in Kenya, Rwanda, and Uganda).

Trucking, with its **anticompetitive** practices, is potentially one of the most problematic areas in corridor performance (Arvis et al. 2010; Raballand and Teravaninthorn 2008). The depth and nature of demand, enforcement of regulation of entry, and compliance with technical regulations (especially axle-load regulations) have resulted in very different outcomes in different parts of the world, almost irrespective of the level of development. For example, countries in southern Africa can count on a strong trucking industry, with commercially managed companies operating on the transit corridors with the lowest prices on the continent (table 2.2). In contrast, the industry in West Africa is fragmented among a crowd of individual providers, has low service quality, and lacks enforcement of vehicle standards and load regulations, resulting in gross overloading of trucks. The cross-border transit business is heavily regulated by freight agencies, which guarantee minimums of business to individual truckers.

Other ancillary services to traders tend to be fragmented across borders to maximize revenues. For instance, brokers often have a vested interest in the multiplication of border procedures (see the two examples in chapter 2). In many countries, the profession employs former customs officials, which limits the prospects for reform. Banks in LLDCs have limited appetite for unification of bonds and guarantees for transit cargo as this would suppress a current source of revenue, because the primary bonds would be done entirely by their counterparts in the transit countries. Without a unified transit guarantee, the desired regional integration of transit regime as described in chapters 4 and 5 will not be possible.

Vicious Cycles Limit Quality Improvement

Since trade and transport corridors are sensitive to time and extend over several countries, often with poor governance and business practices, LLDC corridors are especially vulnerable to rent-seeking activities of the kind described earlier. In the political economy framework, the major challenge is that there may not be many agents interested in promoting good service delivery. Furthermore, the services market may not be large enough to naturally allow for both agents interested and those not interested in quality service to coexist, thus limiting creation of a niche for quality-driven supply and demand for logistics services. For instance, in West Africa, traditional trading networks contribute to sustaining an ecosystem of low compliance and poor quality of trucking services, preventing the emergence of the quality services that traders and producers integrated in the global supply chain need.

Countries become trapped in vicious cycles, where inefficient procedures and regulations sustain low service quality (for example, in transport and customs brokering), or even the conduct of informal activities that, in turn, perpetuate unfriendly regimes (figure 3.2) and transport

Figure 3.2   Vulnerability of the Supply Chain to Rent-seeking Activities

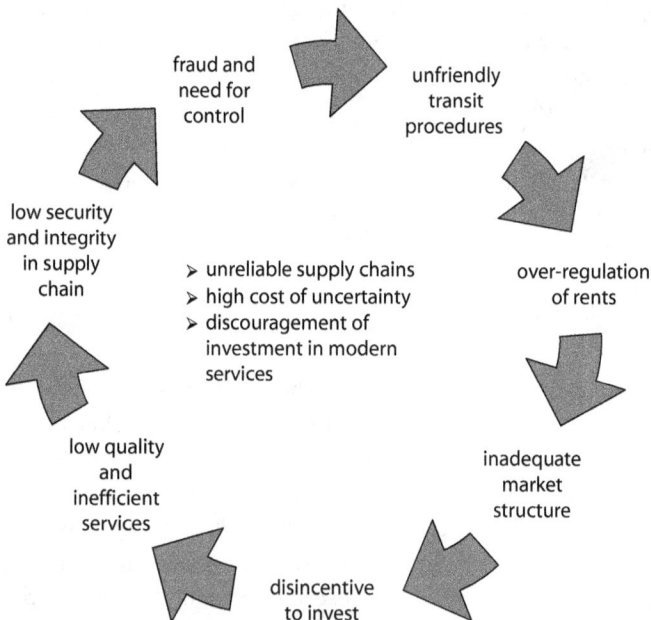

fraud and need for control

unfriendly transit procedures

over-regulation of rents

inadequate market structure

disincentive to invest

low quality and inefficient services

low security and integrity in supply chain

➤ unreliable supply chains
➤ high cost of uncertainty
➤ discouragement of investment in modern services

Source: Arvis et al. 2010.

regulation. Transport is trapped in equilibrium, where a transit system is optimized for certain types of traders and service operators and cannot evolve toward a system compatible with the requirements of global logistics networks, which could then link the country to international markets.

While changing the behavior of all the key agents in the vicious cycle at once is utopic, targeted changes are still possible. A "virtuous circle" can be facilitated by providing incentives for compliance and quality that will enable progressive emergence of compliant behaviors, quality services, trust, and friendly control and regulation.

Transit Corridors: A History of Public-Private Partnership with Mutual Benefits

Overland transit trade has a history as long as trade itself. Current concepts and procedures developed much before the industrial revolution. Over their long history, trade corridors, notably in Eurasia, have faced much the same challenges as those in developing countries today. Changes in speed or technology, despite their huge impact of trade costs, did not radically change the functions of agents, customs, or transport and brokerage companies, nor their relationships with each other, nor the risk of rent-seeking and misgovernance.

The main lesson from history is that an effective transit system is based on the search for mutual benefit between operators, traders, and regulators. Multilateralism in the 20th century may have shifted the attention to the concept of freedom of transit and the development of international law, but it did not alter the paradigm that transit systems should be based on public-private partnership between the transit operators and the country of transit.

Evolution of Cooperation, and Customs

Ancient empires (China, India, Persia, Rome) were confronted with the need to organize the movement of goods within and between provinces (De Laet 1949; Asakura 2005). For instance, in China, long-distance trade was not impeded by internal taxes; transit documents have been found that guarantee "safe conduct" for goods moving along waterways. From an Indian kingdom in the fifth century BC, there is evidence of internal transit systems from the border to the markets in the capital city, similar to modern systems, with bonds and seals for customs transit.

The Roman customs and transit systems have been extensively documented. The *portorium* was a tax collected *ad valorem* on trade from the border of the Roman-controlled territory and also between the provinces, which were separate customs and fiscal territories. Goods exempt from the portorium, such as supplies for the military legions, or in transit from one province to another were duly identified and sealed to avoid multiple taxation.

In comparison, intercontinental movement of goods in the form of caravan trade, such as on the Silk Road between China, India, and Italy, was extremely fragmented in the absence of transit logistics organized on an origin-to-destination basis. Goods moved in a series of buy-and-sell transactions through several (sometimes hostile) territories and trading fairs, resulting in rapidly accumulating costs. Pliny the Elder in his *Historia Naturalis* reports huge markups on the silk goods between India and Rome (a factor of 500!). With the fall of the empires, this type of pay-as-you-go caravan trade became dominant for almost a thousand years.

In the Middle Ages, transit-country rulers in trade corridors often adopted a friendly strategy toward traders with a view to sharing in the benefits of transit trade. The first transit fees (for example, in Persia) were probably levied in exchange for protection against bandits. The lord of the Saint-Gotthard Pass in Switzerland struck a deal with big traders (an early example of the concept of "authorized operators") to create a route between Italy and Northern Europe, which is still one of the most active today. After the fall of Constantinople, Turkey had commercial treaties with western countries to define the conditions of transit in Turkey along the Silk Road, including flat transit fees.

From the 13th century on, modern transit procedures emerged in support of the commercial revolution in Europe as goods began to move between distant buyers and sellers thanks to a new banking and trading system. Formal transit systems were needed to help the transport operators move the goods across a Europe that was highly fragmented territorially. Bonds, seals, and carnets were designed so that traders approved by the authorities could move, bypassing the payments and controls applicable to goods for local consumption.

Most of the current concepts and terminology come from that period and were formalized in the 1697 fiscal reform by Colbert, the reformist finance minister under France's king Louis XIV. Colbert tried to implement a vision of transit facilitation to develop trade and to reinforce the position of French ports as gateways not only to the French interior but also to independent states to the east. However, this vision could not be achieved because it required the unification of transit over a large territory to allow seamless movement of goods. This was prevented by opposition from the provincial tax collectors—who also were influential business people under the French *ancien regime*—who stood to gain from a fragmented transit and tax system.

Evolution of Freedom of Transit

This story is not very different from the problems found in many developing regions today. The industrial revolution did not much change the paradigm and the basic concept, but pushed for "freedom of transit." As railways and canals started to spread, most movement of goods switched to these means. These modes of transport made it relatively easy to secure shipments from interference en route. When the International Railway Union (*Union Internationale des Chemins de Fer*) was set up in the late 19th century, it promoted a framework for rail transit, probably the first example of a multilateral trade facilitation instrument. In parallel, Europe's colonial expansion spread unimpeded transit over large territories in Africa and Asia for the benefit of European traders and investors. But facilitation of transit across those territories often conflicted with the local trading culture and traditional practices, where local rulers engaged in contractual relationships with traders or protected caravan trade, which was a source of sometimes violent tensions.

The period after World War I saw a shift in paradigm, with freedom of transit instituted as a fundamental principle by the League of Nations (1921 Barcelona Convention on Freedom of Transit). This evolution reflected the concern among the promoters of the League of Nations that access to the sea for landlocked countries or areas was a major source of potential conflict, something unfortunately confirmed a few years later at the expense of Poland, Finland, and other Baltic states. However justified it may have been in the international context of the time, the new concept of absolute freedom was a departure from the historical contractual and partnership nature of transit systems and their implementation. For instance, in contrast to previous centuries, 20th-century international conventions banned transit duties as contradictory to freedom of transit.

After World War II, there were two contradictory developments. On the one hand, truly efficient multilateral systems were created in Europe in the reconstruction period, such as the TIR (*Transports Internationaux Routiers*) system, allowing door-to-door international trucking of goods, which has since become a primary long-distance transportation mode. On the other hand, when newly independent countries emerged from former colonial empires or were formed otherwise, they keenly felt the need for border controls and transit systems where there had been none. Hence, while trade corridors in Europe became more efficient, in the rest of the world, they became more fragmented. Ad hoc solutions governed by bilateral agreements were implemented between many independent developing states at a time when less attention was being paid to trade facilitation.

Today, LLDCs' right of access to the sea is protected by various international conventions, notably the 1958 Geneva Convention on the High Seas; the 1965 New York Convention on Transit Trade of Landlocked Countries; the United Nations Conference on the Law of the Sea (first treaty in 1958); and, most important, Article V of the GATT on "freedom of transit" (1949). Even now, lawyers still debate how this "right" can be reconciled with the national sovereignty of the transit country (Uprety 2005). GATT Article V and its jurisprudence instituted principles of nondiscrimination toward originators of transit cargo and banned transit duties as a cost-recovery mechanism. Moreover, freedom of transit does not mean "free of charge" or exclusive of cost-recovery mechanisms. Because access brings economic benefits for the LLDC at some cost to the transit country, the case can be made for the transit country's right to recoup the net cost it incurs from transit traffic.

How LLDC Traffic Benefits Transit Countries

If providing transit for an LLDC is in the transit country's own self-interest, that is, benefits its economy directly, it will have more incentive to facilitate traffic for the LLDC.

Direct Economic Benefits
The costs and benefits to transit countries of LLDC transit fall into five categories:

1. Direct revenues (including fuel taxes) from use of road transport services, railways, and other infrastructure, versus direct costs of wear and tear and capacity requirements attributable to the transit traffic
2. Indirect costs, such as traffic accidents and loss of cargo, air pollution and noise, and propagation of disease (notably those that are sexually transmitted by drivers)
3. Secondary effects because of agglomeration of freight volumes and economies of scale in transport infrastructure, such as increase in port or railroad throughputs
4. Creation of value-adding opportunities, such as assembly operations in export corridors (special economic zones)
5. Political benefits from playing a regional leadership role.

In the few case studies that have attempted a cost-benefit evaluation of LLDC trade, the overriding conclusion has been that the main benefit to the transit country is the business that LLDC trade generates for transport operators—trucking and railway companies—which in most cases are in the private sector. But governments have the option of capturing some part of that benefit through appropriate charges for use of the transport infrastructure.

Box 3.2 describes the main options for user charges for LLDCS, each with its advantages and drawbacks. A vignette scheme is arguably the

Box 3.2

Instruments for Charging Transit Traffic for Road Use

A **transit fee** is generally collected at the border by vehicles entering or transiting a country. Member countries of the United Nations Conference on Trade and Development may charge transit fees only if they are fair, reasonable, and nondiscriminatory, that is, related to the cost of providing the infrastructure service and without discrimination on the basis of nationality.

Road tolls specific to each highway and each journey can be collected from transit traffic at a toll barrier just inside the country. Revenue leakage may be a problem.

A **vignette** is a form of toll paid in advance: a permit giving the right to use a country's roads (motorways and expressways or the main transit corridors) once, a specified number of times, or an unlimited number of times within a defined period (a week, a month, or a year). In the 1990s, Switzerland became one of the first countries to introduce this payment instrument, which has now been adopted by several European countries. All users of these roads must pay; foreign vehicles purchase a vignette upon entry at the border. Rates vary depending on the vehicle's size or weight. Enforcement is by traffic police on the road, which may be problematic where such capacity is limited.

A **fuel tax** is paid by all trucks in transit, independent of the roads they use, unless high local fuel prices compel truck owners to carry with them all the fuel they will need, at least for short trips. Fuel taxes can be either a fixed charge per liter or a percentage of the pump price; in the latter case, revenues will rise or fall with the underlying price of oil.

Annual vehicle license fees can complement fuel taxes and offer the advantage that they can penalize trucks with the most damaging axle configurations. Since the fees are not payable by foreign trucks, they would mainly interest countries where domestic trucks perform much of the transit traffic (as in Tanzania and Thailand).

ideal instrument for cost recovery, but a conventional toll is easier to implement and enforce. Whether these taxes and fees are paid into the central treasury or earmarked to a road fund is immaterial to the estimate of national net benefits.

Taking Advantage of Empty Backhaul Capacity

LLDCs export mostly bulk products, for which rail is the most economical transport. In contrast, their imports are relatively high-value goods that are more suitable to be transferred by road—carried in containers or on trucks as "break bulk" instead of unitized cargo (containers). This flow pattern generates empty backhaul capacity on inbound rail and outbound road services. Liberalizing transport markets, in place of public intervention in freight allocation and contracting, may help take advantage of this excess capacity. It certainly is an argument for eliminating the *tour de role* systems of West Africa (see chapter 7). It may be useful to examine whether bilateral quotas for trip permits and narrowly defined operating permits impede the working of the market to take advantage of backhauls in achieving lower transport costs and tariffs.

Transit Fees for Transit Countries

International law allows transit countries to charge transit fees, but defines them narrowly. For the 153 World Trade Organization members, the internationally agreed upon definition of transit fees was stated in GATT Article V. It refers only to "demonstrable costs" incurred by the provider of a transit or border service, which must not discriminate among goods or vehicles by country of origin. The same principle also applies to international civil aviation law governing overflight fees paid by aircraft flying over but not landing in a territory. This narrow definition aims to prevent a coastal country from taking abusive advantage of its geographical position.

Landlocked Countries Aspire to a Transit Role

Transit offers a major opportunity for a number of inland countries. For example, Afghanistan sees itself as a key transit link between the warm water ports in Iran and Pakistan and the landlocked republics of Central Asia; Kazakhstan sees itself as part of a land link between Europe and China; Bolivia sees itself as a potential transit hub between the Atlantic and Pacific coasts; Nepal sees itself as the land link between the economic giants of China and India. Lao PDR aspires to be a transit country between China and Thailand—and has realized this goal by cooperating with these neighbors in funding a connecting highway that is now nearing completion.

However, the benefits these countries expect to gain may well be illusory. Transit traffic and its fees may help to finance the existing Afghan highway infrastructure. But a transit route between China and India through Nepal would require much higher capacity infrastructure than presently exists and thus necessitate a substantial additional investment. Each case involving construction of new road or rail routes over high and extensive mountain ranges is likely to be prohibitively expensive in competition with sea or lowland routes.

A more promising case is Kazakh Railways, as it has spare track capacity available and would therefore benefit from additional freight traffic. The benefits from allowing increased transit trucks through Kazakhstan will be limited, unless Kazakh trucks are able to get a significant share of the market. Raising transit fees any higher would be problematic, because Kazakhstan would be vulnerable to reciprocal fees on its own transit routes and because the costs would probably outweigh the gains. However, in all three cases—Afghanistan, Kazakhstan, and Nepal—the inland transit country may hope to gain political leverage, which could be used to improve the country's own transit position.

Both Pakistan and Iran seek major economic opportunities as transit countries by becoming the gateway to Central Asia. To do so would require an efficient transit system between the ports and the Central Asian republics that would allow vehicles to use transit routes with minimal delays en route. Transit traffic will necessarily cross through Afghanistan, which would play a pivotal role in providing access and should be able to improve substantially its own transit arrangements to Pakistan's ports as part of a wider regional transit solution. Similarly, Nepal may be able leverage its position as key link in an Indo-Sino transit route to convince India to streamline its own transit-transport to the ports. For Kazakhstan, developing an efficient land bridge between China and Europe, with streamlined procedures and operating agreements, not only could generate direct economic benefits but could also provide Kazakhstan itself with access to efficient land bridges to both China and Europe. In all these cases, the main advantages of becoming a transit country might have less to do with the direct benefits of providing transit—although some may possibly mistakenly perceive them as significant—and more to do with leveraging that transit access to upgrade or streamline the transit arrangements for its own trade.

Transit Systems: From Vicious to Virtuous Cycles

Chapter 2 listed the extra costs incurred by traffic en route to or from LLDCs and identified the main causes. Recognizing the nature and extent of these extra costs is an essential first step to seeking a solution. But taking action to reduce or eliminate them can be discouraging and difficult. LLDCs often find themselves struggling to break out of vicious cycles, also known as chicken-and-egg situations. Low-quality and inefficient services between the seaport and the LLDC destinations do not offer much security and integrity in supply chains, and widespread fraud creates a need for control. The result is overregulation, which leads to unfriendly transit procedures and encourages rent-seeking (informal payments) as the only viable way to conduct transit. These practices undermine the competitiveness of the market and discourage investment, leading back full circle to the low-quality services.

When the transit country fails to recoup infrastructure use costs, such as through a minimal fuel tax, or under-prices its rail services, it is likely to neglect to maintain the infrastructure or to fail to offer attractive services. This neglect then discourages transit traffic, giving the transit country even less reason to allocate resources to improve its transit facilities—another negative cause-and-effect cycle. Also discouraging to countries seeking transit routes is a prevailing corrupt culture in which transit traffic is subject to widespread informal payments.

Such vicious cycles are found in transport relations, for example, between Nepal and India and between Mongolia and China, where full offloading of goods from the trucks of the one country and reloading into the trucks of the other country is required at the border. Such highly inefficient transshipment is indicative of mistrust on both sides.

It is not uncommon for customs agents and truck drivers (or the owners of the cargo being transported) to regard each other as crooks and to behave accordingly. Customs tightens controls, keeping trucks waiting in line longer while conducting checks on every vehicle, and it may seek informal payments in exchange for overlooking "minor errors" in the truck's documentation. In response, shippers may feel justified in understating the value of their shipments and offering bribes to avoid long and unpredictable delays. Furthermore, these transit impediments encourage outright smuggling—evading the formal border crossings altogether. Afghanistan and Bolivia are two examples of countries where smuggling is believed to be widespread and relations between the trading community and customs agencies are traditionally highly adversarial.

Who is more to blame? Who needs to make the first move toward reform? Whatever the origin, the challenge is to find ways that can draw both parties away from the traditional mindset toward setting in motion a virtuous cycle, where constructive actions by one party encourage the other to comply more closely with the rule of law and, thereby, consolidate a cooperative rather than combative behavior pattern.

Public voice can play an important role. If momentum for change is to be created and sustained, stakeholders need to be mobilized who have the most to gain from reforms that make trading systems more efficient and less corrupt. At an early stage, governance mechanisms need to be identified that will protect their interests. Those with most at stake are the import and export community and transport companies operating internationally. Along with other civil society bodies, they need to promote and encourage champions for change.

Changing the Incentives for Cooperation and Mutual Benefit

Game theory offers some basic tenets that are highly relevant to this problem. The classic example is the prisoner's dilemma in which two prisoners would be able to minimize their sentences if they both told the same alibi. But if neither knows what the other will say, each prisoner's options will lead him to betray the other, with the result that they both lose. This is a "win-win" game, in the sense that both can gain if they coordinate their actions, compared to the outcome if they act independently. Win-win games require that the parties have information about what the other party intends to do and have mutual trust that they will stick to the agreed plan.

The same logic applies to trading relationships. For instance, customs endeavors to enter in a trust-building relationship with compliant operators in which facilitation of trade will be the counterpart of some verifiable commitment to compliance. The resulting trade expansion and increased revenue will be a win-win situation. This concept, called "authorized operator" by the World Customs Organization, will be introduced in chapter 5.

Unfortunately, the political economy of corridors is too complex for the win-win paradigm to apply to all agents. It is not likely that the incentives of all agents can be aligned. For instance, not all traders or service providers would be able to participate in cooperative schemes that would require and provide compliance standards and regulation of entry. Not all traders, especially small-scale importers or traditional networks, might be interested in the quality-based regulations that would be of interest to exporter and logistics companies that were part of global supply chains. It is impossible to change the market structure of trucking services overnight. Few LLDC governments will take the risk of antagonizing—by breaking a freight allocation system or opening it to foreigners—a business group so essential to the country as the trucking companies and drivers.

Hence, feasible implementation strategies of corridor improvement are extremely constrained. On the one hand, a reform package should change the paradigm of corridor organization and introduce quality-based regulation of incentives. On the other hand, it should offer options to those numerous operators who are unlikely to meet the requirements of the reformed freight and transit system. Typically, the transition in market for services may involve some form of dual market structure, with a modern sector open to international competition and meeting the standards of a fast-track system, while the old procedures and control may remain available for the rest. Such duality is typically the default solution for trucking reform (for example, recent reforms for new European Union members or in Turkey); it may be complemented with incentives for regrouping of operators from the "old" sector (for example, fiscal incentives for trucking cooperatives or capacity building programs to improve the managerial skills of small trucking companies). Differentiated approaches rewarding compliant operators have also made way in customs procedures, including those for transit (see chapter 5).

However, reform strategies based on duality and differentiated treatment may not be easily acceptable in developing countries' corridors, as they are a clear departure from the traditional regulation of the services operating on trade corridors. Most corridor and bilateral treaties go back to the 1970s to early 1980s, designed at a time of state-led development and intervention in transport that preceded deregulation. These policies were marked by the notion of private market failure in the freight business and the need for the government to intervene in the freight market. Governments were also willing to maximize employment opportunities, notwithstanding competitiveness objectives. Hence, many of the current market transit systems, all three or four decades old, are based on very egalitarian, and often labor-intensive, organization of trucking and brokerage services, with limited entry requirements and freight allocation systems that favor small independent operators, independently of the quality of service. Examples include the queuing arrangements for truckers or the monopolies given to brokers to lodge customs declarations at borders. Although Organisation for Economic Co-operation and Development countries deregulated market transit in the 1980s, such deregulation of freight markets is still lagging in several subregions, notably in Western and Central Africa and the Middle East and Central Asia regions, where it is most problematic, and in Latin America and Southern Africa, where it is less so but still the norm.

Note

1. Nepal and Bhutan must transit through India. The Central African Republic river corridor is not always usable, and transit must go through Cameroon as an alternative. Tajikistan depends primarily on Uzbekistan, itself a double-landlocked country; the alternative route goes through Afghanistan and Iran.

References

Arvis, J.-F., G. Raballand, and J.-F. Markan. 2010. *The Cost of Being Landlocked.* Washington, DC: World Bank.

Asakura, Hironori. 2005. *World History of the Customs and Tarriffs.* Brussels: World Customs Organization.

De Laet, Siegfried J. 1949. *Portorium Etude sur l'organisation douanière chez les romains, surtout à l'époque du Haut-Empire.* Brugge: De Tempel.

Fahrer, Chuck, and Martin Ira Glassner. 2003. *Political Geography,* 3rd ed. New York: Wiley.

Gallup, John Luke, Jeffrey D. Sachs, and Andrew D. Mellinger. 1998. "Geography and Economic Development." NBER Working Paper W6849, National Bureau of Economic Research, Cambridge, MA.

Raballand, Gaël, and Supee Teravaninthorn. 2008. "Transport Prices and Costs in Africa: A Review of the Main International Corridors." Directions in Development, Washington, DC: World Bank.

Uprety, Kishor. 2005. *The Transit Regime for Landlocked States: International Law And Development Perspectives.* Washington, DC: World Bank.

World Bank. 2007. "Burkina Faso—The Challenge of Export Diversification for a Landlocked Country: Diagnostic Trade Integration Study for the Integrated Framework Program." World Bank Foreign Trade, FDI, and Capital Flows Study 43134, World Bank, Washington, DC.

———. 2009. "Malawi Country Economic Memorandum 2009: Seizing Opportunities for Growth Through Regional Integration and Trade." Publication 47969, World Bank, Washington, DC.

———. 2010. *World Development Report 2010: Development and Climate Change.* Washington, DC: World Bank.

CHAPTER 4

Moving Goods on Corridors: Transit Regimes

Transit trade for developing countries has gained new recognition and is now a major topic in global forums and a new subject of regional initiatives. During the past 50 years, a number of trade, transportation, and transit agreements have been put in place around the world as instruments for economic development. However, there has been much less focus on implementing these plans, especially the mechanisms that make transit services possible over long distances and across several borders.

The heart of the transit system is the transit regime, which is the set of rules and regulations that govern the movement of goods from their origin in the transit country (often a seaport) to their destination (such as a clearance center in the destination country). The efficiency of the corridor supply chain depends on its design and above all its implementation. The aim of this chapter is to clarify the conceptual framework for transit regimes and to examine why they do or do not work. Three main arguments are made here. The first is that at the heart of a functioning tran-

Chapters 4 and 5 are based on the authors' original research with contributions from Pilar Kent and Gerard Luyet. An abridged version (Arvis 2011) was included in the *Border Management Handbook* as chapter 17, "Transit Regimes." The content here is an overhaul of the corresponding chapter in the *Customs Modernization Handbook* (De Wulf and Sokol 2005).

sit regime is a public-private partnership, a relationship, contractual in some cases, between competent logistics operators and the authorities of the transit country. The second argument is that the principles of working transit procedures are essentially universal and low-tech, the fruit of millennia of evolution, and they vary depending on the degree of regional integration not only of the agreements but also of their implementation. The third argument is that, while managing transit is part of each country's sovereignty and responsibility, there are huge gains to be had from integrating transit systems within a region.

This chapter presents the foundation and workings of a transit regime, including the very efficient systems developed in Europe after World War II, which are the de facto benchmarks for transit regimes. The last section of the chapter summarizes the contribution of global standards. The next chapter will look at implementation challenges and ways to remedy what seems to be a widespread failure to implement trade-friendly transit regimes in developing regions.

Role of the Transit Regime

The term "transit regime" specifically refers to a set of procedures under which goods are transported through countries from one customs operation to another without payment of duties, domestic consumption taxes, or other charges normally due on imports and exports. These procedures were instituted to prevent goods intended for transit from "leaking" into the domestic market, thus protecting transit countries from loss of fiscal revenue. Transit procedures should be simple, transparent, and efficient to avoid unnecessary delays and extra costs. A poor transit regime is a major obstacle to trade.

Moving goods through a customs territory without payment of duty and taxes in the countries of departure and transit is in accordance with the "destination principle" of taxation. This principle states that indirect taxes should only be levied in the country of consumption. Such legislation should be included in the customs code of the country of transit. In its absence, transit can be regulated by an agreement between customs agencies and the different parties involved in the transit operation.

It is useful to distinguish between *international* and *national* transit. International transit refers to crossing one or more national borders. National transit occurs when goods, having entered the country of destination, are transferred from the point of entry into the country within the national borders to a location where they clear customs (for example, a dry port or inland container depot). These two types of transit can be combined; in fact, it is standard practice for many land-locked developing countries (figure 4.1). Imported goods arriving at national borders from transit countries are rarely cleared at the border, but instead are shipped under national transit to a major city near the intended destination.

The Basics of Transit

A transit regime is, in essence, a mechanism by which operators are authorized for transit when they meet a set of criteria and provide financial guarantees. In exchange, customs allows unimpeded transit for trucks or trains. The key requirements of a well-functioning transit system, developed over centuries and universal, are as follows:

- Customs should make sure the cargo is secure by sealing modified vehicles (closed trailers or containers).
- The principal of the transit operation—the owner of the goods, or, more often, his agent (freight forwarder or trucker)—should deposit a guarantee (or a bond) covering the value of taxes and duties that would be due in the country of transit.
- Customs should properly manage the information on goods in transit and, specifically, should reconcile information on the goods' entries and exits from the customs territory (or during clearance in the case of national transit). This is necessary to identify violations and potential leakages, as well as to release bonds.

The typical transit procedure is implemented as follows (see figure 4.1):

- At the initiation of transit (at the entry post), customs issues the transit manifest and affixes the seals against a guarantee provided by the principal.
- At the termination of transit (at exit post or an inland clearance destination), customs checks the seals and manifest and discharges the guarantee after reconciling information on entries into and exits from the customs territory (inbound and outbound manifest information).
- When the cargo is high risk—or when not enough security is offered by the seals and the guarantee—goods may move in convoys guarded by customs officers.
- It is common and acceptable practice to impose (reasonable) specified routes and a maximum transit time.

Figure 4.1 The Transit Regime: International and National Transits and Final Clearance

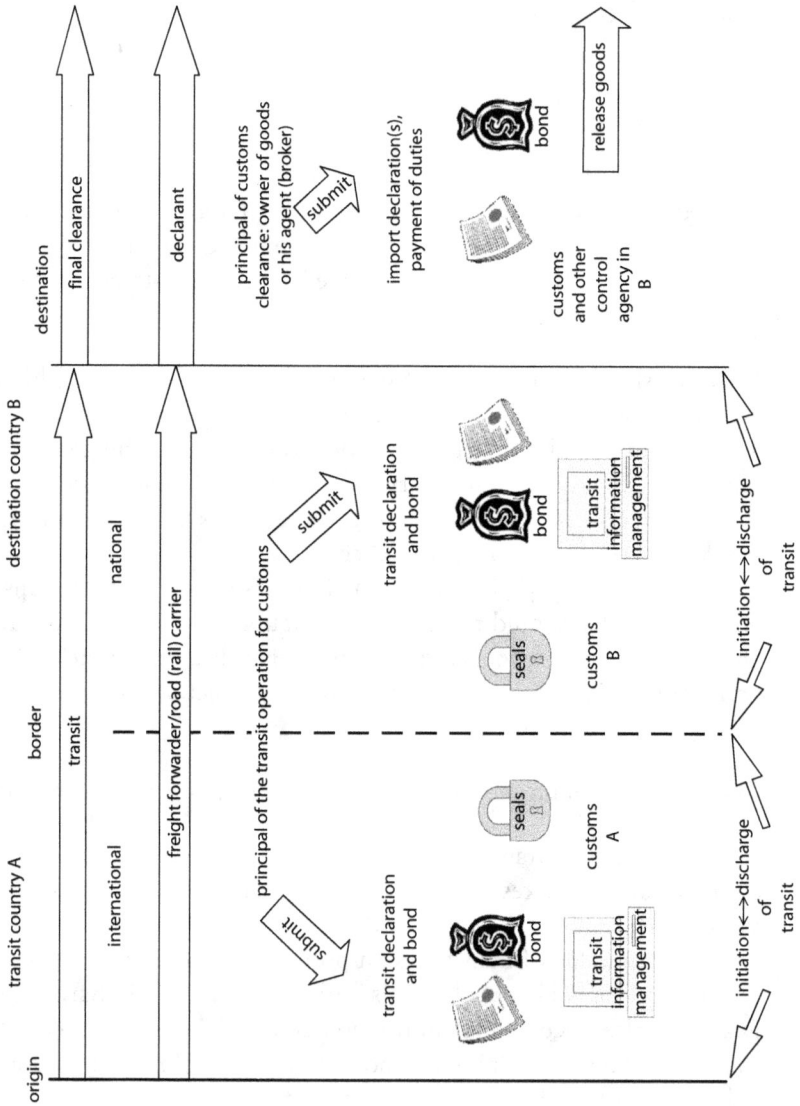

Source: Authors.

A Public-Private Partnership

Transit essentially relies on a public-private partnership: the private sector provides financial guarantees and applies operational procedures that make transit trade possible, and in return it obtains freedom of transit under minimal supervision. This dynamic has the following implications:

- Operating transit should not be perceived as a right, but rather a privilege given to authorized operators on the basis of professional competence and compliance (criteria include proven existence as representative of the transport sector, proven financial standing, absence of serious or repeated offences against customs or tax legislation, and proven staff member knowledge in the proper application of the Transports Internationaux Routiers (TIR, International Road Transport) Convention.
- Transit should be based on trust between the vehicle operators and the public agencies.
- In applying controls, customs may differentiate depending on the quality of the operators and their vehicles, the sensitivity of the goods carried, or both.

It may be hard for small-scale trucking firms to meet the requirements of the transit regime, but in practice, few small firms operate in cross-border markets anyway. Operating transit over relatively long distances (for example, beyond a thousand kilometers) can be done only by firms with a sizeable network of affiliates, agents, and maintenance facilities.

Transit by Rail

When available, transit by rail can offer the advantage of simpler customs procedures. Rail transit is widely used in central Asia and is being rejuvenated in West Africa and between the United States and Mexico. However, a lack of commercial orientation among many railways, exacerbated by poor coordination between the railways of one country and the next, often prevents this potential from being realized. That said, one of the main reasons for the growth of rail transit is the simplicity of the rail transit regime.

The advantage that railways offer for transit traffic is that, in almost all circumstances, governments exempt them from the obligation to provide a transit guarantee. As large, well-known enterprises with continuing business, they are deemed a low risk. Customs agencies are confident that they can have legal recourse to the railway in the event of "leakage." Furthermore, most rail cars used for high-value goods are closed and sealable.

Key Concepts and Practices in Transit

Key to a discussion of transit regimes are the following concepts:

- Seals
- Documentation flow
- Principal and guarantor
- Guarantees.

Seals

World Customs Organization (WCO) "International Convention on the Simplification and Harmonisation of Customs Procedures" states that there should be a physically secure mechanism so that goods present at the start of the transit operation will leave the transit country in the same quantity, form, and status. The easiest and best way for customs to guarantee this is by sealing the truck[1] to ensure that goods cannot be removed from or added to the loading space of the truck without either breaking this seal or leaving visible marks on the loading space. Seals and trucks approved for use in the transit operation therefore must conform to well-specified criteria that ensure their effective and secure operation (see box 4.1). New transport seals are being studied; prototypes already in use include a microchip that is activated when broken and transmits a signal picked up by satellite, which then sends information to the organization

---

Box 4.1

General Requirements With Respect to Seals

The seals and fastening shall

- Be strong and durable.
- Be capable of being affixed easily and quickly.
- Be capable of being readily checked and identified.
- Not permit removal or undoing without breaking or tampering without leaving traces.
- Not permit use more than once, except seals intended for multiple use (e.g. electronic seals).
- Be made as difficult as possible to copy or counterfeit.

Source: WCO 1999, Annex E.1.

or principal of the sealed container (including information on its location). Although the prices of such automated seals are high at present, they are expected to fall in the coming years.

Documentation Flow

To control the start and completion of a transit procedure, a system is needed for monitoring the movement of goods. This system could be based on paper documentation shipped from the customs post at the exit from the transit country—after validation of the valid transit transaction—and issued by the customs post that controls the origin of the transit shipment. Increasingly, however, such documents are sent electronically. When the copies of the documents match, the transit operation is completed and the guarantee is released. When they do not match, the transit procedure is not completed satisfactorily, and import duties, taxes, and other charges are increased by a stipulated fine.

Principal and Guarantor

The *principal* is the owner of the goods—or more often, the owner's representative (such as the carrier). The principal initiates the transit procedure and is responsible for following that procedure—providing guarantees and the necessary documentation. To act as the principal (or agent), companies must be registered, obtain a guarantee to cover the transit operations, use a transit customs document and bill of lading, present the goods and declaration at the relevant customs offices (of departure, transit, and destination), and accept responsibility for the sealing of the transit vehicle.

A *guarantor* is a private or legal person who undertakes to pay jointly and separately with the debtor (in most cases, the principal) the duties and taxes that will be due if a transit document is not discharged properly. A guarantor may be an individual, firm, or other body eligible to contract as a legal third person, usually a bank or insurance company. Guarantors must be authorized by customs, which, as a rule, publishes a list of financial institutes authorized to act as guarantors.

Guarantees

The guarantees acceptable by customs are defined by the regulations of the transit country. Within the open options of financial securities, the choice is the exclusive responsibility of the principal. A guarantee can be provided as a bond by a bank or as a form of insurance by a guarantor, who can be reinsured internationally by well-known and reliable insurance companies (this is the case with the TIR). Nonguarantee forms of security, such as deposits, may still be in place in some transit countries, although they cannot be recommended. At times the principal is also the guarantor—a common practice for rail transport, which grants customs access to more direct recourse mechanisms.

There are two categories of transit guarantee:

- An individual guarantee covers only a single transit operation effected by the principal concerned, covering the full amount of duties, taxes, and other charges for which the goods are liable.
- A comprehensive guarantee covers several transit operations up to a given reference amount, set to equal the total amount of duties and other charges that may be incurred for goods under the principal's transit operations over a period of at least one week.

In general, the calculation of a transit guarantee is based on the highest rates of duties and other charges applicable to the goods, and it depends on the customs classification of the goods. The amount covered by the comprehensive guarantee is 100 percent of the reference amount. If the principal complies with a certain criterion of reliability, then the amount of the guarantee to be specified to the guarantors may be reduced by customs to 50 percent or 30 percent of the reference amount. For high-risk goods, customs can be allowed to calculate the guarantee at a percentage related to the risk of nonclearance.

An international transit regime such as the TIR allows for further savings. For individual guarantees, many countries avoid potentially complex valuation procedures by offering vouchers based on ranges for the value of goods that transit operators carry. Although this system may cost more on average, it is much simpler at initiation. The TIR guarantees attached to the TIR carnet are effectively vouchers. (The costs of guarantees are discussed later in this chapter.)

Transit and Clearance at Destination: Related But Distinct Procedures

The procedure called "transit" is a transport operation under customs control that makes possible a delayed clearance in another country or location. There are essential conceptual and operational differences between transiting goods through the territory of the transit country and their final clearance in their country of destination. These differences are sometimes not recognized, particularly by government decision makers, and as a result, the design and implementation of transit systems in developing countries often do not incorporate good practice. These differences include the following:

- The agent for a transit operation is the carrier or the freight forwarder, not the owner of the goods. The agent furnishes the guarantee and lodges the transit declaration with customs. This agent is usually, but not always, different from the declarant at the final declaration.
- The transit declaration is a simplified document, akin to a bill of lading or a manifest. The transit declaration and final declaration are separate documents serving separate purposes. For instance, a transit manifest might not carry information about the harmonized system (HS) classification of the cargo.[2] Customs does not need to value the goods for each vessel precisely—it needs only to be sure that a proper guarantee is issued by the transit operator for all its goods currently in transit.
- One of the primary responsibilities of customs is to properly account for transit declarations created at the entry point and terminated at the exit point.
- For transit traffic, the due diligence expected of customs is limited to affixing or checking the seals and to verifying the guarantee instrument. As a general rule, no inspection of the goods is required. Other border agencies, such as standards or quarantine, are not party to transit operations.
- The transit should be terminated at its destination before clearance takes place. Typically, another operator will be the principal of the clearance procedure with regard to customs at the destination.
- The transit declaration relates to the container or trailer, which, between origin and destination, may be hauled by various vehicles (for example, a change of truck cab or even multimodal transport, such as by ship or rail, and then road).

Regionally Integrated Transit and Carnet Systems

Authorities in each customs territory along a trade corridor are ultimately responsible for transit in that territory, and they can set their own rules. Legally, the chain is a sequence of independent transit procedures. However, large gains are possible with cross-border cooperation and with the creation of a framework to integrate transit across territories into a single seamless procedure. A key element of the framework is a single document, commonly known by the French term, "carnet," that accompanies the shipment along the transit chain and allows officials to verify the shipment's compliance with the transit regime.

The carnet transit regime or regional single-procedure regime must include the following ingredients to ensure cross border comparability and an effective chaining of transit procedures in each country:

- Harmonized documentation
- Common standards for transit operators
- Common enforcement standards
- A regionally integrated system to ensure interoperability in bonds across countries and consistency in manifest reconciliation (to discharge or call guarantees consistently, customs in country B should be able to call a bond issued by a guarantor in country A).

The most difficult element in a carnet transit regime is regional integration. The only fully developed regional systems to date are the TIR and the European common transit system. Each represents the most logical solution to the bond and manifest problem, but at a different degree of regional integration. The many attempts to copy the TIR and the European common transit system in developing regions have not succeeded.

The TIR Principles
The international transit regime initially known in French as *Transports Internationaux Routiers* (International Road Transport) is now referred to in documentation and legal texts only as TIR. The "Customs Convention on the International Transport of Goods under Cover of TIR Carnets," or TIR Convention (UNECE 2005, section 2, pp. 36–239)—adopted in 1960 and revised in 1975—is not only one of the most successful of the international transport conventions but also the only existing global transit regime (though it is still Eurocentric). So far the TIR Convention has 68 parties, primarily in Europe, Central Asia, the Middle East, and North Africa. It has not yet been enacted in the Americas or East Asia, where TIR membership is spotty. Sub-Saharan Africa has some signatories to the convention.

The TIR system is widely seen as the "best practice" that sets the standard in this domain and should serve as a model for any future regional transit frameworks. Many developing countries, therefore, either want to join the TIR system or design regional equivalents that replicate the factors that make it work.

The TIR Convention allows the temporary suspension of customs duties, excise duties, and value-added taxes payable on goods originating from or destined for a third country while being transported across the territory of a designated customs zone. Such suspension remains in place until either the goods exit the customs territory concerned or are transferred to an alternative customs regime, or until the duties and taxes are paid and the goods enter free circulation.

The TIR specifies five main requirements:

- **Secure vehicles:** The goods are to be transported in containers or compartments of road vehicles constructed with no access to the interior—such that that the vehicle's load can be "sealed," preventing its contents from being extracted without breaking the seal or allowing goods to be removed or added during the transit procedure—so that any tampering will be clearly visible.
- **International guarantee valid throughout the journey:** Wherever the transport operator cannot (or does not wish to) pay the customs duties and taxes due, this system ensures that the customs duties and taxes at risk are covered by the national guarantee system of the operator.
- **National associations of transport operators:** National associations control their members' access to the TIR regime, issue the appropriate documents, and manage the national guarantee system.
- **TIR carnets:** This is the standard international customs document accepted and recognized by all signatories of the TIR Convention.
- **International and mutual recognition of customs control measures:** The countries of transit and destination accept control measures taken in the country of departure.

In essence, TIR operations can be carried out in participating countries by a truck operator who is a member of a national association, with the association's network acting as guarantor. Both the national association and the body that issues the carnets—the International Road Transport Union (IRU)—are private, and in this sense, the TIR system embodies the concept of a "win-win" working partnership between public and private entities.

In most cases, the association represents the transporters and is the national international transporters' union. It guarantees payment within that country of any duties and taxes that may become due in the event of any irregularity occurring in the course of the TIR transport operation. The national guarantee association is not a financial organization;

therefore, its obligations are usually backed by insurance policies provided by the market. The IRU arranges for a large international insurance company to provide a guarantee of last resort.

The TIR system has been a success. The number of TIR carnets issued rose from 3,000 in 1952 to 3.1 million in 2007. The main reason for its success is that all parties involved (customs, other legal bodies, transport operators, and insurance companies) recognize that the system saves both time and money because of its efficiency and reliability. The TIR Convention is simple, flexible, and cost-reducing, and it ensures the payment of customs duties and taxes that are due with the international transport of goods. Furthermore, it is constantly being updated according to the latest developments, mainly in stopping fraud and smuggling.

Types and Functions of TIR Carnets

There are three types of TIR carnets, depending on how many countries are to be crossed, described as follows:

1. The regular carnet, which provides coverage for tax and duty up to US$50,000 (€65,000).
2. The multimodal carnet, introduced in 1987, which specifically caters to the needs of regional and intercontinental multimodal transport; it contains an additional sheet identifying the people who make up the transport chain.
3. The tobacco and alcohol carnet, which provides coverage up to US$200,000, became an integral part of the TIR Convention in 1994.

To qualify, each trucking firm (or other transporter) needs to be a member of the national guarantee association, which includes the obligation to meet all requirements set out in the TIR Convention. For each TIR operation (see figure 4.2), the truckers use the carnet at each border as a transit declaration and a proof of guarantee. The operator returns each used TIR carnet after completion of the TIR transport. In case of fraud, it will repay any amount of duties, taxes, and other charges on demand by the national guarantee association. The TIR system is only applicable to containers or road vehicles with load compartments to which there is no interior access after a customs seal has secured it.

At present the TIR carnet is still a paper document. However, steps are being taken to make it electronic. The IRU has developed an Internet-based application allowing TIR carnet holders to electronically send their

Figure 4.2 The TIR Operation: Sequence of Procedures

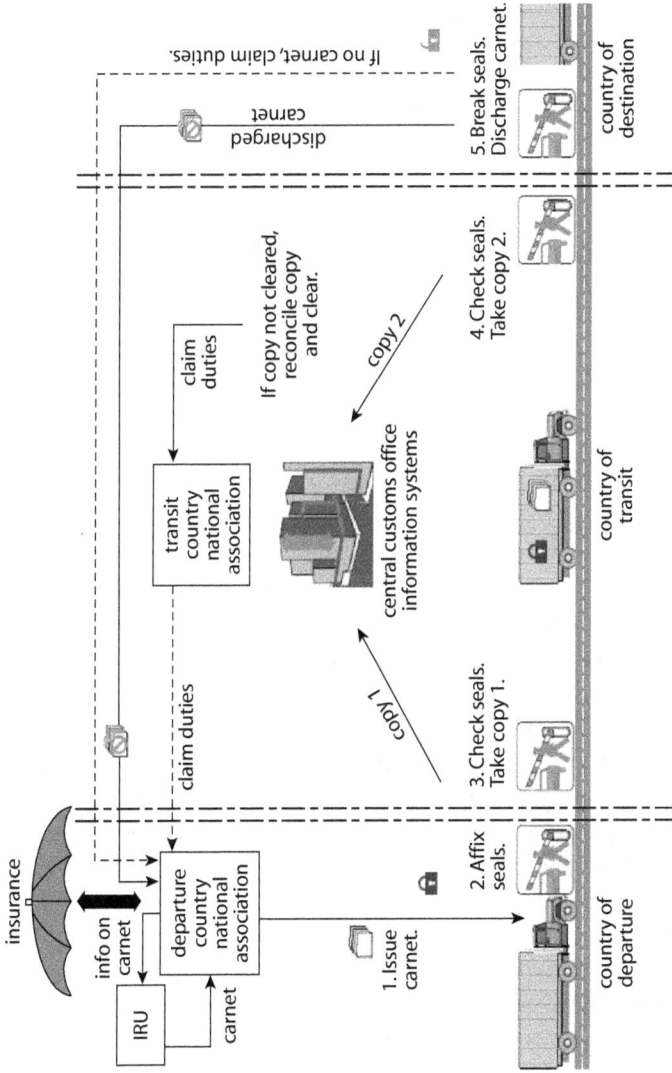

insurance

info on carnet

IRU

departure country national association

carnet

1. Issue carnet.

2. Affix seals.

country of departure

claim duties

claim duties

transit country national association

central customs office information systems

copy 1

copy 2

3. Check seals. Take copy 1.

country of transit

4. Check seals. Take copy 2.

If copy not cleared, reconcile copy and clear.

If no carnet, claim duties.

discharged carnet

5. Break seals. Discharge carnet.

country of destination

Source: Arvis 2005.

carnet information to the relevant border control agencies before they arrive at the offices of departure or entry. In early 2009, this software was being tried out in several central European countries.

Some regional initiatives to join the TIR system have so far failed because the trucking firms in a given country have been unable or unwilling to meet the entry conditions set by the IRU. The IRU carnet system is a private monopoly that sets the price for entry into the system— what it costs the operators and their nation associations to satisfy the professional and financial standards. It also sets the price for each transit operation through the wholesale price of the carnet from the IRU to the national guarantee association. The latter adds a markup to cover its own costs in setting the retail price of the carnet to the individual transport operator. As with any monopoly, there is a potential for abuse. Governments should therefore exercise regulatory oversight at national level over their respective national guarantee association, just as the United Nations Economic Commission for Europe, the international body charged with overseeing implementation of the TIR Convention, should exercise oversight over the IRU.

In short, the TIR system offers a "top of the line" service by virtue of its potentially global coverage and large risk pool, but at a price that some transport communities in developing countries are reluctant or unable to pay. Furthermore, the TIR system has also been criticized for its apparent centralization under a Geneva-based organization. Because of this tension over the cost of entry into the system, some regional initiatives—such as the Greater Mekong Subregion Agreement for Facilitation of Cross-Border Transport of Goods and People in Asia and the Transit Routier Inter État in West Africa—have tried, usually in vain, to replicate the key working features of TIR, but under regional rather than global frameworks. These attempts and the reasons they failed are covered in chapter 5.

The European Common Transit System

European common transit system is the term used here for the European Community and Common transit systems between the 27 EU member states and other countries: Common transit applies to the movement of goods between EU members and the four European Free Trade Association countries (Norway, Iceland, Switzerland, and Liechtenstein), and Community transit applies to trade between European Union (EU) members and third countries, under essentially the same rules. The transit declaration manifest is known as T form. Imports are subject to duty in the destination country in accordance with the EU's common external tariff and to value-added tax in accordance with national tax rates. The European common transit system has been recently automatized in all member countries and is also known as the New Computerized Transit System.

Guarantees can be of three kinds: a cash deposit, guarantee by a guarantor (who vouches for the trader), or a guarantee voucher (a multiple of the standard €7,000) valid for up to one year. For a regular procedure, the guarantee must apply specifically to an individual trip. Authorized transporters (and other principals) may present comprehensive guarantees that are valid for multiple trips and longer periods, but covering only the total duty expected to be at risk in an average week—the so-called reference amount. The coverage of the comprehensive guarantee or guarantees can be less than 100 percent of the reference amount, and it can even be waived if the principal meets conditions that imply low risk.

The European common transit system is a streamlined evolution of a regional carnet system. It is now fully computerized, it does not require the soft infrastructure of the TIR (the IRU and national associations), and it allows competition for guarantees. There is also less intermediation by brokers. In essence it is like a national transit system, but expanded into an economically integrated region. However, the European common transit system is more demanding than the TIR, and its preconditions are less easily met.

The TIR was designed to help connect national transit systems without the preconditions of harmonization and integration. In contrast, the European common transit system requires a high degree of customs and financial integration—and trust—within the region where it is implemented (see figure 4.3). The most binding requirement is that a bank in one country must be willing to routinely issue bonds that another country's customs can confidently call. That requires a high degree of integration—yet it may be possible within small, or very homogeneous, groups of developing countries. The same standards should be applied to authorized operators. Finally, common transit should be backed by harmonized transport policies.

Bonds are applied for in the first country (A) with a guarantor in that country. Customs in the next country (B) can call the guarantee (depicted as 1 in the TIR), through the national guarantee association and the clearing mechanisms between national associations set up by the IRU. Instead, in the Common transit (depicted as 2), customs in country B can call the

Figure 4.3 Conceptual Difference of Bond Management between TIR and European Common Transit

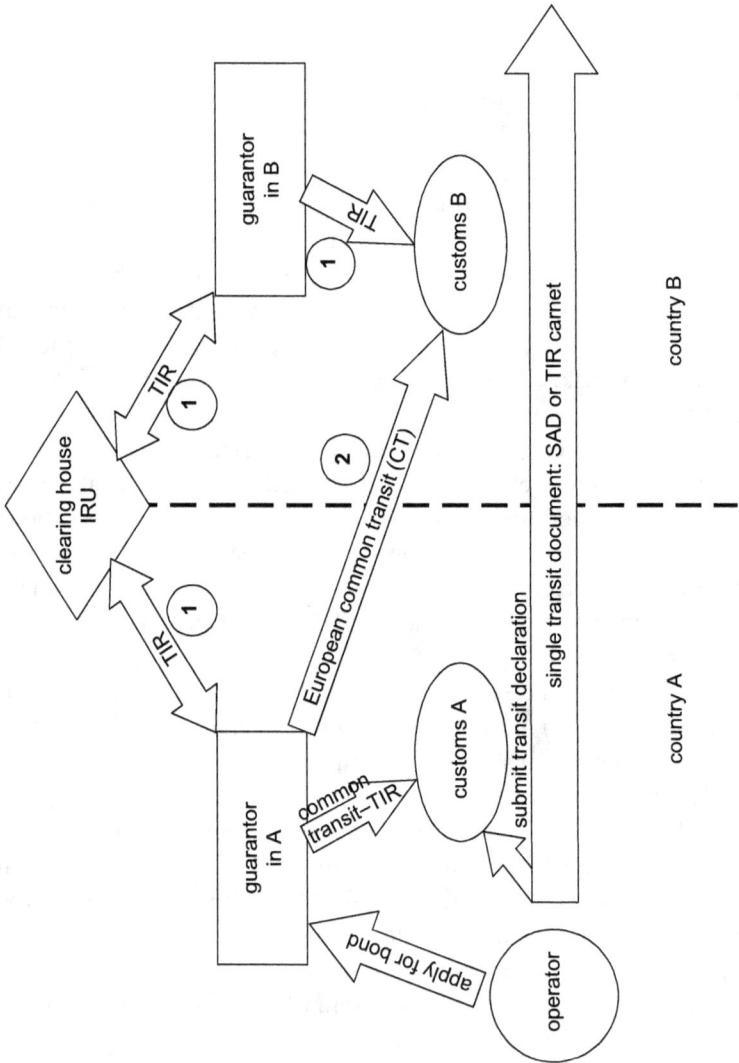

Source: Authors.

guarantee directly from the guarantor in the first country (a commercial bank or an insurance company).

Global Standards and International Legal Agreements Relevant to Transit

Over the years, transit provisions have been codified by various international conventions. United Nations Economic and Social Commission for Asia and the Pacific (UNESCAP) identifies seven important agreements related to transit (box 4.2). The legal agreements most directly applicable to the transit regime are the following: (1) General Agreement on Tariffs and Trade (GATT), which includes agreements on transit; (2) 1999 WCO Revised Kyoto Convention (International Convention on the Simplification and Harmonisation of Customs Procedures); and (3) 1982 International Convention on the Harmonization of Frontier Controls of Goods (sometimes called the Geneva Convention; UNECE Inland Transport Committee 1982). These conventions set broad objectives and core principles underlying the notion of freedom of transit (Grosdidier de Matons 2004). Key principles derived from these international instruments are summarized in table 4.1.

Article V of the GATT specifies that "there shall be freedom of transit through the territory of each Contracting Party, via the routes most convenient for international transit, for traffic in transit to or from the territory of other Contracting Parties." Further, it affirms that ". . . except in cases of failure to comply with applicable customs laws and regulations, such traffic coming from or going to the territory of other Contracting Parties shall not be subject to any unnecessary delays or restrictions and shall be exempt from customs duties and from all transit duties or other charges imposed in respect of transit, except charges for transportation or those commensurate with administrative expenses entailed by transit or with the cost of services" (Grosdidier de Matons 2004, p. 16).

The Kyoto Convention came into force in 1974 and was revised in 1999 (WCO 1999). While the convention is worded very broadly, its annexes define customs terms and recommend certain practices. An annex section in the amended convention (WCO 1999, annex E, section 1), focusing on applicable customs formalities and seals, informs the discussion of these topics later in this chapter.

The 1982 International Convention on the Harmonization of Frontier Control of Goods (or Geneva Convention) is very much about transit

Box 4.2

Legal Instruments Governing Transit Regimes

UNESCAP resolution 48/11 identifies seven international conventions related to transport facilitation that constitute the legal backbone of transit regimes:

1. **Convention on Road Traffic (Vienna, November 8, 1968):** Proposes to facilitate international road traffic and to increase road safety through the adoption of uniform traffic rules. Parties shall be bound to admit to their territories in international traffic motor vehicles and drivers that fulfill the conditions in the instrument.
2. **Convention on Road Signs and Signals (Vienna, November 8, 1968):** A convention on road signs and signals to replace the 1949 Protocol established under the Geneva Convention on Road Traffic.
3. **Customs Convention on the International Transport of Goods under Cover of TIR Carnets (TIR Convention) (Geneva, November 14, 1975):** Goods carried under the TIR procedures in sealed road vehicles are not as a general rule submitted to examination in customs offices en route. But they may be inspected when an irregularity is suspected. Customs authorities shall not require vehicles to be escorted at carrier expense on the territory of their country. Contracting parties authorize agreed professional associations to issue TIR carnets, which guarantee the payment of import or export duties and taxes, including penalty interest in case of irregularities. Customs authorities discharge TIR carnets after conclusion of the transport operation.
4. **Customs Convention on the Temporary Importation of Commercial Road Vehicles (Geneva, May 18, 1956):** Provides that commercial vehicles shall be granted temporary admission without payment of import duties and taxes, subject to their reexportation.
5. **Customs Convention on Containers (Geneva, December 2, 1972):** Contracting parties shall grant temporary admission to containers, whether empty or loaded, for a period of up to three months, which may be extended and reexported. Containers under temporary admission may be used for domestic traffic. Containers approved by a contracting party for transport under customs seal and meeting the conditions set forth in the regulations shall be accepted by the other contracting parties for any system of international carriage involving sealing of containers.

(continued)

Box 4.2 *(continued)*

6. **International Convention on the Harmonization of Frontier Controls of Goods (Geneva, October 21, 1982):** This convention appears as a useful complement to the Kyoto Convention. Its aim is to facilitate the international movement of goods by reducing the requirements for completing formalities and the number and duration of controls. Contracting parties shall endeavor to use documents aligned on the United Nations Layout Key. Documents produced by any appropriate technical process shall be accepted, provided they are legible, understandable and compliant with official regulations. Contracting parties are obligated to provide staff and facilities that are compatible with the traffic requirement (Article 5), to organize joint border processing to ease controls (Article 7), and to harmonize documentation (Article 9). The contracting parties shall whenever possible provide simple and speedy treatment of goods in transit, especially for those traveling under cover of an international transit procedure, limiting inspections to cases where they are warranted by the actual circumstances or risks.

7. **Convention on the Contract for the International Carriage of Goods by Road (CMR) (Geneva, May 19, 1956):** The CMR is basically a European Union affair ratified by European, Middle Eastern, and Central Asian countries to elaborate uniform conditions of contract for international road transport of goods. It is usually used as an international transport instrument and does not apply to either domestic transport or multimodal transport. The shipper is responsible for specifying the particulars of the goods to be carried and for a number of statements. The carrier is responsible for checking accuracy of statements whenever possible. Documentation for customs purposes is the responsibility of the sender. The shipper may dispose of the goods by issuing instructions to the carrier as to the location of the delivery or the delivery to a consignee other than the original consignee. All expenses pursuant to changes in instructions, requests for instructions, and others are charged to the shipper. The carrier is prima facie liable for damages, and the convention details the grounds on which a carrier may be relieved of its liability. The burden of proof that loss, damage, or delay was due to one of enumerated causes rests upon the carrier. The shipper is liable for any damage caused by inadequate information given to the carrier. The CMR sets forth which courts have jurisdiction for hearing cases between carriers and shippers.

Source: UNESCAP resolution 48/11, April 23, 1992.

Table 4.1.   General Provisions of International Conventions Applicable to Customs Transit

1. General	• Freedom of transit • Normally no technical standards control • No distinction based on flag or owner origin • No unnecessary delays or restriction
2. Customs diligences in transit	• Limitation of inspection (especially if covered by an international transit regime such as the TIR) • Exemption from customs duties • Normally no escort of goods or itinerary • No duty on accidentally lost merchandise • No unnecessary delays or restriction In addition, under an international transit regime such as the TIR: • The transit regime applies to multimodal transport when part of the journey is by road • Flat rate bonds are used for transit goods
3. Health and safety	• No sanitary, veterinary, or phytosanitary inspections required for goods in transit if no contamination risk
4. Security offered by the carrier	• Declarant may choose the form of security, within the framework afforded by legislation • Customs should accept a general security from declarants who regularly declare goods in transit in their territory • On completion of the transit operation, the security should be discharged without delay.

Source: UNECE and UNCTAD 2001.

facilitation by recognizing the importance of transit for countries' economic development. It promotes joint customs processing through the simplification of customs procedures and the harmonization of border controls, drawing heavily on the European experience. Article 10 applies to goods in transit: "contracting parties are bound to provide simple and speedy treatment of goods in transit, especially for those traveling under an international transit procedure," and parties should also "facilitate to the utmost the transit of goods carried in containers or other loads units affording adequate security." Contracting parties are bound to the following:

- Provide staff and facilities that are compatible with the traffic requirement (article 5).
- Organize joint border processing to ease controls (article 7).
- Harmonize documentation (article 9).

Conclusions

In summary, transit regimes govern and make possible the movement of goods from their origin to their destination. At the heart of the regime is a public-private partnership, a relationship between logistics operators and the authorities of the country of transit. The principles that rule transit regimes are universal, and procedures involve a transit document and a guarantee scheme that prevent multiple taxation of the goods in transit, also precluding revenue losses associated with leakage of the goods into the transit country. Several legal instruments aimed at facilitating transit have been developed in the past decades. Despite these efforts, achieving an effective and working transit regime has been elusive in all regions outside Europe. The next chapter will revisit these implementation challenges and possible solutions.

Notes

1. For illustrative purposes we focus on trucks; however, the same applies for other modes of transport, such as wagons, barges, and so forth. In practice, the procedures may be simplified for trains.
2. HS is an international goods classification system for describing cargo in international trade under a single commodity coding scheme.

References

Arvis, Jean-François. 2005. "Transit and the Special Case of Landlocked Countries." In *Customs Modernization Handbook*, 243–64, ed. Luc De Wulf and José B. Sokol. Washington, DC: World Bank.

Arvis, Jean-François. 2011. "Transit Regimes." In *Border Management Handbook*, 279–96, ed. Gerard McLinden. Washington, DC: World Bank.

De Wulf, Luc, and José B. Sokol (eds.). 2005. *Customs Modernization Handbook*. Washington, DC: World Bank.

Grosdidier de Matons, Jean. 2004. "A Review of International Legal Instruments." Sub-Saharan Africa Transport Policy Program Working Paper 73, World Bank, Washington, DC.

European Commission. 2001. "New Customs Transit Systems for Europe." Directorate-General for Taxation and the Customs Union, European Commission. Luxembourg: Publications Office of the European Union.

UNECE (United Nations Economic Commission for Europe) and UNCTAD (United Nations Conference on Trade and Development). 2001. *Compendium of Trade Facilitation Recommendations.* Geneva: United Nations.

UNECE. 2005. *TIR Handbook.* ECE/Trans/TIR/6/Rev.1. Geneva: UNECE.

WCO (World Customs Organization). 1999. "International Convention on the Simplification and Harmonisation of Customs Procedures" (Revised Kyoto Convention), as amended. Brussels: WCO.

CHAPTER 5

Improving Transit Regimes and International Cooperation

This chapter reviews the main implementation issues of regional transit systems experienced in the developing world. For the majority of developing countries that do not take part in TIR (*Transports Internationaux Routiers*), many obstacles remain to implementing regional transit regimes or their own national regimes. However, a new focus of reform and technical assistance aimed at the transit regime may help.

This chapter will cover (1) common implementation issues; (2) the reason attempts to implement regional systems have largely failed, even when they mimic the successful European systems; (3) the benefits and limitations of information technology; and (4) recommendations for revamping transit regimes.

Implementing Transit Regimes in Developing Regions

Even when a trade corridor crosses several countries, the basic transit procedure is implemented at the country level. In most cases—especially in

Chapters 4 and 5 are based on the authors' original research with contributions from Pilar Kent and Gerard Luyet. An abridged version (Arvis 2011) was included in the *Border Management Handbook* as chapter 17, "Transit Regimes." The content here is an overhaul of the corresponding chapter in the *Customs Modernization Handbook* (De Wulf and Sokol 2005).

low-income economies and corridors serving landlocked developing countries (LLDCs)—there are too many deviations from core transit principles for the transit regime to support efficient supply chains.

Weaknesses in Information Systems and Guarantee Management

In most cases in developing regions, weak information systems and poor guarantee management are the major problems in implementing transit regimes. Unlike clearance, which happens in one place, transit requires an exchange of information from at least three places: transit initiation, transit termination, and the guarantor (to validate and discharge the bonds). The management and tracing of the transit declaration is not always properly and rigorously implemented and, in many cases, is not automated. This means that transit operations initiated in the transit country are not properly accounted for and closed when the cargo actually exits the country, causing major errors and delays (such as in the discharge of bonds). Moreover, the tracing and reconciliation of manifests can be very difficult. According to the International Road Transport Union (IRU), 95 percent of reported TIR-related customs claims arise from the nonreporting of carnet pages in customs systems—not from fraudulent behavior.

Bonds and guarantees are basic financial products—universally available from the local banking and, ultimately, insurance industries. Regular transit operators have a comprehensive guarantee, equivalent to a standing line of credit, which, among other benefits, should make the guarantee available at the time the transit declaration is introduced. Pricing may vary, but fundamentally the cost of the guarantee is proportional to the time between its initiation and its discharge. Hence, inefficient information exchange and delayed discharge entail significant costs. The authors even observed instances where the logistics companies had to arrange for the return of validated manifests (for example, from Chad to the Central African Republic)—an obvious conflict of interest.

On African corridors, the comprehensive guarantee may cost as much as 0.25 percent or even 0.5 percent of the value of the goods for each country crossed. Voucher guarantees, adequate for occasional operators, avoid this problem, as they are not time-sensitive—but typically they do cost more. Contrary to widespread opinion, the TIR carnet (a voucher by nature) is fairly cheap in such circumstances, because on average it is priced at 0.2 percent of taxes and duties (or typically 0.1 percent of value of the goods) for the basic guarantee. In any case, the cost of the guarantee is much less than transportation costs.

There is no evidence that the requirement of a transit guarantee or its pricing are direct causes of cost and delays. On some corridors, the authors found that traders were blaming availability of guarantee for other causes. For instance, small independent brokers handle trade documentation at borders in Eastern Africa, for example, in Tanzania and the Democratic Republic of Congo. The fact that those have limited financial and borrowing capacity means that they can only have a small guarantee line open with customs. At the border of Tanzania and the Democratic Republic of Congo, this constraint creates delays, because the broker may have to wait to process new shipments for which the previous bonds have been cleared.

Transit Initiation Often Lengthy, Especially in Ports

Along virtually all the developing country corridors visited by the authors, the time to initiate transit in a port is similar to the time to clear goods for local consumption in a coastal country. In some instances, it can take even longer—in 2008, for instance, it took four weeks in the Dar es Salaam Corridor in Tanzania and two in the Beira Corridor in Mozambique. There is no simple or single explanation for this problem, which affects both large and small transit operators. However, it seems that in many cases, customs does not clearly separate clearance from transit procedures, but applies the same process to both. In reality, transit goods should not be subject to the same risk management and control as locally cleared goods. Document checking classification and valuation should not be sticking points for transit goods. In theory, transit can be initiated in a port using the information already available in the shipping manifest.

Effects of Lax Entry Regulation

Lax regulation of entry discourages quality and compliance in services. Of particular importance are the regulations applicable to transit operators (truckers and freight forwarders) and customs brokers. Better services may be encouraged by creating thresholds for the operators authorized to participate in transit operations—for instance, in company size (number of trucks, equity), professional requirements, and deposits (for brokerage operations). Although often the aim is to keep requirements low and the market open for small operators, the problem is that lax regulations encourage the development of low-quality services—services that cannot cover the full transit supply chain and undermine the development of good, comprehensive services.

Lax regulation of entry may encourage rent-seeking behaviors. In most British Commonwealth countries, liberal regulations make customs brokers *de jure* or *de facto* mandatory intermediaries for customs operations, resulting in an overly intermediated supply chain. According to recent research, transit cargo from Durban (South Africa) to clearance in Blantyre (Malawi) had to use eight different brokers—one on each side of every border—essentially to fill and submit the same information on the same document used by the Common Market for Eastern and Southern Africa (COMESA) and Southern African Development Community (SADC). In addition, different domestic banks were covering the transit in each of the four countries on the corridor.

Queuing systems for trucks or *tours de role* for individual truckers are still very prevalent in Francophone Africa and in some countries in the Middle East. They push costs up, lower service quality, and prevent the emergence of organized companies having long term commercial relationships with shippers and freight forwarders.

Transit regimes in developing countries today rarely provide incentives for compliant transit operators offering the best services with minimal fiscal risk. In Syria, a guarantee ceiling limits the number of trucks in transit that a company can operate to two or three. Conversely, the European Common transit system relies largely on the concept of authorized economic operators who have specific incentives—such as reduction in or even a waiver of the comprehensive guarantee—for their operations. On most corridors in developing countries, the same principle of incentives (lower guarantee, fast track) could be applied, since much of the trade is managed by large global and regional companies delivering comprehensive logistics services.

Control Mentality and Convoys

As already exemplified by the problem of initiation in ports, customs agencies often are suspicious with transit. They may resort to the use of convoys during the transit trip, where the transit vehicle is escorted by police officers and a customs official. When the risk of leakage is high and securing cargo with seals is not feasible, convoys with a customs escort is the logical solution, for instance when goods are carried in open trucks. Otherwise, in normal circumstances, there is no reason to have sealed containers or trailers moving in convoys.

The convoys can be several kilometers in length (if there are 300 transit trucks per day entering at land border, each 20 meters in length and with half that distance between them, they would form a convoy 9 kilometers long) and so need to travel at night to avoid disrupting other road traffic. Having to wait until a typical 8:00 p.m. convoy departure imposes a long time penalty on the trucks. The cost of the escorts is typically borne by the trucks in the convoy. Convoys need time to be created (up to four days wait) and are slow.

Though convoys tend to be less prevalent nowadays, they still exist, notably in Western and Eastern Africa, the Middle East, and South Asia. In the absence of convoys, control points and checkpoints may be imposed.

Is the risk of fraud in transit overestimated? The experience of the authors taken from observations on corridors and interviews of customs officials and traders is that the risk for fraud to customs transit is widely exaggerated in general. Customs statistics in LLDCs or their transit countries show that there are very little proven cases of fraud, if any cases are registered at all. On most corridors, bonds are never called by customs of the countries of the corridor. This argument can be interpreted either way to support or not the efficiency of existing control procedures.

In fact, the incentives to commit fraud in transit are not many, even in an environment where smuggling and fraud are common. First, the operator of the transit operation (principal) is, in general, not the one taking advantage of the fraud, because the duties are paid at destination by the owner of the goods, the transit operator has no clear motivation to engage in fraud to transit, quite the contrary (reputational risk and loss of transit operator status). The exception is the case when the merchant is also the transport company, which is not uncommon in Western Africa or Central Asia. Furthermore, in a weak governance environment, a noncompliant trader would find it much easier to fraud the import declaration and to engage in corrupt practices at destination, rather than taking the trouble of setting a parallel clandestine logistics to unload and reload goods before they reach their normal destination. For instance, in African LLDCs, fraud in value is a much higher fiscal risk than fraud in transit.

Transit Facilitation Misconceptions

Transit facilitation initiatives are often influenced by misconceptions. Given the risk of policy makers and development agency putting their efforts into unproductive design and investment, it is worth rectifying some of the most widespread misconceptions.

First, transit does not require a heavy border infrastructure; in fact, transit facilitation reduces the needs for border investment. Since the process at the border should be limited to fairly simple diligence—check the manifest and the seals, no inspection—there is no need for a large transit infrastructure. Transit does not require specific border post arrangements, and transit flows should be separated from the flows cleared at the border. For example, there may be a separate fast lane at a border post with substantial activity (100 trucks a day).

Needs for information technology are very limited, and overreliance on information communications technology (ICT) solutions may be counterproductive (to be discussed in full later in this chapter).

Some simple ideas on where and how to clear, though apparently common sense propositions, simply do not work. As presented in recent reports and project proposals, these ideas include the following:

- For landlocked countries, clearance at the port of entry in the gateway country. Beyond the obvious issues of territorial jurisdiction, the main problem with this idea is that the transit country, to prevent fraud or fiscal loss, still needs a system to make sure that goods are consumed in the destination country. At best there can be preclearance, with the risk of adding a layer of procedures. In rare instances, this is feasible, for example, where there is a very short transit corridor and a dominance of transit trade over domestic trade at the port of entry.[1]
- For a customs union to dispense with transit procedures entirely. In fact, since value-added taxes (VATs) or sales taxes are collected in the country of consumption, some transit mechanism must be maintained even if a collective mechanism is agreed for the collection of extra-union duty (as in the European Union [EU] and Southern African Customs Union [SACU]).

Integration of Transit: An Unreached Goal

Regional transit regimes have not succeeded, apart from the TIR and the European common transit system. Typically transit takes place over at least two territories: one or more transit countries, plus national transit in the destination country. The value of integrating the transit systems into a regime over the corridor, or even a subregion covering several corridors, has been recognized for a long time. So has been the fact that the TIR and European common transit system are the natural references for transit at the regional level. However, no other regions have succeeded so far at passing beyond harmonization to the integration of national transit.

With the enormous success of the TIR system, its concept has been made the basis for attempts to establish bilateral and multilateral agreements among countries elsewhere, for example, in Africa, Asia, and

South America. A 2001 UNCTAD (United Nations Conference on Trade and Development) report on corridors in Africa points out: "[T]here has not been any shortage of measures and initiatives to improve facilitation of transit traffic. COMESA, EAC, . . . and SADC² all have various measures that are in place to address transit facilitation. Unfortunately, the major problem has been poor implementation" (InfraAfrica Ltd. 2003, p. 45). This conclusion coincides with the authors' analysis that outside Europe—with its European common transit system and the TIR—there is currently no fully functional regional transit regime.

Africa's geography and the number of its LLDCs make it highly dependent on transit corridors. It hosts several transit agreements on paper—but implementation has faced various challenges. There are four different regions with separate sets of problems: West Africa (the West African Economic and Monetary Union [UEMOA] plus Ghana); Central Africa (the Douala Corridor); Eastern Africa (the Kenyan and Tanzanian corridors); and Southern Africa.

In many ways the integration of transport and customs policies is most advanced in Africa, at least within the main regional groupings: in West Africa, UEMOA and the Economic Community of West African States (ECOWAS); in Central Africa, the Economic and Monetary Community of Central Africa (CEMAC); in East Africa, the East African Community and the COMESA; and in Southern Africa, the SADC and COMESA.

There are few restrictions on the movement of people and vehicles, and there are common vehicle insurance systems (yellow and brown cards in ECOWAS and COMESA). Furthermore, UEMOA and CEMAC are a monetary union where residents can cross borders with simple identification documents. Unfortunately, all this has not yet created an efficient transit regime.

West Africa has chosen as its common transit system the *Transit Routier Inter-États* (TRIE), based on the TIR. Unfortunately, the TRIE has not succeeded so far, as implementation has departed from an important principle: the regulation of entry and incentive for quality services have been jeopardized by using queuing systems for truckers in the application of protectionist and interventionist bilateral agreements, and excessive overloading has made it impossible to seal cargo. There is no management of the bonds in the TRIE regime that is comparable to the TIR, and de facto there is no real customs guarantee attached to the TRIE carnets. The situation is better in Southern Africa, but—as mentioned earlier—the traditional role of customs brokers and the fragmentation of guarantees prevent the emergence of a regional system.

In South America, despite the soundness of the legal framework contained in ATIT (*Acuerdo sobre Transporte International Terrestre*, or Agreement on International Land Transportation) and transit trade growth in the *Mercado Común del Sur* (Mercosur) countries, the spirit of the rules is not fully reflected in procedures. ATIT, created in the early 1980s, remains a chain of national procedures. Among the Andean countries, integration is significantly lower than in Mercosur, even though a common transit declaration form is in use (also known as the Andean Manifest). East Asia has several agreements such as the Greater Mekong Subregion Agreement for Facilitation of Cross-Border Transport of Goods and People, which has similarities with the TIR, but is not implemented so far.

South Asia is the region furthest away from an integrated transit regime. It is characterized by complex institutional processes and numerous documents. Transit to the LLDCs is organized only bilaterally. The complexity of the system encourages rent-seeking agents and vested interests to maintain the status quo, including labor-intensive solutions such as transloading at borders. Infrastructure issues and lack of equipment at trans-shipment points contribute to the inefficiency of the transit systems. The establishment of the South Asian Free Trade Agreement has created high expectations toward facilitating transit transport of the two landlocked countries in the region, Bhutan and Nepal.

The Economic Cooperation Organization (ECO) Transit Framework Agreement involves countries in Western and Central Asia: Afghanistan, Azerbaijan, Iran, Kazakhstan, Kyrgyz Republic, Pakistan, Tajikistan, Turkey, Turkmenistan, and Uzbekistan. However, TIR is still the main instrument for long-distance transit, and ECO has not implemented its own regime. The same is true with the Arab Manifest promoted by the Arab League: the few member countries active in transit trade (Jordan, Morocco, Syria, and Tunisia) prefer to use national procedures or the TIR.

Regional Transit Regimes: "TIR Lite"

There is no business case to be made for regional "TIR lite" transit regimes. None of the regional experiments launched over the past three decades have produced a truly regional system, where goods can move on transit from origin to destination under a single transit document and a single bond. In most cases, a satisfactory degree of harmonization of documentation and procedures has been achieved within a regional economic grouping but these remain purely national. No serious effort has been made to integrate the transit bonds.

Three lessons emerge from the authors' review of implementation problems and the lack of success in creating regional systems. First, an efficient transit regime depends on the other components of the transit system, including institutional capacities; private sector capacity, notably in transport services; and other political economy constraints. Second, misconceptions in transit design and implementation have appeared, even in environments that were conducive for a successful transit regime. Third, the conceptual differences between the TIR and the European common transit system are complex and not always fully understood.

Most regional experiments, such as the TRIE, have been implicitly based on two principles—principles that clearly depart from the experience of the efficient regimes in Europe. One is that transit should be as open as possible to small-scale operators. The other is that regional systems should be adapted to meet those operators' needs. The resulting approach waters down key design principles and implementation mechanisms (such as guarantees and their management), as is known from history and from the European experience.

The main conclusion is that there is no strong business case for regional "TIR lite" such as the TRIE. Instead, common transit may be implemented within a subregion in the very few cases where regional integration—in transport and financial services, trade, and customs— makes it possible. Between regions, or within regions with limited integration, TIR should be seriously considered as a global transit regime.

Too Many Legal Instruments?

International legal instruments, treaties, or conventions, applicable to trade facilitation, are numerous, especially for developing countries (see table 5.1). They fall broadly into three categories: multilateral instruments, the

Table 5.1   Number of Multilateral Legal Instruments with Relevance for Transit Trade in Africa, 2004

Global instruments	28
Regional (African continent) instruments	8
Subregional instruments	90
Central Africa	16
Eastern Africa	12
Southern Africa	18
West Africa	44

Source: Grosdidier de Matons 2004.
Note: The many bilateral agreements are not counted.

most relevant being already listed in the previous chapter (box 4.2); regional treaties; and the bilateral transit protocols. This legal framework has been reviewed by several authors, including a very comprehensive review for African countries (Grosdidier de Matons 2004).

International legal tools, such as the Kyoto or TIR conventions, provide policy makers in developing countries with principles and global standards that should be implemented in meaningful trade and transit facilitation project. Regional agreements tend to lay down broad goals as policy directions for regional transit systems, but they also spell out some principles of implementation. Grosdidier de Matons and others have observed that there is no shortage of regional agreements (see table 5.1) and that the challenges are with implementation provisions and practices. In fact, much can be achieved within the current legal framework.

The Curse of Bilateral Agreements

Bilateral transit agreements are key building blocks in developing regions that are shaping the organization and the political economy of transit systems. In the absence of implemented regional conventions, bilateral agreements are needed to make transit possible and to complement regional agreements. Box 5.1 illustrates an example of a bilateral transit agreement in the absence of a regional or corridor framework.

Conversely, in the context of regional cooperation, bilateral agreements primarily should be protocols providing practical implementation solutions, such as preferred routes and border crossings and their hours of operation. Unfortunately, in practice, the scope of bilateral agreements also reflects a balance between various interests in the two countries that are not always in accord with the general principles of customs transit and not necessarily conducive to overall transit efficiency.

Many agreements introduce truck quotas or freight-sharing agreements. For instance, in francophone Africa, bilateral agreements have been in place longer than the regional agreements and have maintained old-fashioned, freight-sharing agreements between countries as well as institutionalized queuing systems. These agreements are essentially incompatible with the implementation of a regionally integrated transit regime comparable to the European common transit system or the TIR.

Reengineering the Transit Regime: A Priority for LLDC Corridors

The most promising way to help countries and regions bring about on-the-ground improvements in the conditions they offer for international

Box 5.1

India-Nepal Bilateral Transit Agreement

Together the Indo-Nepal Treaty of Trade and the Treaty of Transit govern transit operations between India and Nepal. Both treaties, renewed every five years, detail the specific procedures required for the transit of Nepalese imports and exports through India. The transit treaty specifies points of entry and exit, defines the 15 mutually agreed transit routes to and from Calcutta and Haldia (the port serving Calcutta), describes the warehouses and open spaces to be provided, and gives detailed guidelines on the simplified administrative procedures.

Several elements that help facilitate transit are as follows:

- Clear description of import and export procedures
- Simplified customs administrative requirements and documentation (in this case, the customs transit declaration)
- Reliable guarantee framework (backed by the government of Nepal)
- Clear distribution of responsibilities and duties among the different stakeholders
- Customs support infrastructure (warehouses, the provision of dry ports)
- Description of the agreed on transit routes.

Source: Uprety 2006.

freight movement is to incorporate into local or regional procedures the elements proved most useful elsewhere—notably in Europe, including TIR. Instituting a proper transit regime—either from scratch or by extensive reengineering of existing systems—is the key to radical improvement of LLDCs' international connectivity. A good transit system will ultimately provide seamless door-to-door or ship-to-door logistics, with improved performance in terms of time and reliability. Furthermore, a good transit regime must incorporate professional requirements, creating incentives for improvement in the level of private sector services, such as trucking and freight forwarding.

For a number of reasons, no fully satisfactory transit regime has been developed outside Western Europe and its TIR-associated trading partners. The first reason is the extortionate rents that exploit the imperfections of the systems on both the private and the public side. For instance, the role of customs brokers present at so many borders, or the role of artisanal trucking for the logistics of LLDCs, would be radically altered if a carnet system were initiated and an "authorized operator" regime were introduced for transit operators.

The experience of World Bank assistance also shows that, in many areas, it is difficult for reform-minded policy makers in transit countries to move from a control mentality and a multiple-clearance system to the public-private partnership paradigm and a relationship of trust with authorized operators. Concepts based on regulation of entry or on authorized operators and traders (box 5.2) go in that direction.

Box 5.2

Authorized Economic Operators (AEOs)

The growth of global trade and the increasing security threats to the international movement of goods have forced customs administrations to shift their focus more and more to securing international trade flows and away from the traditional task of collecting customs duties. Recognizing these developments, the World Customs Organization (WCO), drafted the WCO Framework of Standards to Secure and Facilitate Global Trade (SAFE). Developing an AEO program is a core part of SAFE. These AEOs can not only be exporters or importers but also the logistics services providers handling part of the supply chain.

Operators can be accredited by customs as AEOs when they prove to have high-quality internal processes that will prevent goods in international transport to be tampered with, which means they can provide all of the following:

• Ensure the integrity of the information, that what is said to be in a container is really in the container and nothing else.
• Ensure the integrity of its employees, that they will not put goods in the container that should not be there.
• Secure access to its premises to prevent unauthorized people from putting goods in the container.

As a result of such accreditation, customs will trust the operator and perform fewer or no inspections on goods imported or exported by the AEO. This facilitates the movement of the goods and makes them available more quickly, which lower trading costs. Customs agencies benefit because scarce inspection capacity can be targeted at the suspect cargo of unknown and potentially unsafe operators.

The compatibility of AEO national programs is key to regional and international trade facilitation; for example, such coordination would enable the identification of a load handled by AOEs as it moves through all countries of the corridor.

(continued)

Box 5.2 *(continued)*

Acceptance as an AEO or its equivalent in one country is designed to grant similar status in other countries. This contributes further to the need for high compliance standards; for example, if just one accredited company were found in one instance of noncompliance, all companies on that country's list run the risk of losing their accreditation in other countries. The rules for acceptance as an AEO or its equivalent are determined by each national customs agency, often in consultation with those of other countries and especially those of the United States and the European Union.

The importance of compatible AEO accreditation conditions is that they are a step toward the ultimate goal of having all national programs mutually recognized, which would mean that AEO accreditation would have the same value everywhere. However, this goal could still be far in the future. Establishing regional programs in areas that already have some degree of integration of customs and transport policies, such as existing regional economic commissions, would be an intermediate goal that should be supported by international assistance.

The WCO has launched a number of capacity-building initiatives, such as the Columbus Programme. An example of the application of the Columbus Programme to a LLDC is a three-year technical cooperation agreement on capacity-building between the Customs Administration of Mongolia, the Dutch Tax and Customs Administration, and the WCO in 2008. In addition, 16 memorandums of understanding establishing regional training centers have been concluded by the WCO and the customs administrations of member countries; seminars on AEOs have been held in East Africa, southern Africa, and Central America.

Source: WCO, based on http://www.wcoomd.org/home_cboverviewboxes_valelearningoncustoms valuation_cbcolumbusprogrammeoverview.htm

Implementing a fast-track for authorized operators will face a number of practical challenges, beyond political acceptability (chapter 3). There is little doubt a core group of companies would meet reasonable standards in most subregions for the scheme to be viable: international freight forwarders, multinational corporations, and large modern regional investors are present everywhere. The design of fast-track procedures for authorized operators can rely on global standards and examples, notably from Europe.

The most challenging, from the experience of implementing authorized operators schemes in developing countries, would be to adopt a robust accreditation procedure with specific requirements. First, it should be truly regional. Furthermore, accreditation should be independent and objective, which may be difficult in view of weak governance and low enforcement capacities common to many LLDCs and their transit countries. The example of the TIR suggests a combination of local or regional bodies (national association for the TIR) and a guardian of the integrity of the system that is external to the region (such as the IRU).

Pilot Transit Regime Improvement Program: The Douala Corridor

Conceptually, the architecture of a functional transit regime is universal, whether implemented at the national level or within a regional system. It includes elements such as proper documentation (transit declarations), financial guarantees, information systems and monitoring, and application of the AEO concept.

Outside the operating area of the TIR system, there is a dearth of standards or guidelines to help countries and subregions implement such a reengineering effort (for example, there are no standards for transit declarations or guidelines for the level of guarantees). In fact, the level of awareness of policy makers on what it takes to implement a working system is often low. International organizations (such as WCO, United Nations Economic Commission for Europe, and the IRU) could fill this gap. Technical assistance can also be provided to countries and subregions to promote systemic changes in the transit regime. Until now, aid has focused on partial solutions (for example, reliance on sophisticated information technology) and has rarely addressed change in architecture or taken into account the role of private operators. The challenge is to design a pragmatic sequence to move toward European best practice, which will take into account the political economy and technical constraints and the degree of effective economic and technical integration across countries on the corridor.

Such an approach has been piloted as part of the Central Africa Transport and Transit Facilitation Project, which is being implemented with the aid of financing from the International Development Association, the European Commission, the African Development Bank, and the *Agence Française de Développement*. The main objective is to meet the transit needs of two LLDCs, Chad and Central African Republic. Surveys have often shown these two countries to be suffering some of the highest international transport costs and worst logistic conditions to be found among developing countries (see chapter 2). A TIR-based international road transit convention, signed in 1991, was never followed through to implementation. International transport between the two countries and Cameroon (mainly to use the port of Douala) has been managed under bilateral conventions by freight bureaus enforcing mandatory freight allocation and queuing systems.

The main problems with the old transit regime included very slow release of goods from the Douala port, with seven documents required, all to be cleared by three separate offices. There were also multiple checkpoints and controls on the roads to the LLDCs. Both transport charges and the guarantees required from banks were significantly more costly than for comparable services in other countries. The negotiations of the transit group set up by the governments to develop reforms went through many ups and downs because of the multiple rents that had developed in the system and the reluctance of their recipients to give them up.

Thanks mainly to strong leadership and pressure for reform from the Cameroon government, especially Cameroon customs, agreement was reached on a substantially revised transit system, the Douala Corridor Pilot Scheme, serving Chad and the Central African Republic. The main elements of the pilot program are the following:

- Introduction of a common transit document (based on the model of the EU Single Administrative Document)
- Removal of all checkpoints on the roads
- Use of information technology based on UNCTAD's ASYCUDA (Automated System for Customs Data) system
- Addition of a bar code to the transit document and containers with optical reading at start, destination, and borders
- Introduction of simplified transit procedures for use by authorized freight forwarders who had qualified for the privilege and obtained a standing customs guarantee from the banking system.

These combined changes are expected to yield substantial benefits in terms of reduced delivery times with greater predictability of transit and delivery times, as well as significant price reductions. The project also provides extensive financing for major upgrading of the main transport corridor infrastructure in the three countries.

Technology Helps Manage Transit Trade

While transit systems rely primarily on the public-private partnership, under which compliant and competent operators essentially have freedom of transit, customs agencies need to properly manage the information on transit declarations or carnets, in order to do the following:

- Trace the goods entering and exiting the country, with adequate management of transit manifests or carnets
- Discharge the bonds
- Communicate with other participants, or with an overseeing body (such as the IRU) in the case of a carnet system.

ICT can be of great practical help in all these tasks. Within customs in the transit country, the system electronically tells the exit post to expect the arrival of a shipment within a plausible timeframe. When closed by the exit post, the transit information is input and the guarantee is automatically released.

Automation and Interconnection Across Borders

The automation of customs documentation is now widespread, with several applications now with modules for national transit. For instance, UNCTAD had already developed transit add-ons to ASYCUDA++. Unfortunately, this module has not been widely used. Furthermore, the first-generation custom information technology applications were designed around import and export declarations and had not been adapted to a carnet system such as TIR. Typically, transit data was seized within the same format as import data at each border. This may also have meant that different customs agencies did not recognize the simplified nature of the transit declaration.

The transit module is already built into a new generation of customs and trade documentation systems such as ASYCUDA World and its competitors.[3] Modern system can accommodate the TIR or Common transit format.

The interconnection of national customs is desirable and practically indispensable for a truly regionally integrated system, such as the NCTS (New Computerized Transit System), in Europe. It allows for a seamless exchange of information on a transit manifest or the initiation and termination of a bond. Today, NCTS is the only fully functional application for regional transit that manages both documentation and guarantees.

The e-TIR, which has a different concept, is in its pilot phase (as of the end of 2010). In e-TIR the carnet barcode or Safe-TIR number helps validate a page of the carnet at one of the border crossings, and this information is sent into a central database accessible by each participating country. Radio frequency identification device technology applied to vehicles or trailers may also facilitate the tracing of cargo on a corridor and speed up controls at entry and exit checkpoints.

Several groups of countries, including some in Africa, have been experimenting with transit data interfaces so that the information from the country initiating transit transmitted to the next country's border post where the cargo will cross. For example, South Africa transmits this information to its neighbor on the corridor to Zambia. Ghana's CGNet has a similar project for transit operations with Burkina Faso. Even when countries have not actually integrated their transit regimes, as is the case with many LLDCs, even the ability to pass advance information will have immediate benefits in terms of transit facilitation (see box 5.3).

Goods Can Be Traced, Need Not Be Tracked

Transit goods can be traced through the automation of carnet or transit manifest. Tracking, in contrast, involves electronically tracking the merchandise. The prices of global positioning system (GPS) tracking

---

Box 5.3

Impact of Information Technology: Streamlining Transit Information at Beitbridge

The most active trade corridor in Africa is the North-South Corridor linking South Africa to the landlocked countries in the north and beyond to Tanzania and the Democratic Republic of Congo. For a long time, the crossing into Zimbabwe has been the chokepoint of the corridors with the risk of multiple-day delays.

In 2002, the South African Revenue Commission and the Zimbabwean customs agency allowed the customs agent to submit the transit or import declaration prior to the arrival of the truck. This information was already available electronically from the shipper or the transporter when the cargo left the port of Durban or the Johannesburg area. According to statistics obtained from South African and Zimbabwean customs at Beitbridge, the electronic anticipation of the information dramatically reduces delays in transit times from 20 hours to almost 3 hours, and from 32 hours to 4 hours for the clearance of imports into Zimbabwe (as of June 2010, statistics courtesy World Bank's Olivier Hartmann).

Source: Authors.

devices are falling, and they are ever more popular with large trucking firms that want to know where their vehicles are at all times (so they can alert consignees if delivery is likely to be delayed). Drivers whose trucks break down or are otherwise delayed also want their companies to know where to find them, and GPS devices have become important management tools for logistics operators.

Such tracking for the benefit of cargo owners should not be confused with tracking by customs or other border agencies, which may be done with or without the trucker's knowledge. Currently several suppliers recommend electronic devices to customs authorities, and products such as e-seals with GPS tracking have their high-tech appeal. However, for a transit system to work, there is absolutely no operational need for real-time tracking. Furthermore, no developed country to now has found the need to implement real-time tracking.

There are serious disadvantages to tracking as well, including the reinforcement of the control mentality (with the potential for abuse instead of a partnership approach with incentives for compliant operators offering guarantees). In addition, there is no established best practice or clear guidance for how customs can use tracking information. Customs is not in a position nor does it have a mandate to interpret real-time information received from GPS tracking. For instance, how to interpret a truck being stopped for a length of time, especially on very long corridors. In addition, the limited experience shows that maintenance can be a serious challenge in a development context (the devices should work independently of the truck for a period of several days).

However, GPS tracking initiatives may have indirect benefits. Recent experience suggests that the positive impact of e-seals and GPS tracking may be less to implement tracking as a tool than to help rebuild confidence between customs and transit operators, leading to the disuse of unfriendly control solutions such as convoys. For instance, in Jordan, e-seals have been implemented since 2009 to dispense with convoys on the route from the port of Aqaba to the capital Amman and the Iraqi border. Ghana is implementing the same system, with the support of trucking companies, seeing the opportunity of phasing out convoys.

Conclusions: Progress Toward Global Standards

In summary, transit regimes govern and make possible the movement of goods from origin to destination. At the heart of the regime is a public-private partnership, a relationship between logistics operators and the authorities of the country of transit. These involve a transit document and a guarantee scheme that prevent multiple taxation of the goods in transit, also precluding revenue losses associated with leakage of goods into the transit country. Several legal instruments aimed at facilitating transit have proliferated in the past several decades. Despite these efforts, achieving an effective and working transit regime has been elusive in all regions outside Europe.

As seen today, a single worldwide transit system is a utopia yet to be achieved. A more realistic, yet optimistic, vision would be the development of a transit regime, such as the European common transit, within economically and financially integrated subregions, with the TIR supporting long-distance transit movement between regions. Developing regions, particularly LLDCs should engage in a major effort to overhaul and reengineer their transit regime along the core principles of compliance, regulation of entry, and partnerships.

These principles are essentially universal and do not accommodate well variants that depart too much from the norm, as exemplified by the failure of the many "TIR lite" experiments. The implementation of a transit regime is not different from that of other fiscal instruments, for example, such as introducing a VAT.

One responsibility of the international community would be to even better explicate the global standards of transit. Many elements are already spelled out in several conventions, notably in the 1999 WCO Revised Kyoto Convention (International Convention on the Simplification and Harmonisation of Customs Procedures). However, there are gaps regarding the recommended standards for regional systems—references are only available in the convention defining the common transit and TIR. At a more practical level, such recommendation should deal with the format of regional carnet, management of guarantee, or protocol of data exchange between countries.

Notes

1. The best known example is the Ethiopian transit trade cleared in Djibouti.
2. EAC (East African Community) and SADC (Southern Africa Development Community).
3. CGnet in Ghana, Gainde in Senegal, and Simba in Kenya are among other customs and automatic data interchange systems developed in transit countries serving LLDCs.

References

De Wulf, Luc, and José B. Sokol, eds. 2005. *Customs Modernization Handbook.* Washington, DC: World Bank.

Grosdidier de Matons, Jean. 2004. "A Review of International Legal Instruments." Sub-Saharan Africa Transport Policy Program Working Paper 73, World Bank, Washington, DC.

InfraAfrica Ltd. 2003. "Improvement of Transit Systems in Southern and Eastern Africa." United Nations Conference on Trade and Development, New York.

UNCTAD (United Nations Conference on Trade and Development). 2001. *UNCEFACT 2001: Compendium of Trade Facilitation Recommendations.* Geneva: UN Centre for Trade Facilitation and Electronic Business.

Uprety, Kishor. 2006. *The Transit Regime for Landlocked States: International Law and Development Perspectives.* Washington, DC: World Bank.

CHAPTER 6

Improving Road Freight Transport

Landlocked developing country (LLDC) international trade depends primarily on road freight services. This chapter explains why focusing on the quality of road freight services is so important for the trade of LLDCs and suggests how LLDCs can significantly reduce their access costs by road. It addresses three sets of issues in road freight transport for LLDCs:

- Structure of road freight industries
- Cross border formalities for vehicle and drivers
- Impediments to transiting the coastal neighbors of LLDCs.

The previous chapters examined the transit regime, that is, the policies and procedures that govern the movement of goods. Chapter 4 showed that an efficient transit regime implies the need for regulation of entry for trucking operators and introduced the requirement for international road transport operations to be regulated for service quality. This chapter now focuses on the regulations that affect vehicles, their drivers, and contractual procedures for road freight services. While the movement of goods is overseen by customs and the regulation of trucks is implemented by transport and road agencies, there are important synergies between these agencies.

Importance of Road Transport in Transit Countries

Of the three surface transport modes, roads provide the main transport infrastructure and services linking most landlocked countries to their transit neighbors, and for many, it is the only transport mode available.

Only 15 LLDCs have a rail link to a port in a transit neighbor, two have only a river-to-sea or lake connection, seven have both, while six have neither and rely on roads for all their international land transport (see chapter 7, table 7.1). Even for those LLDCs that do have rail and waterway (or lake) connections to their neighbors, the freight volume using these modes is rarely sufficient to make them financially sustainable.

For a sample of nine Asian LLDC corridors, land transport costs make up more than 80 percent of the cost and 60 percent of the time in getting goods to and from a deepwater port in a transit country, and most of this time and cost is incurred in the transit country rather than the LLDC (table 6.1).

Border crossings and ports together account for only 17 percent of the land transport cost and 39 percent of the land transport time, while land transport in the LLDC itself (including loading and unloading of the trucks) accounts for 27 percent of the cost and 22 percent of the time. The largest share of both cost and time is taken up by land transport in the transit country, 56 percent of the cost and 39 percent of the time.

For selected LLDC trade corridors in Africa, Asia, and South America, only a third of the transport cost (and a little more of the transport time) occurs in the LLDC itself, and in some cases, these shares fall as low as 10 percent (table 6.2). In only one corridor does more than half the transport cost occur in the LLDC (La Paz via Arica to Los Angeles), and in only three corridors does more than half the travel time occur in the LLDC (Mongolia via Tianjin, China; Cambodia via Laem Chabang, Thailand; and Bolivia via Arica, Chile).

Table 6.1   Transit Times for Land Transport in Nine LLDC Corridors in Asia

Source of cost and time	Cost (%)	Time (%)
Land transport in LLDC	27	22
Border crossing	7	14
Land transport in transit country	56	39
Port	10	25
Total land transport	100	100

Source: Author estimates based on data from United Nations Economic and Social Commission for Asia and the Pacific and United States Agency for International Development.

Table 6.2   Cost and Time Penalties of LLDCs Compared to Coastal Neighbors in Africa, Asia, and South America

Country group	Cost	Time
Total LLDC corridor	US$3,900	47 days
Total coastal country corridor	US$2,500	35 days

Source: Author estimates based on data from United Nations Economic and Social Commission for Asia and the Pacific and United States Agency for International Development.

These high land transport costs contribute to making LLDCs' total corridor costs and times about 53 percent and 32 percent higher, respectively, than those of their coastal neighbors (table 6.2). The average cost of exporting a container from an LLDC was about US$3,900 in 2008, while from a coastal developing country it was about US$2,500. The transit time from a LLDC was about 47 days, compared to only 35 days from a coastal country. Although it is impossible to eliminate these penalties, they can be substantially reduced by enhancing the trade competitiveness of the LLDCs.

Given that most transport to LLDCs is by road and most of the road cost occurs in the transit country, any attempt to reduce the additional trading cost to LLDCs needs to start with consideration of the road costs in their transit neighbors.

Reasons for LLDC Corridor High Road Freight Costs

There are three main reasons for the high cost of road freight to and from LLDCs, and these reasons provide the framework in which the land transport issues will be covered in this chapter. The first cause is the structure of the road freight industries in the LLDCs and their transit neighbors, the ways that they are regulated, and the way that their services must be contracted. The second cause is the costs of getting trucks, drivers, and their loads across land borders, which includes the imposition of quotas at many of the borders. The third cause is the payments and time that transit trucks incur (formal and informal) in crossing their coastal neighboring countries to reach a deepwater port.

Road infrastructure is no longer a common source of high road freight costs in corridors to LLDCs. With few exceptions, nonexistent or inadequate road infrastructure linking LLDCs to ports is no longer the impediment that it was to road freight services even just a few years ago. Of the two remaining LLDCs still dependent on rail or waterway transport, Bolivia has recently completed paved roads to Iquique in Chile and

Corumba in Brazil, while Mongolia will soon have paved road access to Tianjin port in China. And now, given increasing volumes of bilateral trade, most transit countries view upgrading roads that are used only for transit and cross-border trade to be as much in their own interest as that of the LLDCs that depend on this access.

Structure of Road Freight Industries

Road freight industries in LLDCs and their transit neighbors are often, but by no means always, highly fragmented, with many individually or family-owned trucks, few medium-size companies, and even fewer large companies. The small-scale operators, often using secondhand vehicles in largely informal markets, provide low-cost, no-frills services that meet a substantial demand. At the same time, shippers engaged in international trade are often willing to pay more for higher standard services. They need services from larger companies that can provide reliable, high-quality operations, that have sufficient physical and managerial capacity to enter into long-term contracts, and that can deal effectively and efficiently with the documentation requirements of international trade so as to expedite border crossings.

Despite the plethora of anecdotal evidence, there are few reliable statistics on the structure of road freight industries. Argentina has an average of only six vehicles per company but about eleven for international companies.[1] In Egypt, two out of three large trucks are owned by individuals.[2] In Mongolia, 73 percent of trucking companies owned fewer than six trucks in 2005.[3]

Regulatory Framework

This fragmented industrial infrastructure is often supported by a regulatory framework whose primary objective is to protect individual and family truck owners against competition from outside companies. Regulations often restrict where a carrier may operate (defined regions or routes), what truck types may be operated, and the kinds of commodities that may be carried. And they may rigidly separate "for hire" (that is, contracted to independent operators) services from "own account" (that is, traders operating their own transport services).

The advantages of deregulation, or at least of reduced regulation, of domestic road freight markets have long been recognized (see summaries in OECD 2001 and World Bank 2009). They include greater use of vehicles, lower tariffs, and improved quality of service (particularly for international services). However, actually carrying out the reforms needed to achieve these ends can take a long time and require skillful negotiations with current transport operators who may fear (perhaps correctly) that they will lose out even if other industries gain from deregulation.

Although the benefits of reduced regulation for transit road freight services are similar to those for domestic road freight services, there are additional considerations and interests that make negotiating such agreements even more difficult than negotiating domestic transport agreements. While it is relatively easy to argue in favor of transport deregulation where the beneficiaries are national companies that use road freight, it is more difficult to justify when it might favor traders and road transport operators in neighboring countries and when road freight operators in the country implementing the reduced regulations are likely to lose business.

Regulating for Quality

For domestic freight transport, reducing regulation in road transport usually involves replacing highly anticompetitive quantity licensing with less economically distorting quality licensing (Rushton, Croucher, and Baker 2006). Quantity licensing—which controls the number of license holders or the total volume of freight they can move—restricts competition and raises freight rates while doing little to encourage better services; when combined with tariff control (often needed to prevent the few licensed operators from charging monopoly tariffs), the negative impact of such licensing on the efficiency of the road freight industry can be devastating.

In contrast, quality licensing—which awards licenses to those who meet a set of standards—does not set any limits on the number of operators and so does not depend on (and does not need) tariff controls. Instead, by demanding higher standards, it raises the professionalism of the industry—and can empower operators with higher standards to charge higher tariffs. Obtaining a quality license requires the operator to meet minimum safety, security, and environmental standards and to show technical skills, accounting, and financial capacity. The freedom of entry to the road freight business that quality licensing provides usually results in an increase in efficiency in the industry—with fewer trucks operating more hours and longer distances, invariably at lower tariff rates. The efficiency gains are so great that even when the lower tariffs stimulate an increase in demand, it can be met with fewer trucks and fewer operating companies, prompting a fear of competition and its consequences among existing companies.

The International Road Transport Union (IRU) offers an internationally recognized certificate of professional competence (CPC) for trucking company managers, their drivers, and mechanics (box 6.1) that can be used in a quality licensing system. For companies engaged in international and transit freight, a higher level CPC can qualify for entry into the Transports Internationaux Routiers (International Road Transport [TIR]) system, providing a significant competitive advantage.

Balancing Regulation and Protection

The need to ensure minimum standards of professional competence raises questions of how a government can best strike a balance between opening markets to competition and encouraging safe, secure, environmentally clean, and professionally competent trucking services, while also fulfilling their political obligations to protect their own industries.

Achieving a balance between openness and regulation requires an understanding of the three broad categories of a country's trucking industry. Each category is aimed at satisfying a different segment of the market for road freight services and, therefore, a different balance between openness and regulation. The categories are described as follows:

- The least demanding of regulation are the small road freight companies or individual truck owners who service the demands of small manufacturing, farming, and distribution companies. This segment has

---

Box 6.1

IRU Training Courses

As part of the implementation of the South East Europe Trade and Transport Facilitation Project, the IRU and the World Bank initiated a training and certification system for truck and bus drivers and managers. The certification process was modeled on the current requirements for drivers and managers of trucking companies in European Union (EU) countries. The training and certification are managed through a network of training institutes approved as IRU Academy Accredited Training Institutes. The full list of training materials from the courses on passenger and goods transport is available from the website of the IRU academy (http://www.iru.org/index/en_academy_index).

Source: Global Facilitation Partnership for Transportation and Trade, http://www.gfptt.org/entities/ActivityProfile.aspx?id=350a3c8e-1b57-420b-abaf-7f2386457cee.

the lowest demands for quality of service and only needs regulation in respect to safety and the environment.

- More demanding of regulation in respect of service quality are domestic road freight companies that meet the demands of medium-size and larger agricultural, mining, and manufacturing enterprises; these companies usually look for transport contracts that can best be satisfied by road transport companies that have substantial truck fleets and can provide a quality and reliability of service beyond that achievable by individual operators.
- It is international road freight companies that benefit most from a more regulated environment, because their clients are much more demanding in terms of service quality and the range of facilities offered. To satisfy the demands of this market, the road freight companies need vehicles that meet international regulations for safety, security, and emissions; drivers who are qualified in multiple countries; and financial resources to support operations over a wide geographic area. Clients of international road transport operators and public agencies responsible for international trade need evidence that these exacting demands can be met.

The quality licensing appropriate for the first category is minimal, while that for international road freight transport is most demanding. The quality requirements can include those for a minimum number of international standard trucks, a minimum capital base to fund long-distance transport, insurance for the truck and its load, and guarantees needed to cover potential customs duties. Carriers that meet the criteria are likely to be incorporated enterprises with a relatively large fleet of large trucks (mostly tractor-trailer combinations with sealable freight compartments), salaried drivers, a sound financial situation, and authorization to operate under the TIR regime (see chapter 5) or its regional equivalent. Such firms typically have well-established commercial relations with agents in the other countries along the transit corridors and may even be part of a multinational group of carriers or logistics service providers.

In all three categories, licensed operators should be free to enter into service contracts with their customers. Indicative freight rates may be published as part of information for the clients, but should not be mandatory. Restrictions on making contracts and required tariff rates reduce competition and push up freight rates to the detriment of the exporters, importers, and final consumers.

Quality licensing leaves open the possibility for operators to "graduate" from one category to another once they meet the higher quality standards. This potential keeps the international trucking market contestable, that is, less at risk of becoming a "closed shop." It also gives domestic carriers incentives to improve their performance.

For international road freight services, quality licensing can be supplemented with extension of the concept of Authorized Economic Operator (AEO), which was introduced in chapter 5. Since 2005, the European Union has allowed road freight companies (as well as other participants in international supply chains) to be designated as AEOs. Accreditation as an AEO adds greatly to the road freight operators' professionalism and increases its market competitiveness.

Contracting Between Clients and Trucking Companies

The freedom of traders to contract with trucking companies is a requirement of a commercial system that allows competition to determine the most beneficial arrangements for both parties, both in terms of price and quality of service. But in many developing countries, other arrangements still prevail for truck operators to find loads for their vehicles. By far, the most common of these systems is queuing.

Queuing Regime

This alternative to freedom to contract requires a client to use the next truck available in a queue of trucks that are waiting for business, a queuing regime, or "*tour de role*" in Francophone African countries where they are common. When there is an excess of trucks or a large directional imbalance of demand, trucks can queue for very long periods, sometimes weeks, waiting for the next load. The situation is worse when the queuing rules give preference to trucks registered in the same city, province, or country in which the queue is formed. A common outcome of this arrangement is that trucks return empty to their origin location rather than tolerate the long wait for a return load. And if they operate within their "home" city, province, or country, they are assured of a similar preferential treatment.

The inefficiencies of such systems are many. Having to wait in line is the most obvious, but not necessarily the most damaging. The greater ill is the barrier introduced between the freight owner and the trucker to directly negotiate their own contracts. Much is to be gained if they can get to know each other through regular service, so that the shipper knows who is carrying his goods and what risk he runs of pilferage or late delivery. The trucker also benefits by getting to understand the shipper's quality requirements: punctuality, special handling, and other quality concerns.

Benefits of Eliminating Queuing

Despite their wide prevalence and recognized negative impact on transport efficiency, queuing systems have been abolished in only a few cases, with resulting benefits for both freight owners and truckers. The port of Aqaba, Jordan, which is not an LLDC but does have substantial transit road traffic, is an example of the benefits LLDCs and their transit neighbors might derive by abolishing a queuing system. In order to change the economy of the city of Aqaba from total dependence on its port to one that attracts commerce and tourism, the long queues of trucks in the downtown area that resulted from the *tour de role* queuing system had to be eliminated. In 2008, the queuing system was replaced with a technologically simple advanced notification system, which permits only approved and licensed truck operators to operate out of the port's container terminal. Trucks are not even allowed to enter the town until they are notified that the container they have come to collect has cleared all its entry requirements and is ready for pickup, and they must use predetermined routes provided to the driver by the notification system based on the current levels of traffic congestion. Thus, traders now contract with transport companies for the transport of their containers rather than having to use the next truck in the queue that is waiting at the container terminal (for imports) or at the free trade zone (for exports).

The impact on the trucking industry of this advanced notification system has been dramatic. The productivity of trucks serving the port has increased by a factor of about three, so they now travel about 100,000 km per year instead of the 30,000 km per year or so they averaged before the change was made. A 30 percent increase in container traffic at the port is being handled with a much reduced truck fleet. Importers are now provided with a reliable and timely transport of their containers at no increase in the tariff.

Procedures for Movement of Trucks and Drivers Across Borders

Once the structure of the international road freight industry and the procedures for its members to contract with clients have been addressed, there remain the issues of getting trucks, their drivers, and their loads across land borders and of reducing the costs and delays attributable to impediments to transit traffic within the transit country.

Trucks Crossing Borders

Although border crossing arrangements for trucks have been simplified for many LLDCs—they now account for only 7 percent of the cost and 10 percent of the total land transport activity—there are still many features that can be further simplified to reduce costs and times.

For trucks to cross the borders between LLDCs and their coastal neighbors in as little time as possible, efficient procedures are needed that allow the vehicle, its load, and its driver to cross as quickly and efficiently as possible. Complications in any of one of these three categories make efficiencies in the other two ineffective. Thus, requirements for all three are included in most bilateral or multilateral transit agreements. However, most simplifications at border crossings have been related to documentation and inspections of the goods being transported. Less attention has been given to simplifying the arrangements for trucks and their drivers, even though these can impose as much border delay as the arrangements for goods.

There are three different systems of allowing trucks to cross international borders. Some bilateral agreements simply do not allow vehicles to cross from one country to the other; instead, all loads must be transferred from a vehicle registered in one county to a vehicle registered in the other. This system is the least efficient and can result in cost penalties of hundreds of dollars and time penalties of several days. Fortunately, such systems are not common, but where they do exist, their impact on the trade competitiveness of the LLDC involved is significant.

The second system allows vehicles to cross the border with a temporary license to import to the transit country. This system requires consistency between the allowable design standards of trucks and the insurance requirements of both countries. If there is no consistency, it is almost impossible for a truck to cross a border. This problem is unresolved at many border crossings in East Africa as well as between China and its neighboring countries, but less so in Central Asia. However, in most cases, it is not enough simply to comply with these border crossing standards and requirements. Many countries, especially transit countries, also impose quota systems to protect their trucking industries.

While checks of trucks' compliance with quotas impose time and cost penalties at the border itself, the greatest cost of quotas comes long before the truck reaches the border. It is evident in the need to comply with the quota restrictions when contracting the truck for the transport of the goods, and this infringes on the freedom of contract between the trader and the transporter. If least-cost road freight contracts are offered by companies that cannot comply with quota requirements, the trader is forced to contract with a higher cost transport company, probably in a different country. If all the quotas have been filled, then the international trade cannot take place. While the combination of these cost penalties might be less than a total prohibition of cross-border truck movements, quota systems have been demonstrated to impose this set of very high cost and time penalties.

In the third system, trucks from one country can enter the other by means of a carnet, which requires only a demonstration of their registration and insurance certificates. The carnet is a relatively simple process that provides the best practice benchmark to which the inefficiencies of the other two systems can be compared. Several regional trade associations (such as the League of Arab States) allow this easy transit of trucks among their members.

As quota systems are by far the most common and most troublesome for trade, they are dealt with here in more detail than the other two systems.

Quota Systems and Bilateral Transit Agreements

Bilateral transit agreements enable two neighboring states to analyze their trade needs; to compare the strengths and weaknesses of each countries' road freight transport companies; and, on the basis of the analysis, to set quotas for the numbers of trucks allowed to cross their land borders or to share the total number of trucks between the countries.

While the objective of the quotas is to guarantee a share of the demand for truck companies from each country, a desirable second objective should be to share the quotas in a way that has least impact on the transport tariffs that result. Under the bilateral agreements, quotas are usually renegotiated annually, enabling countries to reconsider from one year to the next any "excessive" benefits that may have been granted to the other country and to freeze any further increase of the quota; that is, each country gets to keep some level of control of the market shares.

Freedom of Transit and Cross-Border Trucking Agreements

Bilateral transit agreements imposing quotas run counter to the objectives of transport efficiency: when trade is not balanced, carriers' capacity use is inefficient, and trucks must make many trips without cargo. These agreements can also be considered contrary to the spirit of international trade commitments endorsed by the World Trade Organization (WTO), specifically Article V on "freedom of transit" of the General Agreement on Tariffs and Trade (GATT), which prohibits duties, quotas, or other nontariff discriminatory practices against goods in transit. It is debatable whether the nondiscrimination principles of Article V apply to vessels and trade in transport services as well as trade in goods (chapter 3). If implemented, the General Agreement on Trade in Services (GATS), which deals with trade in services such as road freight, would certainly prohibit quotas and bilateral agreements. However, most LLDCs have not endorsed GATS, and the economies that have done so have excluded trucking so far.

The authors have observed that international organizations generally recommend that countries not enter into arrangements that are discriminatory not only for goods but also for freight services. The United Nations Economic Commission for Europe (UNECE) resolution reinforces and clarifies the agreements (see box 6.2) in relation to road transport by reiterating that any truck licensing system that is subject to quotas (whether it be bilateral or multilateral) is counter to the principle of freedom of transit, which is the same argument made in GATT Article V. However, these principles are often ignored, even by the advanced economies in the EU, as well as the United States, which otherwise is a strong supporter of free trade agreements.

One of the aims of the GATS is to promote liberalization of trade in services; thus, it adopts the principle that all countries are entitled to

---

Box 6.2

UNECE Resolution R.E. 4

The revised Consolidated Resolution on the Facilitation of International Road Transport (R.E. 4), adopted by UNECE in 2004, asserts that

Without prejudice to other provisions of these principles, freedom of transit should be granted on major international traffic routes (E-roads in Europe, similar roads on other continents). Traffic should not be banned or subjected to such measures as transit duties, taxes (other than user charges and tolls for the use of transport infrastructures) or quotas.

Source: UNECE, http://www.unece.org/trans/doc/2009/itc/ECE-TRANS-2009-10e.pdf.

the same treatment (the "most favored nation" clause). Yet bilateral quota agreements, which by definition are based on reciprocity and grant various market access conditions (in this case, road transport permits) to the different countries, are contrary to this principle. In addition, GATS identifies restrictions on market access that ought not to be maintained, including restrictions on the number of operations and the quantity of services offered, thus proscribing any system of quotas on transport services.

Despite these GATT and GATS requirements, situations arise in which the dominance of the road freight market by the transit country could be seen as a threat to the national integrity of the LLDC that depends on its services. It is also possible that it would take some time for the road freight companies in the transit country to increase their efficiency to become competitive with those of the transit country, supposing that the transit country did not continue to offer financial incentives for its own road freight companies to maintain their competitive advantage. These circumstances favor a gradual relaxation of quota agreements, accompanied so far as is possible by efforts to harmonize rules and operating conditions between companies registered in the two countries.

Effects of Truck Quotas on Trade Relations

A bilateral quota system has consequences not only for the efficiency of road transport, but for international trade relations as well. A shortage (or a glut) of quota allowances can be used to shape trade relations, which are no longer simply a matter of seeking the best product at the best price but also of obtaining a necessary transport permit to carry out the trade. So by limiting the number of quota licenses, the system is often used to limit the volume of trade between the countries, or in the case where one of the countries is an LLDC, to limit the extent to which it can compete with the exports of the transit country that is the other party to the quota agreement.

The fact that negotiations between countries often inject considerations having nothing whatsoever to do with the smooth functioning of road transport into the determination of the level of bilateral quotas would suggest that neither trade relations nor transport relations are what they would be if they had resulted from deregulated markets.

Since the EU is one of the largest trading blocks to continue the use of truck quotas, and at the same time is a fervent supporter of free trade, most of the discussion of the virtues and deficiencies of truck quotas has been in the context of their application by the EU. However, the same arguments apply to all bilateral and multilateral applications of truck quota systems

Truck Quotas in the EU

The EU has two systems of quotas for limiting competition from trucking companies registered in its neighboring countries. The first and longest standing is a system of quotas based on bilateral agreements, which is supplemented by a more recent system of multilateral quotas. No pretense is made that these systems are anything more than protectionist measures for EU trucking companies faced with competition from trucking companies in neighboring countries that may be less efficient but—because of lower wage rates and perhaps less stringent safety and environmental regulations—are able to offer lower tariffs.

The multilateral tariffs were introduced in an attempt to overcome one of the perceived flaws of bilateral quotas, that is, that they result in a high level of empty backhauls because of the prohibition against third country backhaul loads. While there are far fewer multilateral than bilateral quota licenses, the initiators of multilateral tariffs, in their attempt to deal with backhaul loads, have aroused even more opposition from established trucking companies. The multinational quotas only allow trucks to travel empty from the country where they dropped their original load to pick up a return load in a third country. However, the trucks have ended up undertaking cabotage freight (transporting loads between two countries within the EU). Suggestions for overcoming this rule-breaking include requiring the trucks to leave EU territory within a specified time of dropping their original load or limiting the number of cabotage loads they can carry before exiting EU territory.

Truck Quotas and LLDCs

There are many situations in which the dominance of the road freight market by the transit country could be seen as a threat to the national integrity of an LLDC that depends on its services. It is also possible that it would take some time for the road freight companies in the landlocked country to increase their efficiency in order to become competitive with those of the transit country. These circumstances favor a gradual relaxation of quota agreements, accompanied as far as possible by efforts to harmonize rules and operating conditions between companies registered in the two countries.

One-on-one dealings on quotas in bilateral negotiations tend to favor the state that is least dependent on the economy of the other, which is more likely to be the transit country than the LLDC. So, although LLDCs often look to quota agreements to protect their smaller or less efficient trucking companies, this does not often work in practice, and the LLDCs continue to face difficulties defending their haulers' interests.

A recent example of a trading block that has eliminated truck quotas is found in the Greater Mekong subregion (GMS) of Southeast Asia. Under a cross-border transit agreement signed by GMS countries,[4] quotas are issued for transport between member countries on the basis of a number of approved vehicles rather than number of trips. This arrangement offers greater flexibility in responding to varying demand, but still raises opportunities for rent-seeking because quotas are still used. After the quota curbing the number of authorized transit operators (trucking services) between Thailand and Laos was lifted, tariffs fell by 20–30 percent. The dominant operator remained dominant, but the fact that shippers now had the option of going to other carriers gave them market power to negotiate lower tariffs.

Truck Driver Border Crossing Procedures
Systems for allowing truck drivers to cross borders can be almost as imposing as those for vehicles. Where trucks themselves are not allowed to cross the border, there is usually an exception so that the vehicles of each country can travel at least as far as a site where the freight can be transferred from one truck to the other, and these exceptions also specify the nationality of the driver who can take the truck this minimum distance into the other country. But these arrangements can require that two drivers are needed in each direction, either to change roles at the actual border or for a driver of one nationality to operate the vehicle in one direction and the other to operate it for the return to the original country.

These and all other systems require that drivers have a passport and usually a visa to enter and work in the second country. The most efficient systems are those that require a passport only, but because the driver will perform paid work in the second country, a visa is usually needed. A few bilateral agreements substitute a temporary passport entry for commercial drivers, with some requirement that they leave the country within a specified time. Where a multiple entry visa is allowed—and this can be issued at a consulate of the second country—the imposition of border cost and time penalties is minimized. But even where this is the formal system, immigration agencies sometimes insist on an additional visa issued at the border, obviating the advantage of the system. It is border immigration officers who ultimately determine the efficiency of any visa system.

While systems allowing passport only or multiple entry visas for commercial drivers are becoming the norm, many bilateral agreements still require that drivers obtain a separate visa for each entry to the second country, a costly and time-consuming procedure that adds little if anything to the national security or employment protection of that country that could not be achieved with a multiple entry visa system.

A best practice solution can be found in the League of Arab States, where private and commercial drivers who are residents in any one of the member countries can easily cross into another. This requires only the simple presentation of a carnet on which is recorded the date and place of each entry and exit among the member states.

Facilitating Truck Movement Through Transit Countries

Transit countries can adopt three types of measures that can affect the fluidity of traffic on their international land transport corridors: (1) formal checks on the trucks and their loads while they are in transit and charges for their road use, (2) informal checks during the same transit, and (3) charges for the use of convoys.

Formal Checks on Transit Trucks

The principal reason for checks on transit trucks is to ensure that they are not overloaded and that the vehicle owners pay road use fees. A complaint often made by transport ministries in transit countries is that transit trucks do not pay for the damage they cause to road pavement. A logical response is tighter enforcement of axle-load limits (since it is excessive axle loads that cause the most damage) and use of more weigh scales. These measures could address overloading but not the issue of payment for the use of roads. This is usually dealt with by imposing a fuel surcharge such that the total payment is approximately the same as the estimated cost of use of the roads.

The Southern African Development Community (SADC) is one of the regional economic communities that, while still having different charges for each country, has moved further than most in ensuring that charges are levied at the land borders or on fuel as a cost recovery mechanism. To reduce the risk that trucks from outside the community will try to enter with a full tank of fuel to avoid the fuel levies charged at the retail level, at some borders, the trucks are charged the fuel levy on the capacity of their fuel tank (box 6.3).

Axle Load Limits and Road Damage

Developing countries offer very few success stories on the imposition of axle load limits. Weigh scales are purchased and installed, and enforcement campaigns are waged for a month or two, but then political attention

---

Box 6.3

SADC Cost Recovery Mechanism

In the SADC*, the types of charges payable by vehicle operators when entering a country and using its roads vary considerably. There are two types of charges: (1) compulsory access fees, which are all charges payable at border posts upon entering a country and (2) other fees, including charges payable on toll roads, fuel levies, and fuel taxes. Almost all countries considered in the SADC's study charge compulsory access fees: seven of them apply transit charges, fees, or tolls, while the other four rely exclusively on other types of access fees (road transport permit fees, cross-border charges, and so on). However, almost every country considered imposes fuel levies (eight countries) or fuel taxes (three countries). Only South Africa and Mozambique currently apply fees on toll roads; in contrast, the Democratic Republic of Congo and Lesotho do apply tolls, but these are collected at the border.

The SADC study shows significant disparities in charges levied at the border post when entering a specific country. The Democratic Republic of Congo has the highest (US$565 for heavy vehicles), followed by Zimbabwe (US$370), Zambia (US$80), Namibia (US$43–US$136), Botswana (US$36–US$121), and Mozambique (US$100). Lesotho (US$2–US$4) and Malawi (US$8–US$15) have the lowest charges. South Africa is the only country where no compulsory access charges are levied at the border; however, toll fees are levied if transit vehicles travel on toll roads.**

Source: Africon 2007.
*SADC member states are Angola, Botswana, Democratic Republic of Congo, Lesotho, Madagascar, Malawi, Mauritius, Mozambique, Namibia, Seychelles, South Africa, Swaziland, United Republic of Tanzania, Zambia, and Zimbabwe.
**The compulsory access charge considered is the minimum payable for each country and vehicle type (assuming the minimum distance traveled within the destination country). Charges payable in advance for a specific time period are also based on the minimum (for example, per month, such as in the case of foreign vehicle permit fees for light vehicles in Tanzania).

moves on, old habits resume, and little is changed. In very few countries is axle load enforcement anything more than spasmodic and intermittent. These observations apply to the enforcement of axle load limits to all trucks, not just those in transit, but the overloading of transit trucks is seen as more pernicious than that of trucks conducting domestic business.

In contrast, a more rational response in economic terms is to allocate additional funds for strengthening pavements where overloaded transit trucks are believed to do the most damage and then to charge the transit trucks for this additional expense.

For operators, the short-term economies of scale of overloading can be compelling, and they have strong commercial incentives to load their trucks to their physical capacity. Capacity not used is lost—it cannot be stored for sale later on. The short-term gains in revenue are directly proportional to the additional freight carried, whereas the cost to the operator in terms of additional truck maintenance or shorter vehicle life do not become apparent for some time and are often lost in the overall costs of the business. Unless the truck operators are charged for the damage the overloading causes to the road pavement, they can completely escape the highest cost of overloading.

From a national economic perspective, the total operating costs of all trucks using a road, when added to government expenditures on pavement rehabilitation and strengthening, are lower than the sum of the truck operating and road pavement costs with trucks loaded only to their legal axle load limit. World Bank studies in the 1980s (Harrall and Faiz 1988) demonstrated that on all but the most lightly used roads, stronger pavements were economically justified, because the savings in truck operating costs of carrying more freight outweighed the extra construction or repaving cost.

It is routine practice for trucks engaged in international transport to be weighed at the border post of entry. Transport ministries can and do use the same information to verify axle loads. To avoid multiple weighing on a single international trip, the UNECE has designed and is promoting an International Weight Certificate that, if issued by authorities in the country of origin, will be accepted by all border agencies in transit and destination countries.

Trucks engaged in international transport are rarely to blame for deterioration of road pavement because they can readily be controlled upon entry into the country. If taxes on diesel fuel are set at appropriate levels, these trucks can be made to pay taxes roughly commensurate with the wear and tear they incur. A rough rule of thumb is that 10 U.S. cents per liter of diesel will cover normal wear and tear. In most circumstances, the best solution for weakened pavement is to spend more on road maintenance, which provides its own reward by delaying pavement deterioration and by allowing for fuller use of domestic trucks.

Informal Checks on Transit Trucks

Although it is reasonably easy to address formal checks on transit trucks and to replace convoys, often the informal checks imposed by local authorities or police are much less amenable to remedies. By their very nature, these informal checks are of many different types and impose different levels of cost and time delays. The uncertainty involved in encountering them, as well as the uncertain monetary cost and time delay for negotiation, can often be a greater impediment than the actual cost and time. The practice of imposing informal checkpoints on transit trucks is global and not restricted to one region or continent.

A study of informal checkpoints on road corridors in West Africa (USAID 2008) found the following:

- Most of the informal checkpoints were operated by the customs agencies, second-most were operated by police.
- The Ouagadougou (Burkina Faso)–Bamako (Mali) Corridor had the most informal checkpoints at 24, while the Lomé (Togo)–Ouagadougou Corridor was least obstructed, with "only" 18 checkpoints.
- Payments were highest in Mali, averaging the equivalent of about U$25 per 100 km, and the time penalties were also highest in Mali at 38 minutes per 100 km, closely followed by Burkina Faso at 33 minutes per 100 km.
- In Togo, the delays were least at "only" 16 minutes per 100 km.

A World Bank study (2006) of transit corridors in Central Asia found that customs intervened less frequently but demanded higher informal payments than traffic police. On the Bishkek–Osh highway in the Kyrgyz Republic, transit trucks were stopped more than 20 times and had to pay more than US$35 equivalent in informal payments.

For Rwandan trucks transiting Tanzania, *informal* payments at *formal* weigh stations were a greater impediment than informal checkpoints, with more than a dozen such locations in a transit of less than 1,000 km (USAID 2008). Even empty returning trucks are weighed to check for overloading, or they have to make an informal payment to avoid excessive time lost waiting to be weighed.

The uncertainty of informal payments makes the cost to traders several times greater than the cost to the trucking company. The transport tariff charged has to be enough to cover the maximum out-of-pocket cost to the driver and the maximum time delay to the truck, or else the trucking company will have to fund the difference from its profit margin. To avoid this risk, the tariff charged usually must be much greater than that actually incurred during the transit of the truck.

Recommendations

Trucking is bound to remain the main mode of transportation available to developing country corridors for the foreseeable future. Unfortunately, until recently, the role of the sector for corridor performance and the urge to modernize it was not fully recognized by policy makers and development institutions active in low-income countries. In virtually all regions, much needs to be done when it comes to incentives for quality, economies of scale, introduction of competition, and consistency of enforcement of regulations within and across borders. The following areas are especially important.

Structure of the Trucking Industry

Both LLDCs and transit countries could improve the structure of their trucking industries by replacing quantity with quality licensing, with high-quality requirements for international road freight companies that are compatible with the demands of clients in that market. Provision should also be made for licensed international road freight companies to accede to any system of AEOs that might be operating in the country.

Meanwhile, but more difficult to implement, the domestic road freight market could be liberalized, with quality requirements for individual and small transport companies limited to safety and environmental standards. For medium-size transport companies, quality requirements could be more demanding to include managerial and financial standards.

Queuing Systems

Queuing systems impose such high costs on trading companies that the harm outweighs any benefit from the employment generated by maintaining a larger than necessary trucking industry. It is easier to reform the queuing system for transit road freight than for domestic road freight in either an LLDC or its transit neighbor. It is recommended that queuing systems be abolished for international freight operators and be replaced by freedom for traders to contract with any licensed operator.

Quota Systems

Quota systems that restrict free contracting should be abolished. However, their short-term continuation could give road freight operators in small LLDCs time to prepare for greater competition from operators. Therefore, quotas should be allowed to continue where they can be expected to have short-term restructuring benefits, but any such continuation should be time bound to less than five years.

Continuing quota systems should only be used to guarantee minimum market share for each country, not to limit volume of trade. Minimum quotas for each country are preferable instead of trying to control total road freight by quotas. Such systems can issue a fixed number of quotas for each country (enough to ensure viability of the industry), with any additional road transport being open to companies in either country (or even from third countries to better comply with WTO requirements).

Procedures for Moving Trucks Across Borders

Truck specifications and vehicle insurance requirements should be made compatible between LLDCs and their transit neighbors. Once this is achieved, the only necessary restriction on trucks crossing borders would be a verification of their documents.

Procedures for Moving Drivers Across Borders

The recommendation in respect to commercial drivers is that multiple entry visas, valid for at least one year, should be used where single entry visas are now required. Multiple entry visas would not impose any security or commercial threat to the country issuing them, but would facilitate bilateral transport movements. Where both the LLDC and transit country are members of a regional regime, the use of driver carnets would be even more efficient that multiple entry visas.

Facilitating Truck Transit

To facilitate the movement of transit trucks through transit countries, two areas are recommended for change: checks on overloading and informal checks on transit trucks.

The recommendation with respect to checks on overloading of transit vehicles and charging for use of roads is that both need only be made at borders for exports from LLDCs and at ports for trucks transporting their imports. A border or port weight certificate should be accepted to avoid intermediate en-route checks and payments, even where they are used for trucks transporting national goods only. The truck should be reweighed at the destination port (for exports) or at the border crossing (for imports) to verify the certificate.

There are no satisfactory solutions to the problem of informal checkpoints and informal payments for transit trucks. Any potential solution lies more in changes in social attitudes to observance of laws and avoidance of bribery and other types of informal payment demands than it does to specific measures within the transport and trade sectors.

Notes

1. *Universidad Tecnológica Nacional,* Argentina, 2007.
2. Based on 2009 data from Egypt's Ministry of Transport.
3. Mongolia Infrastructure Strategy, World Bank 2006.
4. The GMS agreement is formally known as the Agreement Between and Among the Governments of the Kingdom of Cambodia, the People's Republic of China, the Lao People's Democratic Republic, the Union of Myanmar, the Kingdom of Thailand, and the Socialist Republic of Viet Nam for Facilitation of Cross-Border Transport of Goods and People.

References

Africon. 2007. "Implementation of Harmonised Road User Charges System in the SADC Region: Final Report." Report to SADC (Southern African Development Community) Secretariat.

Harrall, Clell G., and A. Faiz. 1988. "Road Deterioration in Developing Countries: Causes and Remedies." World Bank Policy Study 13370, World Bank, Washington, DC.

OECD (Organisation for Economic Co-operation and Development). 2001. "Regulatory Reform in Road Freight Transport." Proceedings of the International Seminar on Regulatory Reform in Road Freight Transport, European Conference of Ministers of Transport, February.

Rushton, A., P. Croucher, and P. Baker. 2006. *The Handbook of Logistics and Distribution Management.* London: Kogan Page.

Universidad Tecnológica Nacional, Argentina. 2007. *Transporte Automotor de Cargas en la República Argentina, Centro Tecnológico de Transporte, Tránsito y Seguridad Vial* (C3T), *Universidad Tecnológica Nacional,* Argentina. http://www.utn.edu.ar/secretarias/extension/c3tlibro.utn.

USAID (U.S. Agency for International Development). 2008. "Improved Road Transport Governance Initiative on Interstate Highways." USAID West Africa Trade Hub.

———. 2009. *Freight Transport Development Toolkit: Road Freight.* World Bank Energy, Water, and Transport Department, Washington, DC.

———. 2010. "Success Story: Civil Society Tackles Road Corruption." USAID West Africa, June 29. http://www.watradehub.com/sites/default/files/resourcefiles/jun10/transport-success-story.pdf.

CHAPTER 7

Alternative Transport Modes and the Role of Logistics Intermediaries

Road freight is the primary mode of transportation on trade corridors and the primary mode in nearly all landlocked developing countries (LLDCs), but other services such as river or rail are also important for LLDCs' connectivity to trade. However, although the availability of alternative modes does reduce the vulnerability of being dependent on only one transportation mode, it is not as important as the availability of back-up corridors (chapter 3).

Furthermore, trade relies on ancillary services provided by brokers and forwarders to clear goods in transit or at destinations and can benefit from the development of storage and distribution services such as container depots. Although not exclusive to LLDCs, these topics may be of greater significance because of LLDCs' relatively small freight volume and shallow markets, which make implementation of sound policies even more challenging and economies of scale on the modal infrastructure difficult to generate.

The main alternatives to roads as transport modes for LLDCs are rail, air, and waterways (rivers and lakes). Fifteen of the LLDCs have, in addition to road connections, a rail link to a port in a transit neighbor; only one has river-to-sea or lake connection; eight have both; and five have neither and rely exclusively on roads for all their international land transport (table 7.1).

Table 7.1   LLDCs with Rail and Water Transport Connections

Region	Rail	River, Sea, or Lake	Both rail and water	Neither rail nor water
Sub-Saharan Africa	Botswana Burkina Faso Ethiopia Lesotho Malawi Mali Swaziland Zambia Zimbabwe	Central African Republic	Burundi Uganda	Chad Rwanda Niger
South America			Plurinational State of Bolivia Paraguay	
Central Asia	Kyrgyz Rep. Tajikistan Uzbekistan		Azerbaijan Kazakhstan Turkmenistan	
East Asia	Mongolia		Lao PDR	
South Asia	Nepal			Afghanistan Bhutan
Eastern Europe	Armenia			
Totals	**15**	**1**	**8**	**5**

Source: Authors.
Note: The former Yugoslav Republic of Macedonia and the Republic of Moldova are not included in this list, because they are de facto connected to the European Union transport network.

Each of the alternatives to road transport has different characteristics and applications: railroad and waterways bring substantive cost reductions over long distances and favor the exports of bulk commodities: minerals, cotton, and timber in Africa and soy in Bolivia and Paraguay. None of the alternative modes is likely to be a determining factor in the economic development of LLDCs, although they do offer some security against disruption of a sole transport source as well as protection against monopolistic exploitation by sole-source operators. These transport modes are typically slower and induce more delays than trucking and, hence, are unlikely to help the diversification into new, and likely time-sensitive, value-added production.

Even so, these alternative modes do have the potential to make a significant contribution to LLDCs success as traders by simply providing competition to road transport operators and, in many corridors, by offering a genuine alternative blend of service quality and price to road transport. However, they are rarely given the opportunity to achieve this role, given their lack of attention in the trade and transport policies of LLDCs.

This chapter illustrates the main features of these alternative transport modes and suggests ways they could realize their potential of expanding trade opportunities for LLDCs. The second part of the chapter highlights what are sometimes considered ancillary players in freight transport: the intermediaries between traders and transport operators, such as freight forwarders and customs brokers. Since these ancillary operators play a large role in the actual mode choices of exporters and importers, they help determine whether the availability of an alternative mode will make any difference to the trade and transport operations of an LLDC. Their role is important because their competence and efficiency are a determining factor in how competitive a trader's business will be. However, their experience and capabilities in most LLDCs is often less than that of their colleagues in coastal and more developed countries; thus, this chapter will suggest how this difference can be reduced to the benefit of traders in the LLDCs.

The third part of this chapter provides a brief review of the role in LLDCs' trade procedures of inland container depots (ICDs), a term that has become standard in the industry, but more accurately referred to as inland container terminals or "dry ports." They have a potential that has not yet been realized to assist the clearance process of imported goods far away from the transit country border and to consolidate exports.

Rail Transport: Underused Potential

For LLDCs, rail transport has potential advantages over road transport in terms of lower tariffs and shorter, more reliable transit times. These advantages can come in part from higher speeds, but mostly from shorter border-crossing wait times and fewer en-route delays. However, the extent to which these potential advantages can be realized is a subject of debate, with conflicting evidence from different trade corridors.

Many LLDCs export mainly low-value bulk products, which a well-run railway could serve at substantially lower cost than road transport. This is a possibility especially in cases in which domestic rail freight is in decline, leaving railroad capacity underused (which means marginal operating costs for transit freight would be low). However, many LLDCs' and transit countries' railway infrastructure and services are in poor condition. This makes railways unattractive to transit traffic, which, in a vicious cycle, further reinforces the decline in railway activity and in the railway's finances. This has been the situation for many railways that service LLDCs, although concessioning of services in some corridors has brought about improvement in service quality. The next section presents an analysis of the potential for breaking the cycle of declining demand, service quality, and financial success and suggests the circumstances needed and the potential outcomes that might be expected.[1]

Thresholds for Rail Competitiveness

There are two thresholds that railways would find it very difficult, if not impossible, to compete with road freight: traffic volume and transport distance.

Traffic volume. Given their high proportion of fixed costs and low variable costs, railways can be financially viable (that is, with revenues covering both infrastructure renewal and maintenance, as well as costs of operating the trains) only when their traffic volume is above a minimum threshold. Where freight traffic is less than about 250,000 net tons per year, it is unlikely that services can be maintained, even in the short term; where traffic is less than 1 million net tons per year, it is unlikely the railway can be maintained in the long term.

Between these two levels, it might be possible to keep a reliable and cost-effective service operating, perhaps long enough to attract additional traffic to generate more revenue and to enhance the long-term viability of the service. If the government (or governments, where the line links to an LLDC) is prepared to invest in track rehabilitation, even when it is not directly financially viable, then the line could continue operating much longer. The nonfinancial justifications for such investment could include providing a least-operating-cost route for international trade or keeping a second trade corridor available in case of monopoly exploitation or physical interruption to the main corridor (for example, public funding of the maintenance of infrastructure on Uganda's railway link to Kenya can be justified on both arguments).

Transport distance. With the exception of the few instances where railways have a direct link to the final destination of their freight (such as to a mine or an industrial site), their clients also have to bear the costs of transfer of their freight to another transport mode to reach that final destination. Railway transport, therefore, has high terminal costs (the costs of this transport by another mode to their final destination or from the origin of the freight). Competing road transport does not have an equivalent high terminal cost.

Thus, there is a minimum distance threshold that railways need to satisfy so that their lower en-route costs can overcome these terminal costs. The use of unit container trains and efficient loading and unloading of container wagons has reduced this distance threshold,[2] but it is still on the order of 400–500 km. Most LLDCs are located farther than this distance from the port in their transit neighbors (as shown in table 7.2), thus there are only a few transport corridors to LLDCs where this threshold limits the competitiveness of rail transport. One of these corridors is La Paz, Bolivia, which is about 470 km from the nearest seaport of Arica, Chile. The container service on this corridor proved unsustainable and was suspended several years ago, indicating that the distance was too short to sustain a railway service.[3]

In addition to operating cost advantage, railways can offer faster transit times because their border delays are much shorter than those for road freight. Rail transport also avoids the informal road checkpoints that hinder and add to the cost of road transit freight. Security in transit is another advantage of rail over road transport. Rail-borne containers are less susceptible to theft than those transported by road. Two or three containers can be loaded onto a single rail flatcar with no space between in such a way that the doors of one container are right up against the next, making it impossible to open them en route.

Table 7.2   Rail Distances of Selected LLDCs to a Port

City in inland country	Deepwater port	Mode	Distance (km)
Bamako, Mali	Abidjan, Côte d'Ivoire	Road/Rail	1,150
Bamako, Mali	Dakar, Senegal	Rail	1,200
Bobo-Dioulasso, Burkina Faso	Abidjan, Côte d'Ivoire	Rail	850
Kampala, Uganda	Mombasa, Kenya	Rail	1,400
Kapiri Mposhi, Zambia	Dar es Salaam, Tanzania	Rail	1,870
N'djamena, Chad	Douala, Cameroon	Road/Rail	1,900
Asunción, Paraguay	Buenos Aires, Argentina	Road/Rail	1,100
La Paz, Bolivia	Arica, Chile	Rail	470
Santa Cruz, Bolivia	Paranagua, Brazil	Rail	1,700
Almaty, Kazakhstan	Hamburg, Germany	Rail	4,900
Almaty, Kazakhstan	Shanghai, China	Rail	5,630
Nepal	Kolkata, India	Rail	700
Tashkent, Uzbekistan	Lianyungang, China	Rail	6,600
Ulanbaataar, Mongolia	Tianjin, China	Rail	1,690

Source: Authors.

Even with these advantages, railway documentation for international movements is still quite complicated. Border crossings by rail trigger complex operational processes and procedures, including changes of locomotive and crew, break-of-gauge operations (as at the border with China), marshalling (classifying and separating railcars), technical inspections, and transfer and acceptance of railway documents on the rolling stock and the freight. Customs agencies, meanwhile, have to check railway bills of lading against wagon lists and cargo documents, and certain physical inspections may be conducted by customs and plant and animal controls. Because the railway company often has reason to hold incoming trains in a marshalling yard at the first major rail junction inside the country of entry, time could be saved if customs and the other border controls could perform their documentary and physical inspections at the same location, rather than at the border. In addition, a broken seal or a documentation problem could delay a whole trainload of consignments, compared to just the truckload in the case of road freight; thus, though rail freight delays are less frequent, each incident can be more costly.

Studies done under the auspices of TRACECA (Transport Corridor Europe–Caucasus–Asia)[4] (2004) show that border crossing procedures can be simplified and streamlined and have recommended performance indicators to establish common standards (box 7.1). In particular,

---

Box 7.1

Railway Border Performance Indicators

The processing time for railway border-crossing operations depends on the number of railway cars and the extent of the inspections. However, good practice suggests that a target processing time of 120 minutes (divided as shown) should be achievable, even on the largest international trains:

- Railways: registration of documents, approximately 30 minutes
- Customs: registration of documents, approximately 60 minutes
- Railways: final preparation of documents, approximately 30 minutes.

Inspection by both railways and customs should be completed within two hours.

Source: TRACECA 2002.

procedures could be simplified and standardized if the railway company were to organize its traffic in the form of block trains (that is, uniform in the origin and destination of all wagons in a given train) operating to a timetable between the seaport and the main destination in the LLDC and vice versa. Better still, if this traffic were largely containerized, the control procedures could be kept to a minimum.

Commodities for Railway Transport to LLDCs

Most imports to LLDCs are manufactured consumer and industrial goods, often containerized, whereas most exports are bulk grains and minerals. The possibility of backhaul loads is what makes any transport enterprise financially feasible. The ability to transport backhauls depends on a certain level of compatibility among the products being transported. Many of the constraints that once made products incompatible for backhaul have been overcome. For example, for the transport of export grain, fertilizer as a backhaul product was once considered infeasible because of its contamination of the bulk wagons. But contamination can now be avoided by using collapsible polypropylene liners, thus bulk fertilizer is now a possible backhaul product in grain wagons.

Compatibility between containers and bulk products is more difficult to address. Given that the containers must be backhauled anyway, it is sometimes financially and operationally feasible to load grain and minerals into them, at least for the rail transport to the deepwater port. As an example, copper ingots exported from Zambia are loaded into what would otherwise be empty backhaul containers, not only a saving in transport cost but also an increase in security for an otherwise high-risk product. Even chilled or refrigerated products can make use of regular backhaul container wagons through the use of clip-on refrigeration units, rather than needing specialized refrigerated wagons. This approach is used for the transport of fresh mangoes grown in Burkina Faso and exported via Abidjan.

So, given enough imagination by and cooperation between traders and railway operators, most backhaul products can be made compatible with the wagons that are available to transport them. More problematic is the imbalance between import and export volumes. For most LLDCs, there is an excess of exports over imports by volume. Other than increasing imports, which for trade balance and other reasons is an undesirable strategy, there is little that can be done to address this issue. Both rail and road operators offer large discounts for the use of what would otherwise be empty backhaul capacity, but any advantage gained from this is to the detriment of the competing transport mode.

Ownership of Containers

Despite the efforts to increase compatibility between forward and back-haul loads, the high volume of imports compared to exports for most LLDCs imposes another cost on their demurrage charges for overdue containers. Although the relatively long distances involved in rail corridors to LLDCs help to improve their competitiveness relative to road transport, the long transit times and delays in waiting for a return load often result in demurrage penalties. Given the large imbalance of import relative to export containers, there can be a very long delay between the container being unloaded in the LLDC and it being reloaded with an export load. The international shipping lines that own many of the containers in circulation impose time limits enforced by financial penalties on how long a container may remain inland before having to be returned to the port. The limit is often as little as 15 days, and the daily penalty often increases with the number of over limit days incurred. To avoid these long delays, it is often less expensive for the importer to incur the cost of returning the container to the port empty than to incur the time penalties of waiting for a return load. In extreme cases, the importer has to buy the container before it can be transported inland to an LLDC.

Unitized Container Trains

The use of the block trains of containers and multiparty negotiations among the railways of the landlocked and transit countries, the customs and border police of the transit country, and the shipping lines that own the containers can ensure that the containers are returned to the port consistently within the deadline.

A Regional Perspective on Railway Services to LLDCs

The extent to which the potential advantages of rail transport have been realized, and the potential volume and distance thresholds that have impacted on that realization, vary significantly between trade corridors and particularly between regions of the world. This section will review the performance of railways in trade corridors in three different regions of the world—Sub-Saharan Africa, South America, and Central Asia—and will summarize lessons learned from those experiences.

In Sub-Saharan Africa, 11 of the 15 LLDCs have rail access, but all have low volumes of freight traffic, most because they are small countries with few exports. In addition, the poor infrastructure and operation of their railways prevents them from transporting more. South America has two LLDCs, both small countries with few exports, but their railways are performing well and are profitable for their private operators. The LLDCs of Central Asia have more substantial trade volumes and their railways are also performing well with rapidly growing services to Russia, the European Union (EU), and China.

Sub-Saharan African Railways

In Sub-Saharan Africa, many of the transport corridors from LLDCs to a deepwater port are so long that, under normal circumstances, railways would be a preferable transport mode to roads. However, with a few exceptions, railways have been unable to attract significant traffic from the region's LLDCs. This is the case in part because traffic levels in some countries are below the 250,000 net ton per year threshold for even short-term sustainability of a rail line; while in other countries, the condition of railway infrastructure is so poor that the higher traffic threshold of 1 million net ton minimum is needed to generate enough revenue to fund its rehabilitation. Few lines have reached this level, although many have the potential to do so.

Despite having distances long enough to support efficient rail freight services, most railways in Africa suffer different and multiple constraints. With a few notable exceptions, railways play only a small role in the trade of most transit corridors. The multiple constraints include the poor quality of infrastructure, the unrealistic way the infrastructure costs have been shared between the railway agencies (representing the governments) and the concessionaires, and the types of companies that have won the concessions, including their relationship with the operators of the container terminals in the ports that they serve. Together these characteristics negatively impact their competitiveness compared to road transport.

The two West African rail corridors to landlocked Mali and Burkina Faso offer valuable insights into what is needed to make such services financially sustainable. There are two rail corridors, one from the port city of Abidjan in Côte d'Ivoire to Ouagadougou, the capital of Burkina Faso; the other from the port city of Dakar in Senegal to Bamako, the capital of Mali. The first concession is functioning well and expanding its services despite the intervention of a civil war in 2002–04 soon after it started, while freight services on the second have virtually stopped, and freight forwarders are advising clients to use alternative routes.

The coastal countries have comparable per capita incomes (table 7.3), but the international trade of Côte d'Ivoire is a much higher share of its gross domestic product (GDP) than is that of Senegal. In contrast, Burkina Faso (the principal LLDC served by the rail link from Côte d'Ivoire) has a much lower trade share of GDP than has Mali (the principle LLDC served

Table 7.3   Economic and Social Comparison of Four West African Countries, 2008

Country	GDP (US$, billions)	GDP per capita (US$)	Trade as percent of GDP	Population (millions)	Area (km²)
Burkina Faso	15.5	1,170	29	4.8	274
Côte d'Ivoire	4.8	1,551	73	15.5	318
Mali	4.9	989	45	13.1	1,240
Senegal	7.6	1,697	52	11.3	192

Source: Authors' compilation from World Bank database.

by Senegal). So the countries that mostly trade through the first corridor, Côte d'Ivoire and Burkina Faso, have about the same average trade share of GDP (51 percent) as those that use the second corridor, Senegal and Mali (48 percent). However, the total GDP (and the international trade) of the countries using the first corridor, is almost double that of those using the second corridor. The population immediately served by the first corridor (20.3 million) is rather less than that immediately served by the second corridor (24.4 million). While these socioeconomic differences indicate a greater trade potential for the Abidjan-based corridor than the Dakar-based corridor, this difference is not enough to explain the significant difference in performance of their rail services (see box 7.2).

Four significant differences between the ways these two railway lines were established have dictated the outcome of the concessions and the quality of the rail service they offer to the LLDCs that rely on them:

- **Concessionaire responsibility in financing infrastructure:** well assigned in Abidjan–Ouagadougou, but with too much responsibility in Dakar–Bamako, taking into account the volume of freight traffic to support it.
- **Condition of infrastructure when the concession started:** upgraded before it declined to an unrecoverable level in Abidjan–Ouagadougou, but left until the railways had deteriorated so far that the funding was inadequate in Dakar–Bamako.
- **Nature of the concession operating company:** an integrated logistics company in Abidjan–Ouagadougou; a specialized railway operator with limited regional experience and connections in Dakar–Bamako.
- **Port container terminal operator:** an early concession to a consortium including the railway operator with a regional logistics interest in Abidjan–Ouagadougou; but a later concessioning to a specialized port container terminal operator in Dakar–Bamako.

Box 7.2

Contrasting Railway Concessions in Côte d'Ivoire and Senegal

The Dakar–Bamako and Abidjan–Ouagadougou transit corridors are of comparable length at 1,240 km and 1,180 km, respectively, both meter-gauge and long
enough that rail transport should be competitive with road freight if the volumes
are high enough. The origins of the two railways are very similar, both having
been operated as single administrations until all four countries became independent in 1960, but their fortunes since then have been quite different. Freight
services on the Dakar–Bamako rail line have virtually ceased, while the Abidjan–
Ouagadougou railway corridor is thriving despite a civil war in Côte d'Ivoire
between 2002 and 2004.

The route from Abidjan was the first to be concessioned in 1993 to Sitarail,
a consortium in which the governments of Côte d'Ivoire and Burkina Faso each
hold a 15 percent share, staff hold 3 percent; and foreign companies associated with the French-based Bolloré group now holding the remaining shares
(67 percent). The original assets of the railway are still owned by the two governments (through holding companies), and the concessionaire pays a lease
fee for their use. The concessionaire has added assets of its own, most recently
two new 3,300-hp locomotives from General Motors. Although the two governments funded significant rehabilitation before the concession started, now
Sitarail prepares infrastructure investment programs, which, when revised and
accepted, are funded by the holding company, with Sitarail paying a debt
charge to cover this cost. The container terminal in the port of Abidjan was
concessioned in 2003 to a consortium that includes the railway operator. This
link, together with the operator's other logistics interests, results in the railway
being part of a well-integrated logistics service throughout the region and
especially to its LLDCs that are also served by onward road services from
Burkina Faso.

In contrast, the route from Dakar was not concessioned until 2003, by which
time it had been through several changes of administrative structure, switching
between two-country ownership and several versions of joint operation. The
concession agreement made with Transrail differs from that for the Abidjan line,
with the concessionaire buying traction and rolling stock rather than leasing it or
paying the debt charges for new assets. In addition, the concessionaire is responsible for more of the track rehabilitation cost than in the Abidjan Corridor. The

(continued)

Box 7.2 *(continued)*

funding for rehabilitation of the track was delayed so long that by the time it was put to use, the condition of the track had deteriorated so far that the funding was totally inadequate.

Transrail was originally a consortium of Canadian and French companies, but the Canadian railway operating company was taken over by a U.S.-based company, which then sold it to a Belgian railway operator. Another interest is held by Senegalese entrepreneurs. Dakar's port container terminal was not concessioned until 2007, by which time the Abidjan concession had been operating for four years and had gained a strong initial competitive advantage. The Dakar terminal is concessioned to Dubai Ports World, recognized as one of the world's most dynamic container terminal operators. But it is highly specialized in port operations and does not have the logistics connections throughout the region that the Abidjan operator has.

Source: Authors.

South American Railways

Both LLDCs in Latin America, Bolivia and Paraguay, have rail lines to ports in their transit neighbors, and the distances should be long enough to make rail transport a viable alternative to road transport if the volumes are also high enough. Bolivia has four rail links to deepwater ports. One is a 1,700-km line to the port of Paranagua in Brazil, which transports just under 1 million ton per year of soya exports and a mixture of agricultural, industrial, and commercial imports. The line is operated under a concession to a group of Bolivian pension companies and a United States–Canada company (Genesee & Wyoming, Inc.). The same consortium operates services on the Bolivian section of the second line, 1,024 km from Santa Cruz to Buenos Aires. This second line transports less than 0.25 m tons of freight (below the minimum feasibility threshold) and has never transported much more. However, committed investments on upgrading the infrastructure and services on the Argentinean section of the line hold the promise of significant increases in freight traffic.

Services to the third line, to the closer port of Arica in Chile (only 470 km from La Paz, Bolivia) were suspended in 2006 following a disastrous flood and the insolvency of the operator of the Chilean section of the line. Services are still operated at a profit on the 1,870-km privately owned

Ferrocarril Antofagasta Bolivia railway, from the nitrate mines of southern Bolivia to the Chilean port of Antofagasta. In 2003–05, it hauled about 4 million tons each year over average distances of more than 800 km.

The fourth line, from Oruro in southern Bolivia to Buenos Aires, is still in operation but transports little freight because the connecting railway in Argentina (the narrow-gauge Belgrano Railway) was the only one not to be concessioned in the 1990s. Until 2010, the government of Argentina had not found a way of funding its desperately needed physical renovation if it was to continue operation. Freight services had almost ceased to operate. But between 2008 and 2010, Argentina entered into a number of agreements with agencies of China to secure funding for new locomotives and wagons and to rehabilitate much of the track. If these renovations are actually undertaken, the Belgrano Railway could transport much of the soy now grown in the south of Bolivia to the privately operated and specialized soya ports on the Paraguay River in Argentina, involving distances of up to 1,500 km. This upgrading will similarly benefit the second line (that from Santa Cruz) that also depends on the Belgrano Railway for its access to a port. The financial feasibility of such a service would depend on the Argentine government accepting much of the cost of reconstructing the railway infrastructure and not passing the cost on to the railway and its users.

Paraguay's railway closed in the 1990s, but there is still a freight connection across the border near Encarnación to link with the América Latina Logística (ALL) route to Buenos Aires via its Mesopotamica Line, which also has connections to Uruguay and Brazil. The distance from Encarnación to Buenos Aires is about 1,850 km, and the railway transports about 1 million tons of freight per year. ALL[5] is responsible for all the costs of maintenance of the railway infrastructure, and so far, it has found ways of minimizing such costs without compromising the safety or reliability of the freight service while also keeping the service financially viable.

Central Asian Railways

In Central Asia, the railway played a central role in regional transport networks until the break-up of the Soviet Union. The national railways of the Commonwealth of Independent States all benefit in their cross-border rail traffic from a common set of technical standards and operating procedures. Much of the freight volume comprises bulk cargo, such as ferrous and nonferrous metals, coal, cotton, grain, and oil and oil products, that can be carried more economically by rail than by road. The heavy industry of Kazakhstan and its long distances to seaports or international markets played to the railways' strengths. Uzbekian cotton sold to western markets via Riga, Latvia, and Poti, Georgia, is a classic example of long-distance rail freight, being a bulk product with the transport distances of more than 4,000 km and transport cost and time much less than by road.

Since 1992, road transport has taken a rapidly growing share of the regional and international transport market for Central Asia, but starting from a small base. Rail still offers large advantages in principle over the long distances often involved (for example, transit across Kazakhstan alone is about 1,700 km). In addition to their advantages for bulk products, the railways of Central Asia are finding ways to compete for containerized freight as Central Asian markets are opening up to manufactured products from Europe and East Asia and as more of their own manufactured products are finding markets in Europe (box 7.3).

More recently, various consortia of railway companies and freight forwarders have started operating regular container trains to Central Asia from China, Europe, and Russia. While few of these yet offer direct services, the transit times, even allowing for the change of trains at railway hub cities, are still competitive with truck services, and tariffs are lower and reliability higher. There remain operational problems in the longer distance services, particularly gauge changes between Russian and Chinese railways, but these are being addressed by the operators themselves with the support of EU agencies, such as TRACECA, United Nations Economic and Social Commission for Asia and the Pacific (UNESCAP), and the International Union of Railways (UIC).

For some of these services, the railway authority operates the trains, while the freight forwarding member of the consortium buys train capacity on a block basis and on-sells that capacity to its clients. In this way, the railway operator focuses on its specialty of train operations and has a known revenue stream on which to plan services, while the freight forwarder specializes in marketing the capacity provided by the operator and bears the commercial risk of finding customers and applying flexible market pricing.

These services use mostly traditional routes via central Russia and others via the TRACECA route: crossing the Black Sea to Poti, Georgia, then by rail to Baku, Azerbaijan, then crossing the Caspian to Turkmenistan or to the Kazakh port of Aktau, and continuing by rail to Central Asia.

Kazakh Railways in 2007 hauled about 13 million tons of freight in transit and 260 million tons in all. The rate for crossing Kazakhstan by rail, at the equivalent of about 2 U.S. cents per ton-km, was some US$33 per ton (not including loading and other handling charges). That was far

Box 7.3

Rail Container Services to Central Asia

Kazakhstan Railways (KTZ) is the leading operator of container trains between China, Russia, and the LLDCs of Central Asia. KTZ uses Almaty as a hub to connect services from Europe, particularly the Baltic ports, to most of Central Asia. In 2007, it operated more than 1,000 international container trains, connecting Almaty to Nakhodka, a port in Siberia; Lianyungang, a port city near Shanghai; Tianjin, the main port city for Beijing; Moscow; Urumqi in western China; Novorossiysk, the main Russian port city on the Black Sea; and Chelyabinsk, a Russian city close to the northern border of Kazakhstan.

Polzug, a German–Polish railway consortium that includes the Port of Hamburg, operates scheduled rail container services between North Sea ports and Poland, Russia, the Caucasus, and Central Asia. It operates four container trains per day from Hamburg to Lithuania, Poland, and Ukraine, and four weekly services to the same destinations from Bremerhaven and Rotterdam, Germany. All these services provide on-carriage by rail to Central Asia, China, Mongolia, and Russia. While these are all regular services, Polzug has also operated exploratory services, such as one between Shanghai and Hamburg. The downturn in global trade and collapse of shipping rates in 2009 reduced the window in which this service could be attractive—it is much faster but rather more expensive than the sea routes between Europe and China, but slower and less expensive than air freight. But this does not apply to the routes of Central Asia to Europe, Central Asia to China, and Russia for which there is no feasible maritime alternative.

Source: Deliver Journal (http://www.deliverjournal.com/en/) and *POLZUG Intermodal GmbH* (http://www.polzug.de/index.php?id=25&L=2).

less than the cost by road of at least US$150 per ton—with informal payments at checkpoints along the highway estimated to make up about a quarter of this amount.

The rail network developed during the Soviet era crisscrossed borders between republics with minimal train stops and controls at the borders, and the whole enterprise came under the integrated management of the USSR-level Ministry of Railways. Now each republic's operations are managed separately, and substantial controls have been put in place at every border. Meanwhile, only limited progress has been made in modernizing the management structures of the still state-owned railway monopolies and giving them a stronger commercial orientation. Most lack strong incentives to improve performance in the face of the rapidly growing competition from privatized road transport, which is eroding their business.

Kazakhstan, by far the largest of the Central Asian railway systems and carrying five-sixths of the region's rail traffic, has innovated more than its Central Asian neighbors. It has spun off noncore activities and has adopted a plan to create separate companies for each main business segment, that is, freight and passengers—as Russia has done since the beginning of the 2000s. The concept is to give these companies some degree of independence from the infrastructure, possibly paving the way for later allowing private firms to run their own trains over the common infrastructure. All this is with a view to bringing in a more commercial business attitude, to promoting innovation in services, and to attracting private capital to replace aging assets. This will be essential if the railway is to succeed in attracting containers away from road transport. However, implementation of this restructuring has been slow and tentative.

Mongolia likewise has examined such options. Until recently, Mongolian Railways normally hauled well over 10 million tons of freight per year, roughly half of which was oil and timber in transit between Russia and China (but with a gauge change at the border with China) and the remainder was coal from the mines to power stations in the capital, Ulaanbaatar. However, the railway used revenue from the transit freight to cross-subsidize the cost of transporting domestic coal and the few remaining passenger services. The high transit tariff encouraged Russia and China to switch most of the transit freight to a longer, but for them less costly, alternative route via Manchuria that avoided Mongolia altogether.

Two new markets have developed in the past decade. The first for the export of coal and copper from newly discovered (or rediscovered) deposits near the border with China, and the second for the export of iron and other mineral ores to Russia. The first of these involves the construction of short, new standard-gauge lines in Mongolia to link with extensions of the standard-gauge Chinese lines to the border, whereas the second only requires extension of the current Mongolian broad-gauge line to the mine site, as this already links to the Russian network.

Mongolian Railways' monopoly of direct transport services to a deepwater port for this LLDC is about to end with the completion of a paved road from Ulaanbaatar to the port of Tianjin in China, a distance of about 1,700 km. Given this distance, the railway should remain competitive with road transport, but the change of rail gauge at the border and the need to change locomotives and wagon bogies (wheel trucks), combined with difficulty in coordinating the availability of wagons between the two countries, has led many international traders to believe that truck services will be less costly, faster, and more reliable once the paved road is completed. However, that outcome depends on a completion of the two-decades-long negotiations on a transit agreement between China, Mongolia, and Russia. Until this is done, Mongolian and Chinese trucks cannot enter each other's territory other than to access border cities.

Air Freight: A Niche Market for LLDCs

While rail transport can provide an alternative to road transport if the minimum conditions of transport distance and volume are met, air transport offers rather different alternatives under rather different conditions.

One of the main advantages of air freight for trade of an LLDC is that it eliminates the need for land transit to reach international markets. This provides a viable alternative when border crossings and land transport in a neighboring transit country impose high costs and long delays.

The potential for developing new exports based on air freight merits more attention, in light of its advantages in avoiding the complications in dealing with transit neighbor countries. A recent World Bank review (Bofinger 2009) of the air freight market focused not only on LLDCs but also on developing countries in general and identified various cases of strong export growth led by air freight.

The minimum conditions for rail freight to be competitive with road transport have been subject to much investigation and analysis, and this has yielded clear threshold values for distance and volume. In contrast, air freight, at least until recently, has not been subject to the same scope of investigation, and its minimum conditions for competitiveness are still very subjective. The principal conditions relate to (1) the unit value of the products air freighted and (2) the relationship between the volume of freight and the available air freight capacity

Unit Value of Products

The high cost of air freight limits its potential for LLDCs to exports of only the highest value goods, such as precious metals (gold and silver), high-fashion clothing and accessories (very time-sensitive), and cut flowers (perishable), and to imports of urgently needed, high-value manufactured goods.

Examples of typical air freight exports from developing countries include clothing, fresh seafood and fish, and lightweight electronic products (Bofinger 2009). Air transport is also used for high-value and time-sensitive garments and as back-up transport to more conventional clothing markets. Exports of seafood and fresh fish to the United States and the EU have been developed by Ecuador (now some US$95 million a year) and Tanzania (US$70 million), although with some negative ecological consequences in the latter case (specifically, West Nile perch introduced into Lake Victoria, which consumed native species to elimination).

Air freight tariffs are typically on the order of US$1.50 to US$4.00 per kg. Air freight exports from LLDCs that lack sufficient air freight capacity of their own (either as cargo on passenger services or on all-cargo aircraft), also must take into account the land transport cost to a better-serviced airport in a neighboring county. Thus, for air freight from LLDCs to offer a feasible transport option, the export value of the air-freighted goods has to be quite high to exceed these rates by enough to be profitable. In 2005–06, the unit values of some exported air-freighted products (in US$ per kg) were: frozen shrimp, $5.46; fresh Nile perch, $6.50; roses, $3.26; mixed flowers, $4.17; and semiconductors, $12.50.

Freight Volume to Air Freight Capacity Volume

There are two different volumes that determine the capacity constraints for air freight. The first relates to the freight capacity on direct service passenger aircraft to the major markets for the high-value products. At present, these markets are the EU, the United States, and some oil-rich countries in the Middle East. Direct services are needed to these markets because the products are so time-sensitive that transfers of the freight between aircraft at hub airports is likely to diminish the competitiveness of the route. Very few LLDCs have passenger services that meet this constraint, so they need to look for passenger services with similar characteristics in neighboring countries from airports that are easily accessible. The freight capacity of a typical long-distance passenger aircraft is about 15 tons (such as an Airbus 330-300 or a Boeing 767-300), so a year-round daily service could provide for about 3,000 tons per year of cargo.

Kenya was able to develop its flower exports on the basis of the freight capacity on its regular and frequent passenger services to Europe, while Mauritius's clothing exports to the EU also owe their origin in significant part to the cargo capacity in air passenger services. Tanzania's flower exports to the EU use their thrice-weekly service from Arusha to Amsterdam, but when this does not provide enough capacity, the surplus is transported by road to Nairobi for onward air freight by Kenya's more frequent passenger services to Europe.

Where this minimum frequency of passenger service is not available or where the capacity is insufficient, consideration could be given to freight-only services, and these impose the second volume-to-capacity ratio. Here the constraint is not imposed by the available capacity but by the volume of high-value exports from the LLDC.

Air-freighted exports from LLDCs must use airports that are regional hubs large enough to offer frequent, year-round, nonstop flights to U.S. or European hubs, using aircraft large enough to guarantee the availability of the freight space needed—mostly wide-bodied models that meet U.S. and European noise and emissions standards. Typical volume of a Boeing 757-200 all-freight aircraft is about 40 tons, so to fill a thrice-weekly service to 75 percent capacity requires an annual export volume of more than 4,000 tons. An all-cargo DC10 aircraft has a maximum payload of about 70 tons, so would require more than 7,000 tons of exports per year to be profitable.

Not only must the freight volume be sufficient to fill the aircraft, it must also be sufficient to justify the investment in ground storage capacity and provision of prompt and reliable customs processing, including X-ray scanning to meet U.S. security requirements for goods going there. This implies a need for expedited border-crossing for air freight—provided in some corridors—but not many crossings yet achieve this.

Because of the small volume of their high-value exports, few LLDCs can generate sufficient demand to fill an all-cargo aircraft at the minimum three times a week frequency needed to serve major markets (a lower frequency is inadequate for high-value and time-sensitive products). However, there is potential for neighboring LLDCs (such as Uganda and Rwanda) to share regional air freight services, even for dissimilar products such as flowers and fresh fish.

Air Freight Market Development

Given the small range of suitable export products, air freight can at best provide for niche markets that make up only a small share of the total export volume of a LLDC. The private sector has the incentives to develop such niche markets, while the government's role is mainly as a facilitator, since all international operating rights for commercial aviation must be negotiated by governments.

Among the largest current air freight trades are the exports of fresh cut flowers from Colombia to the United States and from Kenya, Tanzania, and Uganda to the EU. Both trades started in the early 1970s or earlier.

The Colombian trade has reached about US$1 billion per year, while Kenya's reached US$400 million in 2005, and Kenya now supplies more than half of the European demand for cut flowers.

The key factors to the development of the Kenya market were favorable year-round weather and good road access from rural growing areas to an airport with international passenger services. Other Sub-Saharan African LLDCs have begun cultivation of flowers for export by air, including Ethiopia and Uganda, and more recently, Rwanda. Despite being its competitor for flower sales to the EU, Uganda depends on Kenya's available air freight capacity and Kenya's rapid border clearance of its trucks (see box 7.4).

Box 7.4

Increased Competition Pushes Kenya to Higher Unit-Value Exports and Air Freight

Kenya has a long-established fruit and vegetable trade: a strong trade in off-season vegetables, such as peppers, especially to the UK, and all-season exports of green beans and Asian specialty vegetables to the EU. Competition is intense for tropical and subtropical fruits in Europe and the Middle East from suppliers in North Africa, especially from Egypt and Morocco; their exports are shipped by sea, often using ro-ro (roll on, roll off) services to minimize delays in ports, with much shorter transit times than Kenya.

These economic circumstances have pushed Kenya to focus on UK markets, where competition from North African suppliers is less intense. The country has also moved to higher value products and increased variety and product differentiation, and it now deals directly with major supermarket chains. These developments have resulted in a change in the nature of the products exported to a wide range of chilled, prepared-food products, including a diversity of whole fruits and vegetables, as well as cut vegetables packaged as high-value mixed salads and stir-fry mixes. This value-added processing (cutting and packaging) contrasts with fruits and cut-flower export sectors, which involve little processing other than grading, packing, and labeling.

Air freight, starting with the large capacity available on passenger services to the UK and later using freight-only aircraft, has allowed Kenya to remain competitive in one of its traditional export markets.

Source: Bofinger 2009.

The example of cut flowers, together with those of fresh fish and time-sensitive fashion exports, illustrate how air export opportunities tend to depend on well-informed entrepreneurs spotting promising coincidences of specific conditions—particularly at the source, in low-cost production potential for particular goods, and at the market, in scale of demand and the prices people are willing to pay. The coincidence can also be in transport, by availability on the relevant routes of air freight capacity not fully used and, hence, available at attractive prices, or in the cost and price equation because of trade preferences or tax subsidies.

The role of governments in developing such air freight markets has been marginal. Their most effective role appears to be in providing information and resources for investigating the potential of innovative new markets, negotiating air transport operating rights attractive to international carriers, and putting in place customs and other export procedures that are rapid and predictable. They have also proven useful in maintaining infrastructure such as airports in relevant areas (preferably with satellite navigation facilities) and good access to potential areas of production.

Beyond providing the basic airport and road infrastructure, LLDC governments need to be cautious about providing more specialized infrastructure, such as airport storage capacity for frozen or chilled export products and should better leave this task to private initiatives. When private businesses do identify a promising potential export opportunity, governments need to be ready to make changes to policies or regulations that would facilitate the realization of such schemes.

An Overview of Inland Waterway Transport

While large rivers or lakes could and, in a few cases, do serve as low-cost transport corridors for low-value bulk commodities—common among the exports from internal regions of large countries—only 11 LLDCs have any capability to develop this transport mode and only 9 actually make use of it: the Paraguay River gives access to Bolivia and Paraguay; the Mekong River to Laos; the Congo River to the Central African Republic (as well as the Democratic Republic of Congo, which is quasi-landlocked); Lake Victoria to Burundi, Rwanda, and Uganda; the Caspian Sea (with the Volga and Don Rivers) to Azerbaijan, Kazakhstan, and Turkmenistan; and the Danube River (that connects to the Rhine) to the Republic of Moldova.[6]

Some of these inland waterways are used for transportation of goods for international trade, while others are not. Moldova receives most of the oil products it consumes through a tank farm on the banks of the

Danube. The three Caspian states make substantial use of the Volga–Don Canal system to export oil, to import cargoes for their oil and gas industries (all three states), and to export wheat (Kazakhstan). In recent years, up to about 15 million tons of cargo have passed through the canal per year. Until 2004, it was subject to draft restrictions caused by one of the locks, but that year a second lock chamber was completed to replace it. Russia and Kazakhstan are now discussing whether a second parallel canal is economically warranted and ecologically acceptable.

In recent decades, Bolivia has become a significant grower of soy for the world market, using river transport for part of its export (1–2 million tons per year). Bolivia's use of the Paraguay–Paraná river system had been restricted by shoals in Paraguay and northern Argentina, as well as by Argentine and Paraguayan regulations mandating that all vessels must hire pilots of the country through which they were passing—which Bolivian barge operators protested as costly and unnecessary. Fortunately, the main months for exporting soy coincide with the highest volumes of flow in the river, so the rock blasting of the shoals was kept to a minimum. At about the same time the shoals were starting to be removed, the piloting restrictions were modified to allow pilots of the vessels' home to be certified to navigate in the other countries on the waterway.

In principle, the "infrastructure" of inland waterways and lakes is provided free by nature, and the energy required to transport heavy loads is minimal because they are generally carried downstream. But overcoming impediments to navigation usually requires large investments, which means that some waterways can be used for transit only on a limited scale. The Mekong has rapids close to where it leaves Laos and enters Cambodia that block navigation at that point, which prevents vessels from southwest China, northern Thailand, and Laos from using the Mekong to reach the ocean. Likewise, the Congo River has rapids throughout its lower reaches below Kinshasa, Democratic Republic of the Congo, that prevent navigation to or from the Atlantic. Despite these restrictions, the waterway agencies of these countries intend to improve their infrastructure[7] to make commercial waterway services a viable and feasible alternative to road and rail transport. In some cases, governments even plan to make these waterways an essential component of an integrated multimodal service, such as that from Uganda via Lake Victoria to the Central Corridor in Tanzania and on to the port of Dar es Salaam.

To make these inland waterways part of international transit, LLDC governments need to decide whether investment to ease physical impediments to navigation, whether by dredging or building canals with locks to get around rapids and dams, can be justified by the likely volume of additional traffic that could take advantage of the waterway. The issue becomes complicated by legal questions when the site of possible waterway projects is in a downstream country, while the main beneficiaries would be upstream countries. By international law, the governments of all countries through which rivers pass have the right to be informed in advance of any proposed projects and to object if they have reason to do so. When the river itself constitutes the border between neighboring countries, the legal issues are even more complex.

Waterway Operations

Waterways infrastructure needs to be appropriate to the type of operations that are most compatible with the physical conditions of the waterway, in terms of the depth and rate of flow of water. The typical configuration for barge trains on large rivers is a set of barges propelled by a powered unit ("tow" or "pusher"). Individual barges can have a carrying capacity of up to 1,000–2,000 tons, and the number of barges is determined by the dimensions of the navigation channel and the power of the tow. An overall capacity of 10,000–12,000 tons per set is not uncommon on the Paraguay River. Compared to road and rail, waterway transport is slow and at higher risk of delays. It is competitive for coal, ores, rock, gravel, and sand for construction.

The former Soviet countries operate distinctive river-sea vessels, powered barges with a capacity of 2,000–5,000 DWT[8] (deadweight tonnage, or how much weight a ship can carry) (average size 2,600 DWT) with a draft of 3.5–4.0 meters that are capable of passing through the locks on the rivers of Russia and Ukraine, but also stable enough to operate in open water in the Caspian and Black Seas.

Because of the free infrastructure and operating economies of scale, the typical operating cost of barge trains in excess of 2,000 tons is very low: 0.1–0.2 U.S. cents per ton-km (even assuming backhauls are empty). Compared to tariffs by rail, the main consideration is likely to be the closeness to the waterway of the mine, quarry, oil refinery, or other point of origin of the product, as well as of the factory or power plant of destination—and the consequent cost of loading and unloading.

International experience on the Rhine–Danube system and in North America on the Mississippi and its tributaries is that traffic forecasts associated with major investments (such as the Rhine–Main–Danube Canal) have proved highly optimistic. Actual demand has fallen far short of expectations. It is believed that such forecasts often fail to take fully into account the "door-to-door" requirements of the potential customers.

Institutional Arrangements for Waterway Management

The international context of waterway transport on international waterways creates very special needs for the institutional arrangements that govern their operations. The main requirements relate to the freedom of navigation and to the responsibilities for development and maintenance of the waterways themselves.

The principles of freedom of navigation on inland waterways date back to the Vienna Treaty of 1815 and later expanded in the Heidelberg Resolution of 1887, which became the basis of all subsequent agreements on the navigation of international inland waterways. The Heidelberg Resolution is concerned with waterways' infrastructure aspects: construction of river ports and mooring facilities; dredging and straightening of the river (including environmental impacts); navigational standards (including minimum clearance for bridges); licensing of pilots, barge operators, and crews; and safety rules (enforced by the national river police, navy, or coast guard). And a consultative body for all the main barge operating companies coordinates operations and lobbies for dredging and ensuring that navigational aids and moorings are installed and maintained (see box 7.5).

International waterway agreements based on the Heidelberg Resolution principles and using the experience of later conventions led to a common method of allocating costs of infrastructure improvements to those who benefit most from them. Although the details might take time to work out, having the principles established shortens and simplifies the process. All eight of the major international waterways and inland lakes and seas already have a waterway commission charged with fair allocation of the water between countries and users and also for establishing the rules of navigation and of charging for improvements (see box 7.6 for the websites of the eight international waterway commissions).

The commission for the Paraguay–Paraná River is one of the least organized and advanced, despite having one of the largest freight transport tasks to administer.

Products, Costs, and Demand Levels for Waterway Transport

Most waterway transport involves the transport of bulk grains or minerals in one direction and no backhauls. In addition, most barge trains or powered vessels transport only one product on a voyage, and many of

Box 7.5

Institutional Arrangements for Managing the Paraguay–Paraná River Waterway ("Hidrovia")

In 1996, Argentina, Bolivia, Brazil, Paraguay, and Uruguay signed the Accord for River Navigation on the Paraguay and Paraná Rivers. It provides for "free navigation, equal treatment, free transit and reciprocity, multi-lateral treatment of cargo reservations, transport and trade facilitation, and port navigational services." In 1989, the Intergovernmental Committee for the Waterway (*Comite Intergubernamental de la Hidrovia*—CIH) was set up by the governments of the five riparian countries to coordinate use of the Paraguay, Paraná, and Uruguay Rivers as an integrated system. A permanent secretariat is based in Rosario, Argentina.

In the interest of safety, CIH regulates barge operators and their pilots and crews for all countries, sets standards for navigation, and provides information to users of the waterway, especially about depth available for navigation, which varies throughout the year. The CIH also coordinates proposals for navigational improvements. Some dredging to deepen the shipping channel has been carried out in the Paraná's lower reaches, between Santa Fe, Argentina, and the Atlantic, and also in Paraguay. Proposals to remove rock shelves by blasting in the Pantanal section of the river basin drew strong opposition from environmental groups. These objections led Brazil to ban dredging in its portion of the Pantanal. But in 1998, Bolivia dredged the short Tamengo Channel that gives it access to the Paraguay River to guarantee a minimum depth of 2.8 meters. Despite the Brazilian dredging ban, the Paraguay River is today navigable at least half the year. Soybean harvesting and shipping in eastern Bolivia occur in April, May, and June, when the river is full and presents little problems for navigation.

The River Plate Basin Permanent Transport Commission (*Comision Permanente de Transporte de la Cuenca del Plata*), set up at the same time as CIH, is a forum for barge operators to meet with CIH and each country's bodies responsible for the waterway. At a recent meeting, for example, the agenda included a proposal by Brazil's Mato Grosso government that barge operators should contribute to the construction cost of structures to protect the piers of the road bridge at Corumba and to serve as moorings (conditionally accepted), and the cost of installing a navigation simulator for crew training in Buenos Aires (rejected).

Source: Authors based on CIH (www.sspyvn.gov.ar/hparana_paraguay.html).

Box 7.6

International Waterway Commissions

1. Central Commission for the Navigation of the Rhine: http://www.ccr-zkr.org/
2. Danube River Commission: http://www.icpdr.org/
3. Mekong River Commission: http://www.mrcmekong.org/
4. Congo Basin Commission: http://www.cicos.info/siteweb/
5. Great Lakes Commission: http://www.glc.org/
6. Lave Victoria Commission: http://www.eac.int/lvdc.html
7. *Comite Intergubermental Coordinador de los paises de la Cuenca de la Plata* (CIC): The CIC (http://www.cicplata.org/) has delegated responsibility for navigation issues to the Comite Intergubermental de la Hidrovia (CIH) but CIH does not have a website. The Secretariat for Transport of Argentina provides information about the CIH: http://www.sspyvn.gov.ar/hvia_com-acta26.html.
8. Niger River Commission became the Niger Basin Authority in November 1980: http://www.abn.ne/

Source: Authors.

them are limited to a single product throughout their operational life. The same considerations for compatibility of backhaul products apply to waterway barge operations as to railways, although since the cost of operation is lower, the cost of any empty backhauls are also lower.

There are also similar volume thresholds to achieve the lower costs of waterway transport as for railways, which are important because they are close competitors where both modes of transport are available. The low operating cost of a powered vessel, such as those used on rivers with a high flow rate or on lakes and inland seas where wave height is a consideration, tend to be reached with vessel sizes of about 3,000 DWT. For smaller vessels, the fixed labor costs for the crew make the unit cost of freight too high, and for larger vessels, the benefits of lower capital costs do not make a large difference to the unit cost. For barge trains, such as those used on the Paraguay River, the maximum barge size is about 2,500 DWT[9] to be compatible with the minimum water depth of about 2 meters. The size of the maximum barge train is largely determined by the power of the pusher vessel and the curvature of the river. Together these tend to impose a limit of about 21 barges (providing about 42,000 DWT), although most barge trains are significantly smaller, perhaps half this size. In addition to the barge train size, the operating cost for a voyage is dependent on the transit time, and this in turn is dependent on the possibility of night navigation and the time taken to break up the barge train to pass rapids, shoals, or particularly sharp curves.

Even with the smaller barge trains and no backhaul freight, and allowing for a few voyage days to pass obstacles in the river, the unit operating cost in a developing country is less than 2 U.S. cents per ton-km. For a single barge train of 12,000 DWT, and a one-way voyage time of about 15 days, the annual capacity is more than 200,000 net tons. Since a single barge train can be profitable, this can be considered as the minimum demand. For a powered vessel of 3,000 DWT, the minimum demand is proportionally less at about 22,000 tons per year.

These minimums are much lower than the minimum thresholds for rail transport because there are no infrastructure costs to be covered. If the cost of investment in port facilities has to be covered, these minimums could double, and if waterway improvements such as dredging are included, they could more than double again. On most waterways with current freight services, the volumes are much greater than these minimums, although on others, such as Lake Victoria, where maintenance of basic facilities such as vessels and berths and connecting land transport links has been neglected, the volume is below the viable threshold for even a single vessel and far below the minimum to make investment financially viable (World Bank 2010).

Development of Logistics Services

Freight forwarders, customs brokers, and third-party logistics providers are intermediate operators between traders and the operators of transport services. Their role is fundamental to both groups—traders cannot deal with all the providers of transport service that are available for the various modes of transport needed between the geographic origin of the freight and its final destination, and similarly the transport operators cannot put together the combinations of transport service that are needed to get the freight from its origin to its destination.

For LLDCs, the transport options and combinations that are available are more and more complex than those for a coastal country, so the efficient functioning of these intermediate service providers is more important for LLDCs. The role of these intermediaries is also more important where transport modes other than trucking are used for the land transport part of the freight journey. Even where road transport is the main land transport mode, it has to be coordinated with the port or airport activity, and this needs to be coordinated with the maritime transport. All these coordination tasks require the services of intermediaries. Where coordination is lacking, the result can be long queues of trucks waiting to deliver their freight to the port, waiting to pick up loads from the port, or simply trying to pass through a land border crossing. When rail or waterway transport is also involved, the intermediaries have additional coordination roles in connecting the rail and waterway transport with the road services needed to collect or deliver the freight to and from its land origin and destination.

In many countries, customs brokers have a special and formal role in the verification of import and export documents prior to their presentation to the customs agency. Many countries require that such documents be presented to the customs agency only after they have been authorized by a recognized customs broker. The role of customs brokers in LLDCs is little different than it is in coastal countries, but dealing with transit freight in a coastal country does require different treatment of freight that is imported and exported to the coastal country. Transit freight is not subject to the payment of customs duties and import and export taxes and is not usually subject to the same inspections as imported and exported freight. For these reasons, customs brokers dealing with transit freight need to ensure that it is not subjected to the more rigorous customs and other agency treatment (such as agricultural and health inspections).[10]

While transport companies provide direct services, between them these intermediate operators coordinate the contracting of transport services for each stage of a freight journey from its origin to destination and, in doing so, need to make sure that all the regulations and documentation required for the transported products to enter or leave the country are complied with and completed.

The differences between these professions correspond to different degrees of integration of services. The freight forwarder integrates the clearance business of the brokers with transport services. Third-party logistics providers (usually referred to as 3PLs), take charge of logistics activities that are otherwise internalized within the trading company.[11] In developing countries, brokerage and freight forwarding are traditional activities, while third-party logistics in many of them is still a niche service industry.

Freight Forwarders

The growing focus on source-to-destination supply chains puts a premium on good freight forwarding services. Because reliable on-time delivery is highly valued, shippers are increasingly willing to pay specialist companies (3PLs) to assume full responsibility for the entire supply chain. By means of a "through bill of lading,"[12] the shipper enters into a single transport contract with the freight forwarder, who in turn enters into separate contracts with trucking firms, railways, and shipping lines to cover each leg of the multimodal journey. Operation of container trains to Central Asia, as well as from Turkey to Europe, is now being managed by consortia that include railway operating companies, port operators, and freight forwarders. One of the principal railway operators in South America is ALL, an indication of an extension of its activity beyond rail operations into logistics.

Either of these models—including logistics companies entering in the operation of railway services or expanding the railways own services to include logistics—could be replicated in several Sub-Saharan African corridors. A similar consortium, in fact, is already operating the container terminal in Abidjan and its connecting railway to Burkina Faso and onward road services to Chad and other LLDCs, and ALL is negotiating taking over responsibility for operating the services of the Rift Valley Railway concession in East Africa.

While the professional capability of freight forwarders in LLDCs is increasing, too many of the countries still lack any formal training or certification for this profession, instead relying on experience to provide the skills to help their clients. While experience is essential, more professional training would result in more capable freight forwarders, and a professional certification would give clients more confidence in the advice of their forwarders. Some of the newer national freight forwarder associations have a conflict with accreditation schemes. Their first objective is to maximize membership, with the quality of that membership a secondary consideration. But they should focus first on the quality of membership to ensure the credibility of this profession in the marketplace.

FIATA (International Federation of Freight Forwarders Associations) also encourages its member organizations to implement accreditation schemes and offers training and examinations to facilitate this policy. To support this effort, it created the FIATA Foundation Vocational Training in 2008, which provides "train the trainer" facilities. Trained forwarders who meet the standards can gain a FIATA diploma in freight forwarding. In some countries, having a minimum number of employees with this diploma is a prerequisite for obtaining a license to be a freight forwarding company. Other requirements may include evidence of financial capacity and standing (for example, needed for the issuance of transit bonds) and lack of criminal convictions on trade or transport matters.

Responsibility for implementing an accreditation scheme for freight forwarders is usually that of the government's trade ministry, but it requires pressure from traders who use the services of freight forwarders and the national associations of freight forwarders themselves to bring this about.

Customs Brokers

Customs brokers do not integrate services on the supply chain; their role is less critical than that of freight forwarders in facilitating trade on corridors, because their narrower task is to facilitate the interaction with customs at border posts and destinations. In fact, as part of the transit procedures per se, brokers are agents of the forwarder or trucker handling the full corridor supply chain. Brokers are professionals regulated by customs, which defines the professional requirement of individuals and financial requirement, both for deposits and bonds (McLinden et al. 2010).

The trend to shifting clearance procedures from border crossings to points of destination (such as the consignees' premises or inland container depots) is reducing demand for customs brokers, because declarations at the destination can now be prepared by the shipper and filed electronically. The introduction of the Automated System for Customs Data (ASYCUDA) World as an update to ASYCUDA ++ as the electronic customs declaration system supported by the United Nations Conference on Trade and Development has also reduced the role of customs brokers, because now traders (if their national laws permit) can enter their own customs declarations without using a broker's services. In 2009, the International Road Transport Union introduced an electronic procedure for submitting "pre-declarations" as part of the Transport Internationaux Routiers (International Road Transport) regime. Some developing countries, among them many of the LLDCs, still require that customs declarations be submitted by a registered customs broker. While this provides some guarantee that documents will be correctly completed, it does not necessarily ensure they will be honestly completed as the brokers depend on information given to them by their clients.

The main policy challenge for customs brokers in the context of LLDCs' corridors is to manage an increasing professionalism of the activity. Unlike the situation where a forwarder manages an entire corridor logistics that takes place at various stages and locations throughout the corridor, brokerage activities occur in one place and so do not require a corporate organization, nor significant investment, as do freight forwarders and 3PL providers. Customs brokerage in fact is often exercised by individuals, and "suitcase business persons"[13] are commonplace. Generous entry requirements in many LLDCs—such as no need for formal training or qualification, only secondary education requirement, and low financial resource requirements—mean that many of them have hundreds of registered brokers. However, such registration is not a guarantee of quality or integrity. In many countries, retired customs officers have privileged access to brokerage licenses, which may tend to encourage entrenched vested interest.

Despite the low formal entry requirements, customs brokers' importance in facilitating international trade has given them a strong negotiating position in preventing reform of the profession. The International Trade and Customs Broker Association (ITCBA), a professional organization similar to FIATA, proposes similar capacity-building programs. Formal support for ITCBA and for its capacity-building programs, perhaps through Colombus programs[14] is one way of bringing about a more professional brokerage industry.

Third-Party Logistics Providers

Companies manufacturing for export now often enter into long-term contracts with freight forwarders in order to break out those parts of the supply chain that are best entrusted to logistics experts or 3PLs. To be competitive, LLDCs and transit countries need to respect standardized international terms of contract, insurance, banking (trade credits), and customs documentation. The emergence of 3PL companies is invariably in response to demands from their potential users, mostly medium to large manufacturing companies that want to outsource their logistics activities. There is only a small role for government, if any, in facilitating this process.

A small but growing contingent of 3PLs has emerged in LLDCs, in particular to support the needs of companies integrated in global supply chains (for example, supermarket, garment, or consumer goods). Production and distribution of goods in these industries have different specific supply chain requirements compared to more mature markets. They typically involve smaller trade volumes, but comparatively large inventories, to ensure availability of the product in highly competitive consumer goods markets and a mixture of time-sensitive and less sensitive products.

Unlike freight forwarders, 3PLs do not yet have an international association, but national associations do exist in some developed countries. In the United States, this role has been taken on by the Transportation Intermediaries Association (TIA). It provides resources, education, information, advocacy, and connections to establish, maintain, and expand ethical, profitable, and growing businesses in service to their customers. As a condition of membership, all TIA members must sign and adhere to the TIA Code of Ethics, and its ethics committee arbitrates disputes. The code is designed to promote and maintain high standards of professional service and ethical business conduct, and it could be used to form the basis of the constitution of an international association.

There is an International Warehouse Logistics Association but this seems to have a more limited scope and to function more as a promotional agency for its members than as a training and accreditation agency, although it does provide training as part of its member services.

Inland Container Depots

In recent years, ICDs have evolved as a convenient intermediate solution between clearance at the border—generally the least convenient option for the freight's owner as borders are rarely close to the economic center of LLDCs—and clearance on the buyer's premises, the most convenient option for the buyer, but least convenient for customs.

The core functions of ICDs are unloading containers from long-distance trucks (and trains) into short-term bonded storage; inspection, duty payments, and customs clearance; and reloading the containers onto local trucks for local delivery. Secondary functions that may be added include warehousing, from which containers, after being cleared by customs, can be stripped and their contents can be delivered to multiple destinations or even broken down, processed, and repackaged for multiple final buyers (for example, for automotive spare parts or pharmaceuticals). Potentially, ICDs help customs clearance and consolidate freight to gain economies of scale on otherwise relatively small transit flows.

ICDs can perform a third function, mainly with regard to exports: the marketing of backhaul capacity in trucks or containers that otherwise would have to return to the seaport empty. In almost all the LLDCs under study, imports substantially exceed exports, especially in truck-borne and containerized cargos. One of the functions of freight forwarders is to organize the market for this backhaul capacity. While the mandatory freight bureau concept impedes direct negotiation and contracting between shippers and truckers, other mechanisms can help bring shippers and truckers together on a voluntary basis, such as through the provision and dissemination of market information about available capacity and prevailing prices. ICDs can play this role by offering office facilities and communications to brokers and freight forwarders.

ICDs are often located on the outskirts of a hub city where the price of land is moderate and arterial highways and railways provide good access and do not interfere with urban traffic. Many ICDs are operated by a single freight forwarding company exclusively for their own business, but the consideration here is for those that have a wider function as multiple user terminals. Some are operated by municipal or regional governments, but many are private enterprises that specialize in ICD operation more than in the full range of logistics services.

ICDs are potentially a huge improvement over the traditional concept of public warehouse for trade. Most LLDCs have, and in some cases still impose, compulsory warehouses where goods are unloaded from transit trucks then cleared for local distribution. These systems were justified originally to overcome the many inconveniences—like no incentive to reduce clearance and lack of flexibility—resulting from the lack of services and facilities. Furthermore, where the only ICDs are publically owned and operated, there is a risk that they will function as public monopolies, with low service quality and high operating costs and charges. Until recently, this was the situation in Rwanda, where a state-owned company (MAGERWA, Rwanda Bonded Warehouses) had a monopoly on bonded warehousing and, therefore, on ICDs as well. In 2008, the first concession for a privately owned and operated ICD was introduced, with the aim of providing competition for the public ICDs and, thus, improving transport services. The recent construction of an ICD at Nguéli, near N'Djamena in Chad, is also an improvement over the previous "enclos douanier" (customs enclosure).

Examples of multiple user ICDs in LLDCs include those in Nepal at Birgunj, just inside the border from India, and in the Lao People's Democratic Republic at Thanaleng outside Vientiane, near the bridge over the Mekong River that is also the border with Thailand. Consideration is being given to other locations for multiple user ICDs, such as Ulaanbaatar in Mongolia and at Dosso, a town at the junction of the main routes to Benin's Port of Cotonou and Zinder, Niger's second largest city.[15] Plurinational State of Bolivia operates ICDs inside nominally free zones in Santa Cruz and La Paz.

A fully consistent picture has not yet developed of what makes ICDs succeed and fulfill their trade facilitation objectives in the context of LLDC corridors—especially when relatively small trade flows prevent private operators from handling large volumes, as in inland logistics facilities in the Organisation for Economic Co-operation and Development or large emerging economies. Some of the most effective examples are tied to multimodal operations in the context of efficient railway concessions. For instance, Cameroon's Camrail terminals at Ngaoundéré and Belabo are handling, with reputedly good performance, import and export containers and bulk shipments (such as timber) for Chad and the Central African Republic. An active ICD is also attached to the terminal of Sitarail in Ouagadougou, Burkina Faso, although the activities there have been slowed because West African LLDCs have reduced their use of the Abidjan Corridor because of Côte d'Ivoire's continued instability.

Recommendations

The following recommendations will help improve logistics for these transport modes.

The potential of alternative modes of transportation, especially rail, has continuously been receiving a lot of interest from government and development agencies. The main message coming from the analysis is that the potential of alternative modes to improve corridors and facilitate access of LLDCs should be taken seriously but not overestimated. In many cases, corridors cannot attract the volumes above the expected threshold for investment or even operations. The priority should be on the best use of existing assets and organizations of service in liaison with private logistics services.

Railways

For railways in LLDCs, the threshold of 250,000 tons per year, if the infrastructure is in long-term sustainable condition, and 1 million tons otherwise, and about 800 km as a minimum operating distance, are useful rules of thumb for assessing the financial viability of any nonbulk freight operation. The thresholds will be higher when the railway faces strong competition from an efficient trucking industry.

For Sub-Saharan Africa and South America, where the basic track infrastructure is in "good enough" condition (that is, no significant speed or axle-load restrictions), the cost of a regular shuttle container train service between the LLDC point of origin and the ocean port that handles most of its trade (as in the Abidjan–Ouagadougou Corridor in West Africa and the Paraguay–Buenos Aires Corridor in South America) is mostly the incremental operating costs of the new schedule, with limited impact from infrastructure rehabilitation costs. Where freight volumes are below the 1 million net-ton threshold, some public financial support for infrastructure costs would be needed in the long term, possibly justified on the basis of providing a viable alternative mode or route.

For the Caucasus and Central Asia, where conditions are more favorable, many regular container train services are already operating. However, for sustainability, further commercial integration of railway companies and freight forwarding companies would be advantageous. Where such integration does not already exist, the railway needs operating freedom to negotiate service contracts with major clients and with its transit neighbor's railways. Further, border control agencies of the LLDC need to facilitate the transit of inbound trains to the national capital (or regional cities) where the containers will be unloaded.

Air Freight

Air exporters can do little to develop direct air freight services, since the product volumes are not enough to justify the high frequency needed for perishable commodities or high-unit-value products. Furthermore, LLDCs do not have frequent passenger service whose freighter capacity can be used. However, LLDCs can take advantage of any such capacity as might be available from either source in neighboring transit countries. For this to be feasible, the transit times cannot be too long—for example, with perishable and time-sensitive products that typically are transported overnight to avoid the high cost of chilling or refrigerating them—and this in turn requires expedited procedures for crossing land borders.

Inland Waterways

The major obstacles to increased use of waterway transport are the impediments imposed by transit countries. These can range from regulations requiring the use of a pilot from the transit country to prohibitions on night transportation. Overcoming such impediments will usually require modification of the relevant waterway conventions, not an easy task. However, this is not always the case; for example, some operators on the Paraná River have implemented their own geographic navigation systems to facilitate nighttime operations and have almost halved the previous transit times. Where it is necessary to revisit the waterway convention, an organization of waterway operators is in a much better position to request this than are individual operators, so the formation of such an organization is highly recommended if it does not already exist.

Ancillary Services

Ancillary operators in most LLDCs have not reached the level of professionalism and organization to exert the influence their counterparts have achieved in transit countries or developed countries. Some of the international organizations that represent such operators (such as FIATA for freight forwarders) already offer training and accreditation schemes, but other types of operators (such as 3PLs) have yet to achieve this role. Therefore, international agencies involved in promoting increased international trade have an important role in facilitating the creation and development of such international organizations and, in the meantime, in fulfilling the training role themselves.

Dry Ports

While international lending agencies can promote ICDs, they are best developed by their potential operators and users. LLDCs have been cooperating with their transit neighbors in establishing ICDs at key LLDC corridor points. The public sector can take a role in assembling the parcels of land for ICD use in the best locations—for example, at the intersection of the transit corridors to a deepwater port in a transit country and a ring road in the main industrial city of the LLDC. The government also has an important role in the development of ICDs in ensuring that trade regulations allow trade contracts to designate the ICD as a final destination (the standard international trade contract allows designation only to and from the deepwater port, so the onward contract to an ICD in an LLDC has to be contracted separately).

Notes

1. The main sources for information on railways in developing countries, in addition to the project's own case studies, are Bullock 2009; Kerali and Rastrogi 2004; and UNESCAP 2003.

2. The minimum viable distance for railways to compete with trucks for freight transport has been variously estimated between 400 km and 800 km.

3. But this line did have severe operating conditions (such as a 6 percent gradient in parts) that would have made its feasible threshold distance higher than most other lines.

4. TRACECA is an international transport program of the EU and 14 member states of the Eastern European, Caucasian, and Central Asian regions. It has a permanent secretariat, originally financed by the European Commission, in Baku, Azerbaijan, and a regional office in Odessa, Ukraine. The organization has been entirely financed by member countries since 2009.

5. ALL has now assumed operating responsibilty for the Uganda to Kenya railway.

6. The Niger River in West Africa, serving Mali and Niger, is excluded as it has no navigable outlet to the sea and is navigable for only about 1,500 km of its total length of more than 6,500 km. There are proposals to ugrade the section

in Nigeria to give it a year-round navigable depth of 2.5 meters, but these would take decades to implement.

7. Details are available from CICOS *(Commission Internationale du Bassin Congo–Oubangui–Sangha)* at http://www.cicos.info/siteweb.

8. Deadweight tonnage—how much weight a ship can safely carry—is the sum of the weights of cargo, fuel, fresh water, ballast water, provisions, passengers, and crew when fully loaded. So it is more than the freight capacity, which also depends on the density of the freight. An approximate guide is that the capacity in tons is a little more than half the DWT.

9. This is the capacity of new barges specifically designed for the Paraguay River. Earlier barges, adapted from those designed for the locks of the Mississippi River, had a capacity of only 2,000 DWT.

10. Some transit countries require the same health and agricultural inspections for transit as for imported freight because the perceived health risk is similar.

11. The definition of 3PL found in the Council of Supply Chain Management Professionals' glossary is thus: "A firm [that] provides multiple logistics services for use by customers. Preferably, these services are integrated, or "bundled" together, by the provider. Among the services 3PLs provide are transportation, warehousing, cross-docking, inventory management, packaging, and freight forwarding."

12. A single bill of lading covers receipt of the cargo at the point of origin for delivery to the ultimate consignee using two or more modes of transportation.

13. Brokers who need access to the Internet to make entries into customs data systems, such as ASYCUDA World, but who do not necesasrily have a fixed office. They can operate from anywhere that has Internet access that is facilitated to use the ASYCUDA World or equivalent system.

14. The World Customs Organization's Columbus Program is a customs capacity-building program intended to promote customs modernization and implementation of high professional standards to facilitate world trade. The capacity building is available to customs brokers, although it is primarily aimed at customs agents. For details see http://www.gfptt.org/entities/TopicProfile.aspx?tid=7f481e53-068b-4dab-8720-492b10cf2020

15. World Bank's International Financial Corporation is advising the government of Niger on this proposed ICD.

References

Bofinger, H. 2009. "Air Freight: A Market Study with Implications for Landlocked Countries." Transport Paper TP26, World Bank, Washington, DC.

Bullock, R. 2009. "Off Track: Sub-Saharan African Railways." Africa Infrastructure Country Diagnostic Background Paper 17, World Bank, Washington, DC.

Kerali, H., and C. Rastrogi. 2004. "Trade and Transport Facilitation in Central Asia: Reducing the Economic Distance to Markets." World Bank, Washington, DC.

McLinden, G., E. Fanta, D. Widdowson, and T. Doyle. 2010. *Border Management Modernization: A Practical Guide for Reformers*. Washington, DC: World Bank.

TRACECA (Transport Corridor Europe–Caucasus–Asia). 2002. "Harmonization of Border Crossing Procedures: Recommendations of Border Harmonization Evaluation Workshop." Baku, Azerbaijan, September.

UNESCAP (United Nations Economic and Social Commission for Asia and the Pacific). 2003. "Transit Transport Issues in Landlocked and Transit Developing Countries." Landlocked Developing Countries Series 1, ST/ESCAP/2270, UNESCAP, Bangkok.

World Bank. 2010. "Assessment of Trade and Transport Corridors Serving Uganda." World Bank, Washington, DC.

CHAPTER 8

Managing Trade Corridors

The efficiency of international transit corridors is critical to the competitiveness of landlocked developing countries (LLDCs). An international trade corridor is a collection of routes linking several economic centers in adjoining countries and bounded by gateways. Its economic function is to promote both internal and external trade by providing efficient transport and logistics services. The primary reason for designating a route as part of a corridor is to focus attention on improving not only the route but also the quality of transport and logistics services in the corridor.

As a spatial entity, a corridor spans different scales: a broad scale, typically regional; a national in which a corridor is part of the planning of a country's space economy; and a local scale in which some specific bottlenecks are tackled. Therefore, in addition to government departments at different levels, several institutions and agencies also play a role along the corridor, including those responsible for infrastructure (ports, roads, and railways); border posts (customs, immigration, security, health, and others); transport operations (roads, rail, and water); and various logistics services (freight forwarders, clearing agents, and so on). The main challenge is synchronizing the actions of these various entities so the result is an efficient system. Where actions are not properly synchronized, the corridors may not function well.

Corridor bodies can address the various aspects of transport and transit of goods along a given corridor, typically based on an agreement signed by the participating countries. Corridor agreements deal with a wide range of issues, including infrastructure, customs, and regulations, and are typically based on a number of legal instruments including treaties (for example, in the Northern Corridor in East Africa); multilateral agreements (for example, the Central Corridor, also in East Africa); bilateral agreements (Afghanistan and Pakistan); memorandums of understanding (Trans-Kalahari Corridor); constitution (Dar es Salaam Corridor); and company registration (Maputo Corridor). Although, there are key drivers to the selection of the agreement instrument, there is still a question of to what extent a corridor actually can be "managed," given the diversity of interests and institutions involved in any one corridor.

Not surprisingly, most existing corridor management arrangements are found in Africa, where the high number of LLDCs makes it imperative that countries cooperate to open up trade routes. The same reasons apply elsewhere where interstate agreements have either been signed or are under negotiation to formalize cooperation on transit corridors. Examples of the latter include Chile and Bolivia, which have a several decades-old agreement in place, and Pakistan and Afghanistan where a new agreement is under negotiation.

Corridor management is about providing a single point of coordination and consultation for the variety of stakeholders and the many government agencies that oversee different activities within the corridor. Both the public and private sectors must cooperate effectively to enhance operational efficiency. Consequently, corridor management is as much about the relationships between different institutions and how they collaborate as it is about ensuring that the infrastructure and services are operational.

The most common approach in developing countries is for the governments to take the lead in corridor management. This is a reflection of both the international nature of corridors and also the relative weakness of the private sector in collaborating and working across borders. Nevertheless, and increasingly in some countries, the private sector or autonomous state-owned enterprises have seen it necessary to exploit the corridor approach to pursue commercial ends.

Four Corridor Management Models

Of the variety of approaches to the development of international trade corridors, Arnold (2006) identifies four general models that have been applied in corridor management.

Legislative Model

In the legislative model, corridor management functions are created by treaties between the countries on the corridor and typically entrusted to a formal cross-border institution. This organization is in charge of producing and monitoring policies and draft legislation for supporting corridor development, for example, bilateral, multilateral, and transit trade agreements; formal recognition of the importance of the corridor; designation of specific routes, border crossings, and connected gateways; and programmatic funding for corridor infrastructure. Such a management model can also be effective for initiating reforms to harmonize standards, to simplify cross-border movements, and to reduce the regulatory impediments to efficient corridor services. This form of management resolves many of the difficulties with coordination among government agencies, but has relatively little impact on the physical and operational components of the corridor. Implementation of investments in infrastructure and facilities and changes in procedures are left to individual jurisdictions and specific government agencies. While the management structure is formal, it tends to be short-lived.

An example of the legislative model is the Northern Corridor Transit Transport Coordination Authority (NCTTCA) in East Africa, an interstate body formed through a treaty signed by Burundi, the Democratic Republic of Congo, Kenya, Rwanda, and Uganda in 1985. The NCTTCA has been particularly effective in driving the implementation of regional transit regimes at the national level. The body is funded through a levy on tonnages passing through the port of Mombasa. However, the very same status would appear to have engendered on occasion overtly political considerations in NCTTCA's decision making. While the governments still have a greater say in decision making, there have been recent moves to involve the private sector much more.

Project Coordination Model

The second model is project coordination as part of a general corridor development plan. Efforts to expand and improve corridors are usually undertaken by government agencies on a project-by-project basis. The government's corridor management authority can coordinate these activities, either through direct interaction with the agencies or by providing oversight at a higher level of the government, such as a senior ministry. This model can be quite effective for providing improvements in infrastructure but is not suited to tackling legal or operational issues. The effectiveness of this model depends on the level of government that is actively involved in corridor management and the scope of this management. Where the scope is limited to a single mode or route and does not cover all the transit or the entire corridor, management of the corridor will be less effective. The project coordination form of corridor management tends to be informal and have a limited time horizon. As such, it relies on committees or similar structures rather than a formal corridor organization.

An example of project coordination comes from the Dar es Salaam Corridor Committee, a body founded on a constitution that brings Tanzania together with the Democratic Republic of Congo, Malawi, and Zambia. It took about five years for the constitution to be signed by all parties following the initial agreement in 2003. In the meantime, the private sector has used the constitution to launch some interventions, starting with setting up a secretariat that they are funding. It is expected that the secretariat will coordinate the development of an action plan and lobby for reforms that could enhance corridor operations.

Another case of project coordination is the CAREC (Central Asia Regional Economic Cooperation) Program. Work in four areas (trade, transport, trade facilitation, and energy) is led by a committee, and senior officials' meetings are held where the options for the future direction of the program are discussed. However, the overall guidance of the program is determined once a year at a ministerial conference, where policy and strategic directions and goals are established. The Asian Development Bank is the program secretariat. This institutional framework also supports broad-based dialogue and consensus-building, and it provides assistance in preparing and implementing these initiatives. But its most important function is mobilizing financial and technical resources. As a proof of this, the CAREC Program has put forward an action plan for the 2008–17 period, combining transport investments with trade facilitation initiatives and focusing on the development of the six CAREC corridors to international standards.

Public-Private Partnership Model

In the same hierarchy as the project coordination model is developing public-private partnerships, or commercial model, for improving the operation of facilities and services in the corridor. The partnership management develops concessions, operating agreements, and other arrangements to involve the private sector in managing the corridor's infrastructure and facilities as well as to mobilize funding for corridor development. This model is effective at the domestic level but has some limitations for addressing problems with cross-border improvements. However, it can be used to develop toll roads, rail concessions, dry ports, and multimodal services that extend across borders.

The Walvis Bay Corridor Group is an example of the latter. This public-private body is one of the most active corridor bodies in Africa. It was founded in 1994 to develop Walvis Bay, Namibia, as a hub port for southwestern and central African countries, most Southern African Development Community[1] (SADC) members, to develop a network of corridors converging on the Atlantic Ocean port. It is oriented toward business development and has been able to commission various pieces of forward-looking research, feasibility studies, and new procedures, as well as to gather regional support for follow-up action. The group is dominated by a few large stakeholders. It underscores the link between infrastructure development and the need to increase traffic volumes to justify some of the investments that have been made or are being contemplated.

Consensus-Building Institution Model

The last model is the consensus-building institution, a facilitation organization created to mobilize support from stakeholders for improvements in the corridor and for reforms in regulations and procedures, especially border-crossing procedures. This model can be used for mobilizing support for the legal, physical, and operational components of the corridor. However, this management model has less scope for direct action because its effectiveness is dependent on the level of participation by public- and private-sector stakeholders, as well as its ability to maintain a professional staff that can address the issues related to planning, regulation, and performance. While its primary focus would be national, it can be used to develop consensus between the countries along the border.

One consensus-building institution, the Central Corridor Trade and Transport Facilitation Agency (CCTTFA), was created through an agreement by Burundi, the Democratic Republic of Congo, Rwanda, and Uganda, with Tanzania to use its port of Dar es Salaam. CCTTFA is a new entity based largely on similar arrangements to those of the NCTTCA. The CCTTFA instrument is clear on the role of the various stakeholders in achieving the expected results. The funding regime also helps to emphasize the critical role that donor funding can play in getting corridor institutions off the ground.

Efficient Corridor Management

It is widely recognized that the efficient management of international trade corridors is critical for the competitiveness of landlocked countries.

A formal management framework has been shown to be strategic in promoting and developing transit corridors serving LLDCs. In addition, empirical and anecdotal evidence indicates that there are many benefits to be derived from efficient corridor management, such as the following:

- Corridor interventions are problem-solving.
- They provide a channel for LLDCs to have a say in the provision of infrastructure and services on routes that are important to their trade competitiveness but lie outside their borders.
- Corridor bodies act as incubators and pilots of reform as they bring to the fore specific constraints in the policy, regulatory, and operational spheres, which, when addressed, can often also have a national application. Corridor management groups frequently play an advocacy role for national and regional reforms. A recent case is Zambia, where advocacy by a regional corridor group led to the review of national axle-load limits and standardization of those limits with neighboring countries.
- Corridors consolidate the generally small volumes of shipments from LLDCs and enable the countries to benefit from economies of scale.
- Corridors increase cooperation between the public and private sectors, hence they can lead to the realization of broad social and economic benefits.

However, upon a review of most corridor management institutions, a number of common characteristics and practices emerge as necessary conditions for these bodies to perform efficiently, including the following:

- Corridor management requires an enthusiastic and strong champion or champions with a vested interest in the corridor who can provide strength and continuity to corridor development efforts. Even then, it may be necessary to have donor funding to get the function off the ground.
- Sustainable funding for corridor management is a special challenge that must be addressed. When there is poor coordination, it is often difficult to draw a direct link between a corridor management function and improvements in the performance of a corridor. The majority of corridor management groups in Africa are either funded by donors, governments, or large shippers.[2]
- Cooperation on corridors requires a coordination body. The status and missions that substantially define the management model are explained in the previous section. This management body is often in the form of a

secretariat capable of advising, planning, and coordinating interventions of member countries and organizing interaction with stakeholders. Eventually it will help to mobilize resources and expertise from corridor group members and regional and international businesses and donors.

- Appropriate ownership and power sharing should be encouraged by the organizational design and operating procedures, because corridor issues by their nature are often solved by interactions between many public and private entities. Collaboration between players is key to effectiveness. In fact, in an ideal situation, each institution would share the same "horizontal" position of power and authority, and each would play an equal role, a situation close to the concept of "heterarchy."

- Monitoring the performance of corridors is important if interventions are to be targeted. Properly designed performance indicators that integrate the data gathered from corridor users and stakeholders are needed to assess the impact of corridor management initiatives. Such assessment is not straightforward, as there are as yet no internationally established benchmarks of performance of corridor management approaches. International comparisons contribute to assessing global competitiveness.

Building Trust Between Public and Private Sectors

Creation of national trade facilitation agencies is strongly recommended to bring together public- and private-sector stakeholders concerned with international trade in each country of the corridor. They are generally referred to as PRO committees after the first body of the sort SITPRO[3] in the UK or National Trade and Transport Facilitation Committee (NTTFC). The latter is the designation from the United Nations (UN) economic commissions and the UN Conference on Trade and Development (UNCTAD), which made recommendations on how to organize these committees (UN/CEFACT 2001). PRO committees offer champions for change who have the incentive to build up, step by step, more constructive working relations with the border control agencies and to join with them in seeking durable solutions. Box 8.1 sets out the objectives, functions, and suggested membership of PRO committees.

Experience has shown that consultation and cooperation between public and private sectors toward a common goal are crucial ingredients for success of such bodies. However, the exact formula for that cooperation—who takes the lead, who is and is not allowed in, and who provides the funding—can vary considerably from country to country, depending on the administrative culture and traditions regarding the respective roles of the public and private sectors.

Box 8.1

National Trade and Transport Facilitation Committees

Goals

Governments establish a national trade facilitation body—NTTFC—with balanced private- and public-sector participation in order to accomplish the following:

- Improve dialogue between different bodies involved in trade and international transport.
- Define solutions to remove impediments to trade and transport at operational level.
- Develop measures to reduce the cost of trade and help to implement them.
- Provide a national focal point for collecting and disseminating information on best practices in trade facilitation.
- Participate in international efforts to improve trade facilitation and efficiency.

The NTTFC can serve as a forum for private-sector managers, public-sector administrators, and policy makers to agree on and implement measures. These bodies generally have no executive authority but serves as an advisory body intended to facilitate consensus and voluntary action by members.

Underlying Organizational Concepts

An NTTFC is fundamentally a consultative mechanism serving as a national forum to propose, discuss, consult, and seek consensus among key players on facilitation measures. The three key players in this task are the following:

- *Government agencies* responsible for regulating international trade and transport (mostly ministries of commerce, transport, and finance, including customs agencies)

- *Trade and transport service providers* such as carriers, freight forwarders, multimodal transport operators, customs brokers, commercial banks, and insurance companies

- *Exporters and importers* who stand to benefit from an improved trading environment created by institutional reforms and greater efficiency in service provision and who will increase their trade volumes to take advantage of these improved conditions and reduced transaction costs.

(continued)

Box 8.1 *(continued)*

The second and third of these groups are mainly private-sector organizations, although among the transport operators and other trade service providers, there are often parastatals, such as the railways and state-owned trading banks, insurance companies, and freight forwarding companies. Thus, the essential partnership between the three main entities usually crosses the public-private sector divide.

Composition and Limits of Authority

A nominated government agency should accept overall responsibility for the NTTFC's activities and provide a chairperson. Ministries of transport, trade, or finance responsible for customs are suitable lead agencies for this purpose, since they can also provide secretariat services to the committee. The chair would ideally be appointed from the highest levels of the designated agency—preferably at the level of minister, vice-minister, or permanent secretary.

A permanent commission of about 10 members should be established to follow up on committee decisions and to provide support for its work program. The permanent commission, therefore, would be tasked with preparing documentation and assisting the decision-making process. It could organize tasks in ad-hoc working groups on the basis of specific requests from the committee. Both the committee and the permanent commission would be assisted by a technical secretariat, which would be responsible for daily operations. The committee should meet quarterly, while the permanent commission may meet more often.

Source: UNCTAD 2000.

Since the overriding objective is to build trust in settings where the point of departure is mutual mistrust, some initiatives can be expected to fail or may work only temporarily with one group of actors and then stumble, for example, when a government changes. This should not be grounds for giving up on the principle, but for possible reorganization or reconstitution of the committee.

The cooperative public-private improved communication and joint effort that are essential can be achieved by engaging in various activities that yield best results in a particular subregion and its countries. Availability and sharing of performance data are particularly important in providing committee participants and other stakeholders with a common benchmark to increase awareness, to prepare facilitation measures, and to monitor their impact. In the context of corridors serving LLDCs, observatories should make publicly available all information pertinent to the corridor, such as changes in procedures, performance indicators, or the status and availability of sections of the corridor.

Monitoring the Performance of Trade Corridors

The overall objective of any intervention in trade corridor performance for LLDCs can be defined as follows:

> ... improvement of the efficiency of the systems for delivering goods to and from foreign markets, as well as to producers and consumers in the domestic market of the landlocked country. Often the major trading partners of a landlocked country are its contiguous neighbors, so delivery systems to markets in contiguous neighboring countries are often the most important (Arnold 2006).

Before it can be determined what improvements are most needed and likely most beneficial, it is necessary to assess the corridor's overall performance, in particular where its performance may be reducing the competitiveness for the products using it. Then the effectiveness of any intervention can be measured against the initial parameters.

Trade and transport performance is usually assessed at strategic, policy, corridor, and project levels. Existing indicators are widely used and broadly accepted for performance at the strategic and policy levels, including the Doing Business Indicators (particularly those related to trade across borders) and the Logistics Performance Index. But it is at the corridor level that performance indicators can have the greatest practical impact, since they reveal where specific impediments to logistics efficiency occur. By the interpretation and analysis of indicators at this level, potential measures to address the impediments can be designed, and their potential impact can be evaluated.

The indicators at the corridor level illustrate performance at each principal stage of a supply chain or corridor. A tradeoff has to be made for the level of detail included in the indicators between the greater detail that typically characterizes a more useful indicator and the maximum level of detail that is comprehensible by those expected to act on the interpretation of the indicators. Less detail usually implies easier comprehension.

Development of corridor monitoring indicators has been addressed by regional international financial institutions, such as those in Africa's Northern Corridor; UN agencies such as UNCTAD; and the regional UN

Economic and Social Commissions (UNESCAP), particularly that for Asia and the Pacific; as well as some bilateral agencies, such as the U.S. Agency for International Development (USAID).

Until recently there has not been a common framework for these indicators. Most of the corridor performance measures have included time and cost, but have not always specified what time and cost are being measured or for what unit of transport (per ton, per consignment, per truck, or per TEU [20-foot equivalent unit]). There is an increasing focus on costs and times per TEU, but in many corridors, the usual measure is still per ton or per consignment. As far as can be determined, none of the systems has attempted to compare total corridor performance with competing corridors or to compare the delivered costs of the export (or import) goods in their intended markets.

Some corridor level measures use minimum times, costs, or both, while others provide averages. Some also provide minimum or maximum values, but again they do not indicate to what extent these are absolute values that include all instances or what proportion of instances, say 95 percent, are covered. Some that do provide a range of times and costs show a conventional normal distribution (with the same variation above the average as below the average), whereas most practical experience shows very skewed distributions, with little variation below the average but large variation above. Larger "tails" in the probability distribution of delays implies that the probability of spending several days waiting for clearance at the port, border, or delivery due to unreliable logistics services within the corridor is far from negligible.

Most indicators measure time or cost at different points along the corridor, such as an international border or a port. With notable exceptions, however, few provide cost and time estimates for a whole corridor, and only rarely are maritime costs included.

Only two methods of assessing trade corridor performance have been widely used, developed by UNESCAP and USAID. A third, more detailed method is being developed by the World Bank and has been used for a few corridors in Sub-Saharan Africa. It is not discussed further here as it is still in an early stage of development and is much more data-intensive than the other two methods.

UNESCAP has developed a graphical method of showing corridor performance that is now widely used throughout the Asia region. A good example of its use, with graphs for several corridors, was recently presented by the Korea Transport Institute in the Republic of Korea for corridors in northeast Asia. The graph shows a time–distance interaction for both road and rail corridors, with time or cost on the vertical axis and distance on the horizontal axis and with lines for the minimum, maximum, and average cost and time (see figure 8.1). In essence, this "cost escalation" graphic method provides information about the relative importance and variability in terms of time and monetary costs of each interface point within the corridor. The CAREC studies of seven trade corridors leading to and from LLDCs in Central Asia are among the current prominent users of the UNESCAP method.

However, alternative methodologies have emerged in recent years to measure corridor performance. One of them is FastPath software, developed for USAID by Nathan Associates (a U.S.-based consulting firm) to identify inefficiencies and to evaluate potential improvements in developing countries ports and logistics chains. It identifies and prioritizes specific areas for improvement with credibility and transparency, so that all stakeholders can participate in modifying the analysis and arriving at a mutually acceptable result (see box 8.2 for a description.)

Figure 8.1   Typical Output of a UNESCAP Corridor Performance Monitoring

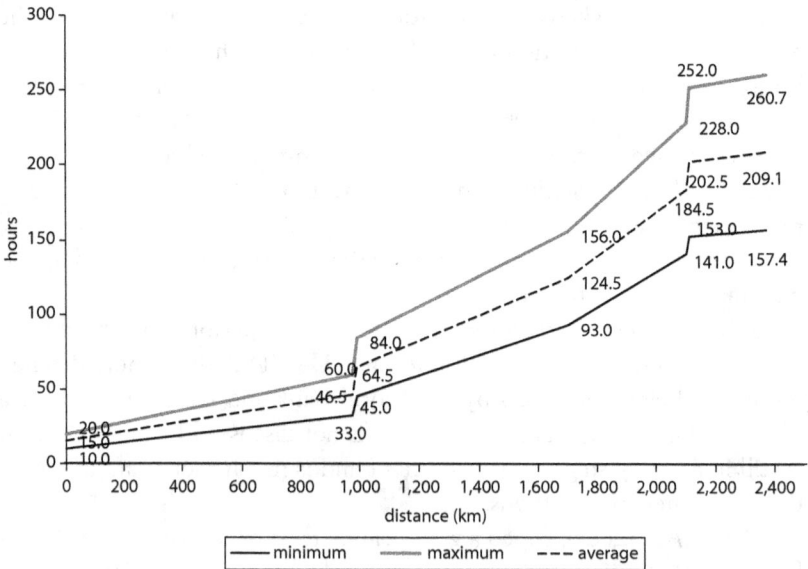

Source: UNESCAP 2006.

Note: The UNESCAP corridor monitoring method is a development of the first one used by UNCTAD for assessing "dry ports." Transit times and distances presented in the figure correspond to the Tianjin–Ulan Ude Corridor by rail (China–Mongolia).

Box 8.2

FastPath Shows Corridor Performance Strengths and Weaknesses

Originally developed for USAID, FastPath software has now been used in assessments of more than 20 trade corridors, usually as a component of a broader corridor analysis. Two of these assessments were of corridors in the ASEAN (Association of Southeast Asian Nations) region, while another was for the Maputo Corridor in southern Africa.

For ASEAN, the two corridors analyzed were Vientiane, the Lao People's Democratic Republic, to Laem Chabang, Thailand, and Danang, Vietnam, to Mukdahan, Thailand, via Savanakhet, Lao PDR. The FastPath analysis showed where each corridor performed well (generally at the ports), not so well (at the border crossings), and poorly (trucking services). A more detailed analyses behind these broad findings made it possible to specify and evaluate various remedies to overcome the corridor weaknesses. Further, an ASEAN logistics strategy was designed, on the basis of assessments of the performance on the corridor of seven sectors—customs and other inspection agencies, ports and maritime transport, rail transport, road transport, inland waterways transport, air transport, and logistics services.

FastPath was also the main analytical tool used in the USAID support for the Maputo Corridor that links Mozambique, South Africa, and Swaziland. The FastPath analysis was not at quite the same detail level as for ASEAN but was still able to identify the components of the corridor that most merited attention. One of the main findings was that the imbalance between imports and exports was a main constraining factor for corridor performance, with the cost of repositioning empty containers largely offsetting the competiveness of the port of Maputo. Time spent at border crossings made up only about 6 percent of the total, while the cost of border crossings was about 8 percent of the total land cost. The percentage variability in border crossing time (58 percent) was only about one-fifth of that of the port and land transport time variabilities (together, about 240 percent). Cost rather than transit time was found to be the main source of competitive disadvantage.

FastPath is an ambitious tool (much beyond what is normally included in a toolkit), and a full application for any corridor requires the entry of a relatively large amount of data compared to the UNESCAP method or the total logistics costs concept, and its outputs are similar to what is proposed in this chapter.

Source: Authors based on Nathan Associates (http://www.nathaninc.com) and USAID 2007, 2008.

Total Logistics Costs on a Transit Corridor

As outlined in chapter 2, transport costs account for only part of the real cost of being landlocked because they do not factor in transit delays and unpredictability. While trying to assess the impact of logistics on LLDCs, practitioners usually choose between the classical approach, based on vehicle operating cost reduction and induced traffic, or in terms of global impact on trade, to try to evaluate logistics costs out of trade statistics. So far, analyses have mainly focused on the transport cost disadvantage of LLDCs, with several shortcomings. It is therefore necessary to determine from a microperspective all the various factors involved in logistics costs.

Expanding upon a model initially proposed by Baumol and Vinod (1970), Arvis, Raballand, and Marteau (2007) proposed a concept of total logistics costs taking the perspective or shipper in the landlocked country of destination or origin. According to this approach, total logistics costs can be decomposed in (1) transportation costs, in fees paid for actual transit transportation services to truckers or rail operators; (2) other logistics costs, in transit overheads (fees, procedures, facilitation payments, and fixed costs of shipments); and (3) induced costs to hedge unreliability in transit, such as inventory costs and warehousing costs, or to shift to faster more expensive mode of transportation. The latter costs are typically internalized and commodity-dependent.

In order to assess the impact of facilitation measures or changes in business patterns related to trade and transport along corridors, Arvis, Raballand, and Marteau (2010) developed a quantitative supply-chain model identifying the impact of cost, lead time, and lead time uncertainty. In this framework, the shipper in the LLDC bears the transit cost of inland logistics operations to and from port and to and from warehouse or factory. The component costs are evaluated by breaking down the transit supply chain into steps using cost and time information: some are transport-related (moving goods between borders), and many are not (storage in port, transit documents, customs processing and warehousing, and so on), using the following equation:

$$\text{Total transit cost} = A + O + \frac{\beta}{\lambda} \times D + w \times T(\gamma) \times V + w \times \frac{S}{2} \times V + \Psi,$$

where $\Psi = \alpha \times T_{trans}$ for an efficient trucking market, and $\Psi = \frac{\alpha}{N\lambda}$ for a cartel or syndicate.[4]

Examples in Arvis, Raballand, and Marteau (2010) show that gains will come primarily from reduction of extreme times in the distribution, change in market structure and operating cost structure of services, and reduction of the rent impact on overheads. Hence, the critical information needed to compute these gains is the following:

- Structure of operating costs of transportation and notably the relative share of variable (for example, fuel maintenance) versus fixed cost (gross margin and monthly use).
- Distribution of lead time of the supply chain, which is typically a log-normal distribution over a baseline minimum feasible time.
- Structure of overheads including unofficial payments.

At the implementation level, a consistent set of indicators should measure the tryptic cost-time-reliability for the full supply chain. Underlying data do not require heavy statistical instruments but do need a sustainable partnership with freight forwarders and trucking operators, who are precisely the ones handling the supply chain from origin to destination and who are in position to provide the data on survey or statistical basis.

Designing the Monitoring System for Corridor Performance

Design of a feasible system for monitoring the performance of a corridor requires careful decisions in four key dimensions: (1) the parameters that need to be measured, (2) the locations for which they should be measured, (3) the types of product and forms of shipment to be covered, and (4) the cost and frequency with which the measurements are made.

Parameters to Be Measured

Comprehensive assessment of corridor performance requires acquiring data in five main parameters: time required, cost of the movement, flexibility, reliability, and safety and security, and then assessing the differences in these parameters for export and import products. Table 8.1 gives an example of the breakdown of results that are sought.

Locations for Which the Measurements Are Needed

The parameters should be measured for each major stage of transport of the freight, including locations where significant amount of time is spent, documents are reviewed, and freight is subject to inspection,

Table 8.1   Cost, Time, and Reliability of Exports on the Vientiane–Laem Chabang Corridor

Component	Cost to shipper (US$)		Time to shipper		Reliability (% variation in transit time)		Overall rating (good to very poor)
	Actual	Norm	Actual	Norm	Actual	Norm	
Port and terminal operations	70	50–150	3.5 days	3–5 days	125	35–50	good
Seaport customs	0	0–50	0.5 hrs	0.5–1.5 hrs	50	35–50	good
Rail transport	35	0–50	3.5 hrs	2.5–3.5 hrs	75	35–50	good
ICD operations	62.5	10–30	2.5 days	1–2 days	75	35–50	fair
Road transport	845	200–300	16 hrs	12–15 hrs	125	35–50	fair-poor
Transloading	50	50–150	2 hrs	2–4 hrs	125	35–50	good
Inland customs	180	100–300	3 hrs	2–4 hrs	199	35–50	good
Export formalities	120	50–150	12 days	3–5 days	59	35–50	poor
Total or Average	1,362	820	18.5 days	10.5 days	100	35–50	fair

Source: Authors.

transshipped, or stored for more than six hours. An export operation involves the following seven major stages of transport; the same ones apply in reverse order for an import operation:

- Loading at origin in LLDC
- Transport within LLDC to border with transit country
- All locations where border transfer between vehicles or inspection of freight or documents may occur
- Transport within transit country
- Unloading and storage in the port of export
- Maritime transport
- Unloading in port of final destination.

Products Carried, Their Transport Unit, and Their Route

Transport conditions and costs differ so much for different types of goods carried that an explicit decision must be made about the types of goods on which to focus the analysis. Bulk products, such as grains and minerals, have very product-specific characteristics and are exported to different markets than are manufactured goods. High-value goods, such as computer components and perishable goods (flowers and fruits), also have very specific characteristics that make them difficult to address in a general performance indicator or set of indicators.

But between these two extremes is a wide range of manufactured products that have a value per TEU of about US$50,000–US$250,000 and a lead delivery time on the order of three to four months. These are the products, mostly textiles and consumer goods, that many developing countries already export and for which production costs are often broadly comparable between different developing countries, so that logistics costs may play a big role in their cost competitiveness at the destination markets.

If the indicators are to be used for overall comparisons between corridors, they need to relate to common origins or destinations. For most products transported in containers, there are, in very broad terms, three major destination markets: Europe and the east and west coasts of the United States. For each of these markets, maritime transport is an important part of the trade corridor, accounting for a significant share of the cost of the delivered products (and for the delivered cost of imports to developing countries from these three sources). For containerized products, it would also be useful for comparative purposes if the indicators were related to specific ports within these three major markets, so that differences in corridor performance are not distorted by the costs to particular ports.

Of course, more specific and focused comparative assessments of particular trades on specific routes can also be useful for particular purposes. But whether seeking broad indications of performance or that of the handling of particular trades, it is always important to also specify the form in which the products are transported (container, bulk solid, bulk liquid, loose), their approximate value, the final destination of export products and the original source of import products, and the port through which they are exported or imported.

Cost and Replicability of the Measurements

Costs of a performance monitoring study can range from less than US$1,000 per corridor, where the assessments are made on the basis of a standard questionnaire sent to freight forwarders in the LLDC and its transit neighbors, up to US$500,000, where a team of specialized consultants undertakes an in-depth, several-month-long investigation of real events in the corridor. For the purposes of comparing corridors or for examining a specific corridor over time, neither of these two extremes is appropriate; the first does not provide sufficient detail, and the second provides too much. To be useful and widely applicable, the monitoring method should have the following characteristics:

- Easy to measure and replicate at different points in time
- Adds marginally to measures that would be made in any case
- Based on consistent and defined parameters that are easily understood
- Able to indicate where in a corridor any excess cost or time is incurred.

To generate broadly relevant indicators of overall performance of corridors, the authors propose a monitoring method that incorporates the best characteristics of both the UNESCAP and FastPath models and is compatible with both. Advantages of the method are that it specifically differentiates between exports and imports, specifies the overseas origin or destination of the freight movements, and includes the maritime segment of the transport. It also provides a readily understood specification of the minimum cost and time, including the shipment size and how the variation above that minimum should be estimated. Finally, it generates an estimate of the total transport cost of using the corridor, thus offering a basis for assessing the extent to which any proposed improvements in the corridor might increase the competitiveness of the exports from the LLDC.

Corridor Monitoring in Practice: Observatories in Africa

The design of all interventions intended to facilitate transit movement requires baseline and traffic flow information. Appropriate data can assist in identifying those components of the regional systems that are not working well so that infrastructure, regulatory, or institutional reform interventions can be better targeted for intervention. Thus, it is very important that data on corridor operations be collected systematically. Overall monitoring activities can take two distinct forms: global corridor monitoring and detailed monitoring at specific locations, or "choke points," within a corridor.

Corridor-wide monitoring involves data collection and surveys covering the length of a corridor, typically between a port and an inland destination. However, choke-point monitoring uses detailed surveys at specific locations that work as bottlenecks to transit movement. Corridor-wide monitoring (also dubbed "observatory pilot projects") has been carried out on Africa's Northern Corridor and along corridors in West and Central Africa. Meanwhile, detailed microscale monitoring has been implemented at Beitbridge (between South Africa and Zimbabwe) and

Chirundu (between Zimbabwe and Zambia) border posts on the North–South Corridor in southern Africa.

Monitoring on the Northern Corridor has been conducted by NCTTCA. Initial activities included a baseline survey on nonphysical barriers along the corridor, which started early in 2004, and subsequent surveys conducted in 2004 and 2005. This was done to raise the awareness among stakeholders from both public and the private sectors of the cost and impact of delays along the corridor. This pilot phase yielded useful lessons in terms of data collection mechanisms (for example, difficulty in obtaining manually filled in data from drivers through trucking companies) and the scope of indicators that could be used to monitor performance. It also pointed to the desirability of and requirements for a sustainable corridor performance monitoring mechanism.

Nevertheless, there have been two separate but related observatory activities in West Africa, one led by the West Africa Trade Hub (WATH) and the second by the Abidjan–Lagos Corridor Organisation (ALCO). In the first case, the Sub-Saharan Africa Transport Policy Program (SSATP) and its regional economic community partners, West African Economic and Monetary Union and Economic Community of West African States, have collaborated with the USAID-funded WATH in collecting information on the number of barriers to movement along three corridors. The data collected include length of delays at road blocks, the agents involved, and total illegal payments made through road surveys to collect the required information. The WATH-led work has contributed to the quantification of the transit delays and costs and causing factors along the three corridors in West Africa.

While not included in the SSATP program per se, the Transport Coordination Committee of the Regional Economic Communities has maintained constant links with ALCO, which, since 2005, has carried out transit time and checkpoint surveys between borders on the Abidjan–Lagos Corridor. The methodology is based on a comprehensive quasi-permanent survey carried out at border crossings with large teams of surveyors, complemented by sample trips to check a number of checkpoints. As a result, the ALCO method is the most expensive of the observatory data collection exercises that have been implemented.

Finally, the type of traffic monitored, data collection processes, and resources are different in each observatory work. For instance, monitoring in the Northern Corridor has only been focused on goods traffic, transit times, delay times, and causes of stops, but not on vehicles, as in the other two corridors.

Conclusions

History and recent experience in developping countries confirm the value of corridor-based initiatives, as opposed to uncoordinated activities in the countries along the corridor. Some form of corridor management is probably a precondition to make a specific corridor a sustainable access solution for LLDCs. It is also a good framework to address some of the political economy constraints, described earlier in this volume, and to build trust between the private sector and public agencies. Corridor management is essentially idiosyncratic, depending on historical development of the corridor and institutions in the countries along the corridor and their political objectives in terms of cooperation and integration. International and development agencies should support capacity-building in corridor management as they have begun to do and should help document success and facilitate experience sharing. However, given the diversity of experiences, there is probably no scope for explicit standards in corridor management, for instance, comparable to existing UN-backed standards for trade facilitation promulgated by the UN Centre for Trade Facilitation and Electronic Business (UN/CEFACT 2001).

The development of corridor performance indicators is also of utmost importance in initiating, implementing, and monitoring the impact of corridor and transit-related reforms and investments. Development agencies should continue to support the development of performance data in the form of pilot surveys and support to corridor observatories. However, even though there has been substantial assistance in this area, it is urgent to introduce more consistency in those efforts to remedy the lack of comparability in methodologies, focus, and output. This could take the form of a common recommendation by the lead agencies, UN and World Bank. The recommendation is to propose a common conceptual framework and definition of indicators consistent with the total logistics costs paradigm, survey methodologies, and business model of observatories that would be both cost-effective and sustainable.

Notes

1. SADC members are Angola, Botswana, the Democratic Republic of Congo, Lesotho, Madagascar, Malawi, Mauritius, Mozambique, Namibia, Seychelles, South Africa, Swaziland, Tanzania, Zambia, and Zimbabwe.
2. In West Africa, the Abidjan–Lagos Corridor Organization started as a World Bank project focused on the human immunodeficiency virus/acquired

immune deficiency syndrome. It is now taking on a wider management role but still with donor and government funding. The CCTTFA in East Africa is receiving support from the African Development Bank in its early stages, with the expectation that a more sustainable funding regime will be developed. A funding system that links traffic to corridor use is in place on the Northern Corridor, where there is a levy on each ton bound for the LLDC that passes through the port of Mombasa. The coastal country, Kenya, opted to make a payment through its treasury. It is likely that the CCTTFA will adopt a similar approach once it is well established. A tonnage levy at least makes a direct link between efficiency improvements and payment for the management function. However and in general, until there are clear benefits, there is usually reluctance to pay directly for corridor use except where the charges are unavoidable, such as road tolls or port charges. But it is precisely in the early stages of corridor management that funding is most needed.

3. Originally called the the Simpler Trade Procedures Board, created in 1970 and terminated in September 2010.

4. O = Transit overheads

A = Administrative costs of organizing transit operations: internal costs or costs paid to logistics providers (for example, to arrange small shipments)

S = Average time (days) between identical shipments required by the level of demand for such shipment (replenishment cycle)

α = Fixed costs of transportation

β = Variable cost of transportation (for example, fuel, maintenance)

D = Average distance covered in the period

λ = Load factor of truck

m = Moving inventory cost

w = Warehouse inventory cost

V = Value per shipment

T_{trans} = Usage of transportation vehicle (including waiting time and return)

$T(\gamma)$ = average lead time for the slowest shipments not delivered within an accepted level γ of non-timely delivery

D = Distance covered in transit (one-way)

N = Number of trips of transit vehicles (per month)

References

Arnold, John. 2006. "Best Practices in Management of International Trade Corridors." World Bank Transport Paper 13, World Bank, Washington, DC.

Arvis, Jean-François, Gaël Raballand, and Jean-François Marteau. 2010. *The Cost of Being Landlocked: Logistics Costs and Supply Chain Reliability.* Washington, DC: World Bank.

————. 2007. "The Cost of Being Landlocked: Logistics Costs and Supply Chain Reliability." World Bank Policy Research Working Paper 4258, World Bank, Washington, DC.

Baumol, W. J., and H. D. Vinod. 1970. "An Inventory Theoretic Model of Freight Transport Demand." *Management Science* 16 (7): 413–21.

UN/CEFACT (United Nations/Centre for Trade Facilitation and Electronic Business). 2001. "National Trade Facilitation Bodies." ECE/TRADE/242, October, UN/CEFACT, Geneva.

UNCTAD (UN Conference on Trade and Development). 2000. "Creating an Efficient Environment for Trade and Transport." Paper presented at Sixth Session of UN/CEFACT, Geneva, March 27–30.

UNESCAP (United Nations Economic and Social Commission for Asia and the Pacific). 2006. *Integrated International Transport and Logistics System for North-East Asia.* New York: UNESCAP.

USAID (United States Agency for International Development). 2007. "Toward a Roadmap for Integration of the ASEAN Logistics Sector: Rapid Assessment and Concept Paper." Summary prepared by Nathan Associates, Inc. http://pdf. usaid.gov/pdf_docs/PNAD1778.pdf.

————. 2008. "Maputo Corridor Summary Report: A Transport Logistics Diagnostic Tool Study." Publication prepared by Nathan Associates, Inc. http://www.usaid.gov/mz/doc/misc/maputo_corridor_summary_report.pdf.

CHAPTER 9

Bringing Together the Solutions

On the basis of the analysis and prescriptions throughout this volume, this chapter has derived 13 key recommendations for policy makers and international organization to improve corridor performance and transit systems. These recommendations are grouped under four general headings:

- Building trust
- Making transport and logistics services work for trade
- Redefining or improving transit systems
- Developing global initiatives to promote common approaches for redesigning transit regimes and monitoring trade corridor performance.

Four main themes emerge as significant potential sources of cost savings and efficiency increase on trade corridors serving landlocked developing countries (LLDCs) and their transit neighbors. First is the concept of building trust in and across countries and focusing facilitation efforts on some active corridors. For this to work requires the mobilization of champions for reform, especially from among parties who can expect to gain from expanded trade. Their involvement is likely to be the only sustainable solution for overcoming entrenched interests, which gain from today's inefficient and corrupt systems.

The second theme is the need for more active policies of improvement of transport and logistics services to achieve better competition and higher professional standards of service, including between different modes of transportation.

Third is the importance of reengineering transit systems with concrete steps forward in the implementation of carnet-based systems and with proper regulation of entry favoring competence and compliance to support information technology infrastructure and adequate border management.

The fourth theme is the role of the international community in promoting global standards that could help the spread of sound facilitation practices in specific regions or corridors. Comprehensive standards for regional transit systems are desirable, at least as a reference to facilitate convergence over a certain period of time. So is the quest for a common performance-monitoring tool that will allow the production of indicators on a cost-effective and comparable basis.

Under the umbrella of these four strategic themes, the study makes 13 specific recommendations, most fairly broad, except the last two, which are addressed mainly to countries—LLDCs and their transit neighbors, as well as their regional economic cooperation bodies. It is envisaged, in fact, that most of the recommendations would be pursued anyway, as relevant to the case, under a program built on a holistic approach to upgrading performance of a corridor or group of corridors in a subregion. This reflects the pattern of some of the initiatives of this type supported in recent years by the World Bank and International Development Association, and it is strongly hoped that other aid agencies and regional banks will continue to play an active part in shaping and helping finance the resultant reform programs.

The two recommendations more specifically addressed to international agencies than to countries are the ones concerning the corridor monitoring methodology and the clarification of standards applicable to regional integrated transit systems. The latter is of great potential relevance to the developing regions to guide their future improvement efforts and to avoid the past proliferation of idiosyncratic solutions that depart in essential ways from the de facto reference systems documented here. Development of the corridor monitoring methodology depends on a collaborative effort among the aid agencies and international bodies that have so far been involved in such work, notably the World Bank, United Nations Conference on Trade and Development (UNCTAD), and United Nations Economic and Social Commission for Asia and the Pacific (UNESCAP).

The recommendations are grouped under their relevant themes, with a reference at the end to the chapter or paragraphs in the preceding text where more elaboration or foundation can be found.

Building Trust

Foster public-private synergy. Ensure achievement of the cooperative, improved, public-private communication and joint effort that are so essential. To do so, adopt whatever instruments can yield best results in the subregion and its countries, such as the establishment of observatories and Web sites, identification of seriously interested and influential champions (at least one private-sector and one government), direct participation of all groups in facilitation committees, and activation of private professional groups (chapter 8).

Focus on corridor performance. Focusing cross-country efforts around individual corridors and the LLDC and transit countries that they serve is a practical way to facilitate trade and transportation on the ground by addressing localized bottlenecks, even when some of the issues, such as regulation and transit regime, need to be dealt with at the regional level. Dialogue and association of key agencies and private stakeholders across countries require adequate platforms and institutions. Collecting and publishing consistent and comparable indicators will support corridor facilitation activities and may eventually stimulate emulation and competition among corridors (chapter 8).

Making Transportation and Logistics Services Work for Trade

Promote service quality and competition in core services. Shift regulatory emphasis in transit neighbors and LLDCs alike toward active promotion of quality standards and requirements for open competition and for the provision of core services, especially trucking and freight forwarding (chapters 6 and 7).

Harmonize or implement cross-border transport instruments. This priority is still high in several regions where lack of integration hinders the cross-border movement of vehicles: insurance recognition, quotas, road and other charges for foreign trucks, and licensing (chapter 6).

Make the most of multimodal and railroad potential. First, consider introduction, at the cost of the LLDC, of a regular shuttle train service between it and the ocean port that handles most of its trade, in the many cases where the relevant basic infrastructure exists and demand allows for at least one shuttle a day (about half a million ton per year). Adequate investment in transfer facilities at inland destinations, such as dry ports (container terminals), should be considered, calling on public-private partnerships with interested logistics operators (chapter 7).

Investigate prospects for air export. Especially where overland transit and related port services present obstacles to improved performance that are hard to overcome, LLDCs should remain on the lookout for air export opportunities. This could include any possibilities of benefiting from spare freight capacity in the cargo holds of international passenger services from neighbor countries (chapter 7).

Redefining or Improving Transit Systems

Focus on improving transit systems. Countries in regional economic groupings should develop a consistent vision of improved transit systems for each main developing subregion. This vision should build on existing efforts, as well as on more geographically focused efforts on specific corridors within the subregion. Any recommended action would not necessarily be to facilitate trade as it is today, but rather to enable or promote a premium level of services by implementing mechanisms, as proposed in chapter 5 that provide the right incentives. A proper sequencing of activities and reforms is essential. Improvement in the transit regime is likely to be the keystone of this vision. Implementation is also dependent on improvement in two areas already mentioned: regulation of cross-border trucking and corridor management. Furthermore, many pairs of countries should address the content of their bilateral treaties, which may be outdated and unduly restrictive and protectionist, as well as incompatible with efforts to build an integrated transit system.

Reengineer the customs transit implementation regime. The objective is to implement a carnet-based system[1] (single document), which supports a unified transit of goods across a region. The redesign should implement procedures by which authorized transit operators meeting certain international standards of quality and compliance will access a fast-track, regionally integrated transit system. The details of the system—documentation, guarantees, similarity to the TIR or other regional transit regimes, and the possibilities of evolution—should be planned in accordance with the growth of local competence and demand. In most regions, this will be a major project requiring substantial inputs from international agencies. Endorsement from the private sector should be sought, especially from the existing logistics sector, including through provisions for those who might find it hard to meet the quality standards of a carnet system (chapters 4 and 5).

Optimize usage of ICT systems to support transit. Implementation of regional transit regimes and, in many cases, improving current national ones may require capacity-building of the implementation agency (customs or other) to adequately manage the data on goods in transit. Information technology transit modules that automate the transit declaration or carnet would serve this purpose. Furthermore, protocols between customs transit modules across the countries on corridors would help keep track of transit cargo along the corridors and release bonds in a timely manner. While automation of the declaration and bonds is always critical, no such recommendation can be made, in general, for real-time tracking systems (electronic seals and global positioning systems). Real time technologies attract a lot of interest, but as of now there is no positive evaluation, nor emerging expert consensus that they do actually provide a robust option to transit facilitation.

Streamline border processing and control. The border infrastructure and management systems should provide for fast-track processing of carnet-based traffic separately from local cross-border trade that is cleared at the border. Processing and control should be reduced for carnet traffic—phasing out inspections, convoys, intermediate checkpoints, and repeated weighing of sealed containers or trailers. Ideally, the long-term objective would be to conduct clearance of goods somewhere other than at the border (as in the European Union), moving it inland and closer to the final destination of the goods.

Give special attention to the initiation of transit in ports. Examining where trade begins is required, because ports are typically the primary source of delays and cause uncertainty for imports bound for inland destinations. Rail freight, which poses little problem of securitization and tracing, should benefit from an expedited initiation of transit. Truck-borne transit should have fast-track treatment ahead of goods for local clearance.

Developing Global Initiatives to Promote Common Approaches for Redesigning Transit Regimes and Monitoring Trade Corridor Performance

Agree on common methodologies for performance indicators and systems. The World Bank should make a major effort to mobilize a coordinated effort among interested international financial institutions, United Nations agencies, and other regional and national bodies to launch and maintain a trade and transport monitoring system for LLDCs. Such a system should be as simple as possible, consistent in concepts, and regularly reported to help stimulate needed remedial actions and to demonstrate the degree of effectiveness of actions already taken, including coverage of all main corridors linking LLDCs with world markets and their key interchange points (chapter 8).

Agree on global standards for an international transit regime. Under the United Nations umbrella, small technical working parties should prepare drafts of agreed upon best-practice standards on at least five topics vital to efficient transit: (1) regulation and designation of authorized transit operators, (2) documentation of transit manifests and carnets, (3) regional guarantees, (4) information systems and the exchange of manifest and carnet information across countries, and (5) border processing of compliant transit trucks. This work can fit into the work program of the World Trade Organization negotiating party on trade facilitation (General Agreement on Tariffs and Trade, Article V) and the United Nations Economic Commission for Europe evaluation of the TIR, but it would benefit from the involvement of the World Customs Organization, UNCTAD, and private sector parties from the International Road Transport Union or its member associations and from the banking and insurance sector (chapters 4 and 5).

Note

1. "Carnet-based" means that all the relevant information can travel with the transport operator (truck driver) across the border preferably in an electronic form that can be read and transmitted by information technology.

Landlocked Developing Countries (LLDCs), Their Transit Neighbors, and Main Trade Corridors, by Region

Table A1.1   Eastern and Southern Africa: LLDCs and Transit Neighbors

Subregion	LLDCs	Transit countries	Main corridors to ports (main hubs in italic), distance	Key regional initiatives and institutions, start date[a]
Eastern Africa	Ethiopia	Djibouti	Addis Ababa–*Djibouti* (800 km)	COMESA (Common Market for Eastern and Southern Africa) 1994 Treaty
	Uganda	Kenya	*Northern Corridor:* Kampala–*Mombasa* (1,300 km)	EAC (East African Community) (2001): Customs Union (2004)
		Tanzania	*Central Corridor:* Kampala–Mutukula–Isaka–*Dar es Salaam* (1,676 km)	Northern Corridor Transit Agreement (1985): Northern Corridor Transit Transport Coordination Authority (NCTTCA) (1985), Secretariat (1988), Stakeholders Consultative Forum (1999)
	Rwanda	Uganda Kenya	*Northern Corridor:* Kigali–Kampala–*Mombasa* (1,700 km)	
		Tanzania	*Central Corridor:* Kigali–*Dar es Salaam* (1,470 km)	CCTTFA (Central Corridor Transit Transport Facilitation Agency) (2006)
	Burundi	Uganda Kenya	*Northern Corridor:* Bujumbura–Kampala–*Mombasa* (1,830 km)	
		Tanzania	*Central Corridor:* Bujumbura–*Dar es Salaam* (1,500 km)	

Southern Africa	Botswana	South Africa	**North–South Corridor:** Gaborone–*Durban* (950 km)	SADC (Southern African Development Community) (1992): Southern Africa Transport and Communications Commission (SATCC); Protocol on Transport, Communications and Meteorology (PTCM) (1996); creation of Free Trade Area (with participation of 11 of SADC's 14 members) (August 2008)
		Namibia	***Trans-Kalahari Corridor:*** Gaborone–Walvis Bay (1,410 km)	
	Lesotho	South Africa	Maseru–*Durban* (500 km)	SACU (Southern African Customs Union) (1969): revised SACU Agreement was adopted in 2002 and includes provision to establish a Technical Liaison Committee for Transport (as also for certain other subjects).
	Swaziland	Mozambique	Mbabane–Goba–*Maputo* (250 km)	
		South Africa	Mbabane–*Durban* (500 km)	
	Zimbabwe	South Africa	**North–South Corridor:** Harare–Bulawayo–*Durban (1,550 km)*	The Ndola–Durban route is the core of the North–South Corridor, which has been chosen by the three regional bodies together for priority effort.[a]
		Mozambique	***Beira Corridor:*** Harare–Bulawayo–*Beira* (850 km)	
	Zambia	South Africa, Zimbabwe	**North–South Corridor:** Ndola–*Durban* (2,500 km)	
		Mozambique, Zimbabwe	***Beira Corridor:*** Ndola–*Beira (1,350 km)*	
		Tanzania	***Dar es Salaam Corridor:*** Ndola–*Dar es Salaam* (1,900 km)	
	Malawi	South Africa, Mozambique, Zimbabwe	**North–South Corridor:** Blantyre–*Durban* (2,300 km)	
		Mozambique	***Beira Corridor:*** Blantyre–*Beira* (580 km) Blantyre–*Nacala* (800 km)	

Source: Authors.

Note: km = kilometer.

a. With regard to all LLDCs and transit countries in Eastern and Southern Africa: 2006 marked the start of more sustained cooperation among all regional bodies. In March 2006, a Tripartite Task Force (from COMESA, SADC, and EAC) was established, which included emphasis on trade and transport facilitation. In May 2007, the task force agreed to make the North–South Corridor, the Durban–Ndola Corridor, and other transit routes in the Democratic Republic of Congo, Malawi, and southern Great Lakes region a joint priority.

Table A1.2   Western and Central Africa: LLDCs and Transit Neighbors

Subregion	LLDCs	Transit countries	Main corridors to ports (main hubs in italic), distance	Key regional initiatives and institutions, start date
West Africa	Mali	Côte d'Ivoire Ghana Senegal Togo	Bamako–*Dakar* (1,200 km)	ECOWAS (Economic Community of West African States) (1975); TRIE (*Transports Routiers Inter-Etats*) (1982), RRTTFP (Regional Road Transport and Transit Facilitation Programme (2003)
	Burkina Faso	Côte d'Ivoire Ghana Togo	Ouagadougou–Paga–*Abidjan/Lomé/Tema* (1,900 km)	UEMOA (*Union Economique et Monétaire Ouest Africaine*) (1994); PACITR (*Programme d'Actions Communautaire des Infrastructures et du Transport Routier*) (2001)
	Niger	Benin Togo	Niamey–*Cotonou/Lagos* (900 km)	
Central Africa	Chad	Cameroon	Ndjamena–Ngaounderé–*Douala* (1,850 km)	CEMAC (*Communauté Economique et Monétaire de l'Afrique Centrale*) (1994); (Predecessor, UDEAC [Union Douanière et Economique de l'Afrique Centrale], had led to agreement on TIPAC [*Transports Internationaux pour les Pays de l'Afrique Centrale*] in 1991, but it was
		Nigeria	Ndjamena–*Lagos* (1,870 km)	not followed through); CEMAC Trade and Transport Facilitation Programme (2006)
	Central African Republic	Cameroon	Bangui-Ngaounderé/ Belabo–*Douala* (1,450 km)	

Source: Authors.
Note: km = kilometer.

Table A1.3 South Asia: LLDCs and Transit Neighbors

Subregion	LLDCs	Transit countries	Main corridors to ports (main hubs in italic), distance	Key regional initiatives and institutions, start date
South Asia	Afghanistan	Pakistan	Kabul–Jalalabad–Torkham–Landi Kotal–Peshawar–*Karachi* (1,600 km)	Afghan Trade Transit Agreement (ATTA) (1965, modified 2004), now to be replaced by Afghanistan–Pakistan Transit Agreement (APTA)
			Kabul–Kandahar–Spin Boldak–Chaman–Quetta–*Karachi* (1,500 km)	
		Iran, Islamic Rep.	Kabal–Herat–Bandar Abbas (1,200 km)	
	Nepal	India	Kathmandu–Birganj–*Kolkata/ Haldia* (1,060 km)	Indo–Nepal Treaty of Transit (1991, renewed with minor modification in 2006 for seven years)
	Bhutan	India	Thimphu–Phuentsholing–Kishanganj–*Kolkata* (800 km)	Bhutan–India Treaty of Friendship (1949)

Source: Authors.
Note: km = kilometer.

Table A1.4   Central Asia and the Caucasus: LLDCs and Transit Neighbors

Subregion	LLDCs	Transit countries	Main corridors to ports (main hubs in italic), distance	Key regional initiatives and institutions, start date
Central Asia	Kyrgyz Republic Kazakhstan	China	Bishkek–Almaty–Korgas–Kuytum–Urumqi–Xian–Shanghai (4,900 km)	ECO (Economic Cooperation Organization) (1985): Transit Transport Framework Agreement (1998, **not yet effective**)
		Russian Federation	Almaty–Bishkek–Kyzyl–Orda–Orenberg–Samara–Moscow–Warsaw–Hamburg (5,200 km)	TRACECA (Transport Corridor Europe–Caucasus–Asia) (1993) UNESCAP (United Nations Economic and Social Commission for Asia and the Pacific) (1992): Intergovernmental Agreement on Asian Highway Network (2003)
	Uzbekistan Turkmenistan Azerbaijan	Russian Federation Georgia	Samarkand–Bukhara–Mary–Ashgabat–Turkmenbashi–Baku–Tbilisi–*Poti* (2,700 km)	UNECE (United Nations Economic Commission for Europe)–UNESCAP joint efforts (1998): SPECA (Special Programme for the Economies of Central Asia) and series of Euro-Asian conferences on transport Shanghai Cooperation Organization (2001)

Region	Countries	Route	
	Uzbekistan Kyrgyz Republic Turkmenistan Iran, Islamic Rep. Turkey	Osh/Tashkent–Bukhara–Mary–Sarakhs–Mashshad–(Bandar Abbas)–Teheran–Tabriz–Erzurum–*Istanbul* (4,500 km)	CAREC (Central Asia Regional Economic Cooperation) (1997): Transport Sector Road Map (2005), Transport and Trade Facilitation Strategy (2007–08), Regional Joint Transport and Trade Facilitation Committee (2009)
	Uzbekistan Turkmenistan Iran, Islamic Rep.	Samarkand–Bukhara–Mashad–Bandar Abbas (4,000 km)	
	Tajikistan Afghanistan Pakistan	Dushanbe–Nijhni Pjanj–Sharkhan Bandar–Pule Khumri–Kabul–Jalalabad–Torkham–Landi Kotal–Peshawar–Bannu–Dera Ismail Khan–Dushanbe–Mazar-e-Sharif–Herat–Bandar Abbas (1,500 km)	
	Tajikistan Afghanistan Iran, Islamic Rep.		
Caucasus	Azerbaijan Georgia Russian Federation	Baku–Alyut–Tbilisi–*Poti* (800 km) Baku–Makhachkala–Russia	Transport Corridor Europe–Caucasus–Asia
	Georgia	Yerevan–Gyumri–Batumi–*Poti* (800 km)	
	Iran, Islamic Rep.	Yerevan–Tabriz–Esfehan–*Bandar Abbas* (2,600 km)	

Source: Authors.
Note: km = kilometer.

Table A1.5 Other Regions: LLDCs and Transit Neighbors

Subregion	LLDCs	Transit countries	Main corridors to ports (main hubs in italic), distance	Key regional initiatives and institutions, start date
Eastern Europe	Moldova	Romania	Chisinau–Leuceni–Birlad–Bucharest (450 km)	Luxembourg memorandum of understanding for development Core Regional Transport Network and creation SEETO (South East Europe Transport Observatory) (2004)
	Serbia Macedonia, FYR	Greece	Belgrade–Nis–Priboj–Skopje–*Thessaloniki* (part of EU Corridor X) (660 km)	
East Asia	Mongolia	Russian Federation	Ulaanbaatar–Naushki–Irkutsk–Krasnoyarsk–Novosibirsk–*St. Petersburg* (3,300 km)	Transit Agreements with • Russian Federation (1991): Road Agreement (1996) that allows transit with both countries • China (1991) for Tianjin as main transit port • Tripartite Framework Agreement being negotiated with China and Russian Federation
		China	Ulaanbaatar–Zamyn Uud–*Tianjin* (1,700 km)	
		Russian Federation China	Ulaanbaatar–Harbin–*Nakhodka/* Vladivostok (6,000 km)	Greater Mekong Subregion program (GMS) (1992): GMS Strategic Framework (2002)
	Lao PDR	Thailand	Vientiane–Thanaleng–*Klong Toey* (near Bangkok) (700 km)	
		Vietnam	Vientiane–*Da Nang* and other Vietnamese ports (600 km)	

Latin America and the Caribbean	Bolivia	Santa Cruz–Cochabamba–Oruro–Arica/Antofagasta (1,200 km)	ALADI (Latin American Integration Association)—Treaty of Montevideo (1980): Agreement for International Land Transport (ATIT) (1990);
			Agreement on River Transport in the Hidrovía Paraguay–Paraná (1992) signed by all MERCOSUR (Southern Common Market) + Bolivia
	Brazil Paraguay Uruguay Argentina	Santa Cruz–Puerto Suárez (Hidrovía Paraguay–Paraná)–*Nueva Palmira/Rosario/Buenos Aires* (3,400 km)	MERCOSUR (1991): adopted ATIT (Agreement for International Land Transport) (1994) as legal basis for international road freight;
	Brazil	Santa Cruz–Puerto Suárez–Corumba–Campo Grande–*Santos* (2,400 km)	Chile and Bolivia became associate members of MERCOSUR (1994).
	Argentina Uruguay	Asunción (on Paraguay River) and Encarnación (on Paraná River)–*Nueva Palmira/Buenos Aires* (1,300 km)	IIRSA (Initiative for the Integration of the Regional Infrastructure of South America) (2000) and MERCOSUR Structural Convergence Fund (FOCEM) (2006), both to channel more funds into infrastructure to reduce asymmetries such as consequences of landlockedness
Paraguay	Brazil	Asunción–Paranagua (1,060 km)	
Paraguay			

Source: Authors
Note: km = kilometer.

Assessment and Policy Recommendations by Region

Actions recommended in this volume fall under four themes:

- **Improve the Transit Regime:** Improve the legal and administrative aspects of the transit regime under which an LLDC imports and exports using its coastal neighbor.
- **Reform Transport Market Regulation:** Reform the regulations governing national and regional transportation markets.
- **Develop Trust and Cooperation:** Develop cooperative agreements among the stakeholders.
- **Monitor Corridor Performance:** Identify priority corridors to implement benchmarking indicators for different transport modes and routes.

These themes will be applied to the different regions in detail later in this appendix. This first section summarizes recent developments and the current status of LLDCs' access problems and transit corridors and suggests how these recommendations might fit with government and private-sector developments and plans.

Eastern and Southern Africa are dealt with together in the first matrix, and Western and Central Africa in the second. Latin America is covered in the third; Central Asia (including Afghanistan, Azerbaijan, and Mongolia) in the fourth; and South Asia (Bhutan and Nepal, but including also bilateral aspects of the Afghanistan–Pakistan corridor) is treated in the fifth. The four remaining individual LLDCs (Armenia, the Lao People's Democratic Republic, the former Yugoslav Republic of Macedonia, and Moldova) are covered in the sixth matrix.

Eastern and Southern Africa

Improve the Transit Regime

Actions taken: Road freight movements are generally faster than in Western and Central Africa, but they suffer from delays that are unpredictable, but can be up to 3–4 days at several key border posts. Ocean ports' release of goods in transit to LLDCs often remains slow. Outside the five-nation Southern African Customs Union (SACU) area, transit still must be arranged one country at a time. Foundations for more progress have gradually been laid. In 2002, Namibia and SACU introduced a Single Administrative Document (SAD), subsequently accepted by Southern African Development Community (SADC) members; compromise is now being sought, and the SAD is being used by some Common Market for Eastern and Southern Africa (COMESA) members. Customs services have been gradually modernizing practices and strengthening IT facilities, including some initiatives to accept electronic payments or process trade movements in advance. Computerized customs management systems, mainly Automated System for Customs Data (ASYCUDA++), are now installed in almost all the countries, at least at headquarters.

After years of discussion, the concept of "one-stop border posts," serving the needs of both countries, is considered close to inauguration of operation, at Chirundu (Zambia–Zimbabwe) and at Ressano Garcia (South Africa–Mozambique) in 2011.

A regional customs guarantee scheme for transit traffic is being tested by COMESA and SADC on the corridor to Lusaka, laying the basis for the follow-on steps of linking up with IT plans, seeking acceptance of as many countries as possible, and obtaining the national legislative changes that would enable use of the scheme. The fact that the region is served by an efficient trucking industry with operating standards comparable to that of industrialized economies makes the implementation of a carnet system a realistic objective.

Current priorities: The first priority is to bring to fruition several concepts that the stronger efforts of recent years have at last brought close to practical utility, especially the regionwide common SAD and the pilot one-stop border posts delivering more efficient border crossing. In addition to effective completion of the final stages at the previously mentioned two sites, these advances will also depend on the extensive IT expansion and improvement that has been under way and on good support from national legislative and administrative systems. A steady program of further conversions of border posts to joint operation should follow.

Rollout of the customs guarantee scheme for transit traffic will depend in part on progress with the common SAD and IT strengthening. Unfortunately, the limited degree of financial integration in the region so far has prevented the feasibility of imposing a single bond and, hence, the implementation of a system similar the European Common Transit. The conditions for an integrated transit regime also exist for the Mombasa corridor, especially within the East African Community (EAC) grouping. Despite conduct of an initial feasibility study and some support by the U.S. Agency for International Development (USAID), a carnet system has not yet been implemented, and will rely on progress in data exchange and harmonization.

Particular effort is needed to resolve the various obstacles to rapid and effective sharing of shipment information between the national customs administrations along the route it is taking. One part of the problem is ensuring effective Internet communication (including the aspect of power supply reliability) among the customs departments and, particularly, among the main border posts. (Chirundu is to pilot a "transit data transfer module.")

Demand appears to be strong among the national customs administrations for wider and more intensive practical training on the actual application of risk management in the work of tax, and especially customs, departments. Greatly expanded effort seems to be needed on ways to ensure sound use of the concept of Authorized Economic Operator certification, which can be valuable for reducing corruption and accelerating transit shipments' progress. Advance processing procedures and post-clearance audits are illustrative of other areas of high demand.

Simplification and harmonization of trade and customs documentation and procedures must be recognized as requiring sustained, permanent attention *and* an imaginative change management approach to their implementation. The COMESA–EAC–SADC Tripartite Task Force is now probably the body that should lead and inspire this vital effort.

Reform Transport Market Regulation

Actions taken: Freight transport services, especially on roads, but also in many of the countries' railways and major ports, are now in the hands of the private sector. Economic regulation is generally appropriately light in road transport, but often too light in major transport services, such as railways that have been, or still are, run directly by national government bodies.

Effective steps in developing regional road freight markets have included bilateral agreements allowing the issue of permits for carriage of trade to or from the other country; harmonization of permitted axle loads within the two main groups (COMESA and SADC); and spread of the COMESA-initiated Carrier License and especially of the COMESA Yellow Card scheme. The Yellow Card is driver insurance against third-party risk, slowly developed since 1987, but now with well over 60,000 subscribers covered for travel in most of those continental COMESA and SADC countries where such insurance is required. In the SADC area, intercountry road freight rates appear to be generally competitive with those of the efficient South Africa market, and only a little higher in East Africa.

Current priorities: An issue most urgently in need of further effort is effective enforcement of axle-load limits, now that they have been largely harmonized among the countries. FESARTA (Federation of Eastern and Southern African Road Transport), the regional trucking industry association, estimates that the share of trucks overloaded varies between 10 and 50 percent. Some control efforts, such as that by the Maputo Corridor concessionaire and SANRAL (South African National Roads Agency), initiated in 2005–06, have been fairly effective. Authorities in the SADC area are working toward linking axle-load control to customs clearance at border posts.

A major contributor to reducing the truck overloading problem should be the revived railways that the region also needs for other reasons. The South African government has been making major efforts to develop the regulatory framework and a degree of competition, which have been lacking during Spoornet's (the former name for Transnet Freight Rail, a South African rail transport company) long decline. Similar efforts are needed to generate a regional capacity to spell out the principles of competition laid out in the Transport Protocols of the regional economic communities (RECs) and help the railways to identify their best potential contribution to the region's economic success relative to those of their competitors. There are other good statements in the various REC protocols that have guided useful efforts toward harmonization and consistency across the region, but it should be understood that conditions in individual countries are sometimes so different that discrepancies are likely to continue, and any convergence, if it occurs at all, will take a great deal of time.

The considerations of slow convergence in policies and harmonization most likely also apply to road transit fees, the aspiration toward elimination of restrictions on cabotage, "third-party" operations by road freight transporters, replacement of present bilateral permits with regional ones, and complete harmonizing of road vehicle standards. It would be valuable to examine the collection of discrepancies from regional norms and analyze adjustments that the country or its neighbors might make to improve their joint efficiency.

Develop Trust and Cooperation

Actions taken: Regional associations of countries have played a major role in promoting and supporting cooperation in transport and facilitation of trade as essential measures for deeper economic integration. To increase follow-up action on that ground, they added initiatives in the 1990s, including focusing change efforts on selected corridors and mobilizing more private-sector pressure for modernization. Such regional groupings include COMESA, EAC, and SADC, with their interlocking memberships. They are now trying to plan their interventions jointly, to bring about the essential synergies among different countries' actions, and to steer members to gradual convergence in transport and trade arrangements. In an October 2008 meeting in Kampala, nine heads of state and many ministers from the region called for moving toward a free trade area embracing all 25 COMESA and SADC member states.

Two corridors in the region have had a formal management organization for at least a decade: the Mombasa Corridor and the Walvis Bay Corridor. A similar management organization is being established in the Central Corridor.

Current priorities: National Facilitation Committees (see chapter 8), or equivalent organizations mobilizing private as well as public support, should be given stronger leadership in facilitation measures on the most active corridors.

The experience of corridor management should be extended to new corridors. Such effort is under way with extensive support from the international community and under the auspices of COMESA for the

North–South Corridor (Durban, Lusaka, and Dar es Salaam). The benefit of cross-border cooperation and corridor management should be considered on the following relatively active routes:

- Zambese Corridor from the port of Beira (and eventually Nacala) in Mozambique to Malawi, Zambia, and Zimbabwe. So far, no feasibility study has taken place.
- The Dijibouti–Addis Ababa Corridor.

Such broad policy-focused efforts need supplementation with greater attention to more individual arrangements with country partners facing special difficulties.

Monitor Corridor Performance

Actions taken: Some performance monitoring records are available for the Northern Corridor, at least from Uganda to Mombasa, Kenya, and some information is available, at least for recent years, for the North–South Corridor from the Copperbelt to Durban.

The list below suggests that it may be wise in some cases to monitor the same route for more than one LLDC.

Priority corridors:
    Addis Ababa–Djibouti (800 km)
    Kigali–Kampala–Mombasa (1,700 km)
    Bujumbura–Dar es Salaam (1,500 km)
    Gaborone–Durban (950 km)
    Blantyre–Maseru–Durban (2,660 km)
    Ndola–Dar es Salaam (1,900 km)
    Ndola–Durban (2,500 km)

Western and Central Africa

Improve the Transit Regime

Actions taken: Freight movements to and from the LLDCs have remained slow and unpredictable, with port dwell times for imports often between 2 and 4 weeks, and transit times, for instance to Bamako or Ndjamena, of 2–3 weeks for what should be a 1-week job.

As in other regions, Western and Central Africa have invested in customs modernization. Some important transit countries have been engaged in major and exemplary modernization drives including in Cameroon, Ghana, and Senegal. These efforts include implementation of IT solutions (single window at ports), risk management, and so on. Customs in LLDCs are typically not as advanced as their coastal counterparts, especially in the two postconflict LLDCs in Central Africa: Chad and Central African Republic.

The customs transit regime has been largely left out of this effort. Customs escorts are still prevalent; computerization of transit cargo is limited. However, the latter problem is being addressed by a regional project looking at interconnection of customs. Beyond a lack of priority given to transit in customs modernization programs, there are three other reasons the transit trade is not much facilitated in Western and Central Africa. One is the proliferation of organizations in charge of regulating trade and transportation, including in the name of facilitation.

Lack of compliance by traders and transporters is also a reason customs maintain a strong control on transit. In all fairness, it is impossible to dispense with convoys when trucks are overloaded and cannot be sealed. Hence, transit improvements are inseparable from progress in other areas, including enforcement and regulation in the trucking industry.

Finally, there is no implementable regional transit regime, despite the efforts by the Economic Community of West African States (ECOWAS) and the West African Economic and Monetary Union (*Union Economique et Monétaire Ouest Africaine*, or UEMOA) to promote the TRIE (*Transit Routier Inter-États*, or Interstate Road Transport). The TRIE is a derivative of the International Road Transport (*Transports Internationaux Routiers*, or TIR), with limited entry requirements and no cross-border clearing mechanisms for the bonds, which are de facto taxes paid to Chambers of Commerce, and not a guarantee with customs. Most experts, including the authors of this volume, have observed that the TRIE cannot work in its current form and have recommended a complete overhaul of its implementation mechanism to incorporate the principles of a working transit system. This need has not been recognized so far by ECOWAS and UEMOA.

Current priorities: As explained in chapter 5, Cameroon, in liaison with Chad and the Central African Republic, is initiating a major overhaul of the transit procedures to implement concepts taken from the European Common transit system. Similarities within the administrative framework and the problems mean that a similar approach should at least be considered within UEMOA. UEMOA, like the Monetary and Economic Community of Central Africa (CEMAC), is a monetary union, which greatly facilitates the creation of a common bond. A working transit regime for the full ECOWAS is probably less realistic than one for UEMOA or UEMOA plus Ghana, given the lesser level of financial and customs integration in the larger REC grouping.

So far, there is no real drive to follow this route, and current trade facilitation efforts are looking at peripheral, yet productive, improvement without addressing the central issue of the transit regime. The main components of the regional trade facilitation strategy agreed on in 2003 include the following:

- Substantial ICT upgrade for the port community, including full application of the ASYCUDA++ system of the United Nations Conference on Trade and Development (UNCTAD), and for information exchange among the three countries' customs and their border stations
- A start on creation of joint border posts (constructed at the Togo–Burkina Faso border)
- Implementation of the TRIE as a regional transit guarantee system to replace the separate national guarantees previously required in each case
- Establishment of corridor observatories, notably to monitor checkpoints and bribes paid en route
- Implementation of targeted corridor-specific action plans to reduce the spread of human immunodeficiency virus/acquired immune deficiency syndrome (HIV/AIDS) and to help users already infected. (Although not a transit issue per se, HIV/AIDS eradication is a major development priority for the bank. Truck drivers, driver assistants, and sex workers have long been identified as populations at high risk of contracting and spreading HIV. This makes the transit corridors one of the drivers of the HIV/AIDS epidemic globally. Almost every World Bank trade corridor project has an HIV component.)

These changes are being accompanied by investment in needed infrastructure upgrades, especially at borders or at interchange points such as the logistics platform at Bamako.

Reform Transport Market Regulation

Actions taken: The two subregions have major issues with the market organization and business practices in trucking. ECOWAS and the two francophone economic unions—UEMOA for Western Africa and CEMAC for Central Africa—have adopted rules and standards very similar to those of Europe and other African regions when it comes to technical and economic regulation of trucking activities.

Regional and national statements of principle generally refer briefly to the role of competition in helping ensure efficiency in the transport sector, as in other sectors. But open competition has been reduced in some cases by heavy regulation and, for transit services to and from LLDCs, replaced with the assigning of jobs, essentially at fixed "recommended" prices and in legally fixed proportions between nationals of the LLDC and the transit country. Fairness is considered to be achieved by assigning the work to the registered trucker of the right nationality who has been waiting longest since his or her last transit job. The mechanism of freight allocation is a queuing system known as *tour de role*.

Regulations on vehicle dimensions and maximum axle loads, agreed upon at regional level and in respect to vehicle condition at national level, have not been strictly enforced. Overloading has been most common in carriage of imports to LLDCs, as a result of the traffic assignment arrangements, unstuffing of most containers upon discharge at the port, and the fact that imports generally exceed exports in volume. The situation is better in Central Africa (Douala Corridor), given that the limited number of routes allows the Cameroonian road fund to exercise better control of overloading than its counterparts in the North.

In 2007–08, the World Bank carried out a thorough study of road freight rates in Africa based on surveys of trucking companies and operators in four major regions. It led to the conclusion that, on all the routes covered in Central Africa and most of those in Western Africa, rates were unusually high relative to costs. Service is poor and the providers' truck fleets are underutilized, but high markups can be maintained because of the freight allocation system (chapter 2). The situation is worse on the Douala Corridor, as compared to Western Africa where the number of competing corridors mitigates in favor of more competition and lower markups.

Current priorities: It is very important to correct the lack of competitive conditions and heavy regulation because, if allowed to continue unchecked, these conditions will severely limit the benefit to the shipper (as opposed to the trucker) of other improvements in the transit system that are now in jeopardy. However, the issue is politically sensitive, because some of the organizations involved (truckers union, shippers' councils, and chambers of commerce) have not been trusted with the management of some function of the trade logistics of corridors (such as transit documents, guarantees, and allocations). So far, there have been no serious efforts to overhaul this organization.

The most difficult issues to anticipate in the transition to market-driven logistics, such as those in southern Africa, would be that far fewer trucks and drivers would be needed than now. Hence, the transition, when it comes, would have to put in place measures to compensate truckers who prove unable to compete successfully once the market becomes more open, just as many of the staff taken on by railways had to be assisted to retire early. Tax adjustments and financing facilities—similar to those already introduced in some countries to encourage the emergence of more reliable, efficient, and secure fleets—will probably need to be adopted more widely, especially in support of transit work.

Develop Trust and Cooperation

Actions taken: In the 1980s, major regional agreements on the measures needed to secure better transport services were reached, as a result of research and negotiations sponsored by Africa's regional economic bodies. But countries applied little effort on the ground. This was because their attention was diverted by overriding political issues, shortage of relevant skills, lack of confidence that other parties would actually fulfill their commitments, and doubts about priorities.

At the country level, public and private forums to discuss priorities in trade and transport facilitation exist nominally (National Trade Facilitation Committees) in the countries of the region. Shippers' councils also play a role. However, these organizations are very much state-appointed bodies, with limited roles for the private sector, including international investors.

The regional bodies, ECOWAS, UEMOA, and CEMAC, over the past decade have developed and adopted their own trade and transport facilitation programs. The aid agencies have promoted wide dialogue with all stakeholders in shaping the plans, to strengthen support and make it more sustainable.

The programs developed thus far have been regional and multicountry in nature, as has support provided from the several foreign agencies, with each participating country receiving some assistance. This approach has been important in helping achieve and sustain compromises that are essential but may be unpalatable to vested interests. The regional level may also be more appropriate for such programs, given the level of trade between the countries and the relative importance of transit in the volume of ports in the transit countries. However, this effort has helped revamp and reactivate trade and transit facilitation committees, with private- as well as public-sector participants, in some West African countries.

Current priorities: Program developers should continue to pay particular attention to designing a reliable monitoring system as well as to establishing baselines and dated targets for a few carefully selected performance indicators: transit times and their variability, border crossing times, and customs performance (the latter on a monthly basis in Central Africa). Results should be published as soon as available, because they are very important both for the managers and for sustaining of support from other government and business circles. Provision has also been made for periodic user surveys, to gather the views and advice of the trading community generally.

Monitor Corridor Performance

UEMOA is already conducting significant monitoring work with assistance from the USAID-financed West Africa Trade Hub on the Bamako–Ouagadougou–Tema Corridor. The Trade Hub's work now intends to expand beyond the road barriers aspect, which has been its focus so far.

Priority corridors:

Bamako–Dakar (1,200 km)
Niamey–Cotonou (900 km)
Bamako/Ouagadougou–Tema (1,900 km)
Monitoring work on this road and on the overland portions of the two Central African corridors listed below is being strengthened under the ongoing multidonor projects in support of their further development.
Ndjamena–Douala (1,850 km)
Bangui–Douala (1,450 km)

Latin America

Improve the Transit Regime

Actions taken: The International Land Transport Agreement (ATIT), signed by the Latin American Integration Association (*Asociación Latinoamericana de Integración,* or ALADI) in 1990 and adopted by the Southern Common Market (MERCOSUR) in 1994, is the main legal instrument governing international freight movements by road or rail for Bolivia, Paraguay, and their transit neighbors. ATIT rightly stresses three keys to success: professionalization of service providers, acceptance by member countries of internal documents issued by other members, and reciprocity and flexibility in the application of standards. It includes an MIC/DTA (International Freight Manifest/Customs Transit Declaration) form, modeled on the United Nations' SAD.

The MIC/DTA, backed by eight other standard documents for a trade consignment, secures transit rights. Under ATIT, carriers have full responsibility for compliance with the international transit regime and are guarantors for customs: their own vehicles are the guarantee in the event they cannot produce evidence of the goods and vehicle leaving the country. The MIC/DTA is sometimes supplemented with specific local provisions. For instance, in Bolivia, a bank guarantee up to US$20,000 must be given for each truck, using a smart card with an embedded chip.

While the transit and guarantee arrangements are considered to have worked quite satisfactorily, with fraud levels believed to be fairly low, border-crossing time requirements are very large, ranging anywhere from 12 to 24 hours for transit, and up to 3 days for customs clearance, at major MERCOSUR crossings. A thorough review of the costs of moving Paraguay's international trade in 2005 concluded that about US$40 million per year, or a third of all the cost savings that might be obtained from efficiency measures, should result from border-crossing improvements. It must also be noted that both Bolivia and Paraguay score lower than almost any other country in Latin America and the Caribbean on the Customs dimension of the Logistics Performance Index.

Current priorities: Improvements are being introduced that should reduce border crossing time. For instance, joint one-stop border crossing stations are being developed at key points on Bolivia's borders with Chile and Peru. Greater use is being made of e-mail, including for communications between Bolivian and Chilean customs.

Much more must be done. A major factor in the time required for clearance appears to be poor coordination among the many agencies, other than customs, which do not use electronic documentation but can still hold up the progress of a shipment. Some of the countries' customs departments are introducing modern risk management approaches in their work, but it is unclear whether there are regionally agreed-upon procedures and criteria for identifying qualified transit operators who could be given accelerated treatment.

In Central America, the Inter-American Development Bank piloted in 2008–09 the *Tránsito Internacional de Mercancía* (TIM). The TIM implements, in the countries of SIECA (*Secretaría de Integración Económica Centroamericana*, or Central American Secretariat for Economic Integration), some of the principles of the European Common transit system. So far, their efforts have focused on improvement and data exchange at border crossings; however, there is not yet a single bond or the equivalent of a regional carnet.

Reform Transport Market Regulation

Actions taken: Operation of the major transport installations, such as Bolivia's two railway systems and Chile's ports, has been concessioned to private operators, while road and river transport services are provided almost entirely by the private sector. These arrangements appear to have yielded generally satisfactory and efficient results.

A major achievement of the early 1990s by ALADI and MERCOSUR was to establish regulations enabling the development of the Hidrovía on the Paraguay and Paraná Rivers, allowing open competition in provision of international river transport services.

To solve its historic shortage of river port infrastructure, Paraguay introduced laws in 2001 to permit private investment. But so far, this has led only to development of numerous private terminals with uncoordinated siting and operation, the result being that vessels can easily spend as many as four days loading from different jetties.

Current priorities: Further major development of the Hidrovía depends on fundamental major decisions on difficult environmental and other issues, to be reached by Brazil and the other concerned governments. But the regulations drawn up nearly 20 years ago must be revised, in particular to permit more adequate channel maintenance and better coordination of operations at the numerous public and private terminals around Asunción, and to generate user contributions to the costs of maintenance and development. It is also desirable to give cabotage rights now to vessels other than those belonging to the immediate riparian state, since this would permit significant cost savings through better use of backhaul capacity of international barge-trains. The river transport offers very competitive costs for transport of Paraguay's bulk agricultural exports (as well as for import of some inputs such as fertilizers). But it is slow, underlining the need to squeeze out avoidable loss of time at any stage.

Develop Trust and Cooperation

Actions taken: In their efforts to overcome the development constraints resulting from their landlocked situation, both Bolivia and Paraguay have benefited from particular geographical-historical factors: the ocean-access provisions of the 1904 peace treaty between Bolivia and Chile and the location of Paraguay surrounded by the three largest South American economies. Argentina, Brazil, and Chile have led the way in developing intraregional trade and liberalizing transport to support it.

The persistence of historic animosities and traditional prejudices in political quarters, and as a strand of public opinion, in all the countries, has nonetheless continued to slow integration and facilitation of transport.

Current priorities: Illustrative of the problems arising from long-term lack of international trust are the many controls and inspections on transit traffic through Argentina, considered by the Paraguayans as excessive and ill-motivated and by the Argentinians as essential protection against fraud (especially trademark forgery). The solution must be devised by combined effort, with better control of illegal activity in Paraguay and better training of provincial officials in Argentina.

Relations between countries should benefit from the high-level political decisions of the past decade to channel some funds from the better-off countries of the region into projects intended to reduce asymmetries of countries that are landlocked or otherwise disadvantaged. These include the IIRSA (Initiative for the Integration of the Regional Infrastructure of South America) initiative and FOCEM (*Fondo para la Convergencia Estructural del MERCOSUR,* or the MERCOSUR Structural Convergence Fund). Relevant projects, such as one to improve important border crossings, are now starting.

There remains a widespread need for more effective communication mechanisms on trade and transport facilitation between the public and private sectors and among the various levels of government. Communication is needed to gather views and shape consensus, to inculcate more effectively the respective responsibilities that public and private bodies each have to fulfill, and to keep people up to date on new developments and procedures. Strongly led national facilitation committees are badly needed.

Monitor Corridor Performance

UNCTAD ran a small technical assistance project in 2005–07 to encourage stronger public-private collaboration, and substantive private contribution, to improve the operation of trade corridors. One of the more successful applications was the Latin American case, the Asunción–Montevideo Corridor, which was supported jointly with ECLAC (Economic Commission for Latin America and the Caribbean). Sustained monitoring was not the purpose, but the promising local efforts to identify and apply cost- and time-saving improvements make this a useful corridor to include in the monitoring effort.

If the effort must be limited to one corridor per LLDC, the first two listed below are recommended by the authors. The third corridor, originating at the eastern border of Bolivia, should be added if feasible.

Priority corridors:
Santa Cruz–Cochabamba–Oruro–Arica (1,200 km)
Asunción (on Paraguay River) and Encarnación (on Paraná River)–Nuevo Palmira/Buenos Aires (Uruguay) (1,300 km)
Santa Cruz–Puerto Suarez–Corumba–Campo Grande–Santos (2,400 km)

Central Asia

Improve the Transit Regime
Actions taken: Carriage of freight across borders, though improved, remains unpredictable in terms of money and time required and is very expensive (including a large component of informal payments). Central Asian countries inherited from the Soviet Union membership in European institutions, including the United Nations Economic Commission for Europe (UNECE). Hence, the countries are parties to the TIR. However, the latter is mainly used only for very long-distance, high-value shipments that are carried by operators from outside the region (Western or Eastern Europe). Other cross-border movements take place in a framework of bilateral or trilateral agreements, so separate arrangements must be made for each border crossed.

At the end of the Soviet Union, countries in Central Asia had to rebuild capacities to support trade, and these capacities remain weak, especially among the poorest counties and in the area of customs and border management. The European Union (EU) and international agencies, especially the World Bank, have provided significant assistance to customs modernization and border management reforms, and they continue to do so. Improvement and expansion of infrastructure at border crossings (for example, to separate lines for transit traffic from those for vehicles requiring customs clearance) are still much needed.

Current priorities: The UNECE/IRU (International Road Transport Union) TIR system provides an adequate framework for major international shipments to Europe, Turkey, or the Islamic Republic of Iran. Although the TIR infrastructure is available for regional trade and transit, much of regional trade is operated by small-scale truckers who are unlikely to meet TIR standards or are unwilling to use the TIR.

To fill this gap, the Asian Development Bank (ADB) and the CAREC (Central Asia Regional Economic Cooperation) have considered a transit system for intraregional movements that would apply most of the procedures developed under TIR, but with significantly lower charges because of the lower cargo values, lower duty liability, and less sophisticated transport equipment used. This project was not supported by other key organizations, including the UNECE and the World Bank. Indeed, international experience confirms that the "TIR lite" approach is unlikely to be robust. As of the beginning of 2011, no technically advanced proposal of a regional regime is in existence.

Reform Transport Market Regulation

Inherited situation: Major services are in the hands of public bodies, without independent regulation. Domestic trucking and passenger transport are now mostly private, though the environment for business often remains poor.

Current priorities: A main concern at this stage is to modernize the management structure and practices of the countries' railways, clearly separating out regulatory functions, opening the way for private-sector initiative in railway activity, and encouraging strong competition with the other transport modes on a level playing field.

Development of private initiative in provision of transport-related and logistics services, including freight forwarding, insurance, and warehousing, should be much more strongly encouraged to help achieve the cost reductions and traffic increases aimed at.

The most effective way to bring about freight transport services best suited to reducing the region's economic isolation would be to replace the national protectionist approaches now followed with agreed-upon regional regulatory arrangements aimed at ensuring fair and open competition among the modes across the region. Viable starts in that direction would include liberalization of access to each country for trucks registered in any other country of the region and encouragement of cross-border investment in transport services (for example, by the Kazakh private sector in trucking companies benefiting from the lower wage levels of some of the other countries).

Develop Trust and Cooperation

Inherited situation: There is distrust among national governments, which is exacerbated by security fears. The countries have no tradition of private-sector initiative. In addition to being landlocked, all the countries of this subregion (and especially Kazakhstan, due to its location between Asia and Europe) must also act as transit countries for their neighbors.

The CAREC program, which the ADB started 10 years ago with participation of four Central Asian republics and Azerbaijan, now also incorporates Afghanistan, China, Mongolia, and six international aid agencies (including the World Bank), which are also providing support for particular elements.

Current priorities: The Transport and Trade Facilitation strategy and action plan agreed upon by CAREC country governments in 2008 aim at halving border-crossing time by 2012 and reducing it a further 30 percent by 2017. Lower freight costs are expected to attract a larger share of Europe–East Asia trade and a major increase in intraregional trade.

The aim is to develop and apply the innovations on six corridors linking world regions on opposite sides of Central Asia, and initially on six specific routes (within the corridors), which will be subject to detailed performance monitoring.

Management of the program and of the corridors running through each country is in the hands of a National Transport and Trade Facilitation Committee, with a regional committee of the same sectoral scope for the overall program.

Monitor Corridor Performance

The corridors that the participating countries selected for inclusion in the CAREC program were chosen in large part to improve links with other regions; however, they are defined only within the borders of CAREC countries. They all also run from one side of the region to the other, linking the LLDC with two foreign markets.

From the subcorridors identified in the CAREC Program for "pilot performance monitoring" (starting in 2009), the authors identified a few main sections which, with the addition of a link outside the region, could contribute to the objective of providing performance information on at least one complete corridor (to a major world market) for each LLDC.

Priority corridors:

Kazakhstan and the Kyrgyz Republic, with focus on markets in the Russian Federation and China and beyond: Moscow–Samara–Orenberg–Novomarkovka–Zhaisan–Aktobe–Kyzyl Orda–Shymkent–(Bishkek)–Almaty–Khorgos–Urumqi–Xian–Shanghai.

Azerbaijan, Turkmenistan, and Uzbekistan, with focus on markets reachable through Poti, mainly Europe and Mediterranean: Samarkand–Bukhara–Mary–Ashgabat–Turkmenbashi–Baku–Tbilisi–Poti.

Kyrgyz Republic, Tajikistan, and Afghanistan, with focus on markets in the Islamic Republic of Iran, Turkey, and beyond: Osh–Sary-Tash–Karamik–Dushanbe–Saryasia–Termez–Hairatan–Mazar-e-Sharif–Herat–Islam Qila–Dogharoun–Teheran–Tabriz–Erzurum–Istanbul.

Uzbekistan, Tajikistan, and Afghanistan, with focus on Pakistan and markets reached via Karachi: Tashkent–Khavast–Istaravshan–Dushanbe–Nijhni Pianj–Shirkhan Bandar–Pule Khumri–Kabul–Jalalabad–Torkham–Landi Kotal–Peshawar–Bannu–Dikhan–Karachi.

Mongolia, to Russia and China and their ports: St. Petersburg–Novosibirsk–Irkutsk–Ulaanbaatar–Zamyn Uud–Tianjin.

South Asia

Improve the Transit Regime

Inherited situation: Transit takes place on essentially two corridors: the first from Karachi to Afghanistan and eventually beyond to Central Asia, in the West. The second corridor, the east transit through India, serves Nepal and Bhutan, while India itself is interested in moving goods through Bangladesh to its northeastern provinces (the Seven Sisters).

Surface freight movement to and from the LLDCs has been governed by bilateral treaties between each LLDC and its transit neighbor (India or Pakistan). Much Nepali or Bhutanese trade is with India itself, but international freight is still handled entirely through Kolkata (and Haldia), with the overland portion by Indian Railways or by Indian or Nepali truckers. Transit remains slow and expensive.

Bhutanese trade, comparatively tiny at present, is handled by Indian truckers between Kolkata and Siliguri, India, where it is transferred to Bhutan's own trucks.

The now-very-large registered commercial freight flows to Afghanistan has been moving more smoothly since 2005, when the Pakistan government authorized the National Logistics Cell, a parastatal trucking company, to share responsibility with the very overloaded Pakistan Railways for transit between the country's ports and the Afghan border. Afghanistan also has an important traffic flow through the Islamic Republic of Iran, including transit from the port of Bandar Abbas (the

Islamic Republic of Iran). As the Islamic Republic of Iran has developed a friendly national transit system, and also has active TIR flows, this route, although less direct, is a very viable alternative to Afghanistan and even Central Asia.

In practice, this region has probably the least modern transit systems due to a combination of weak capacities in the LLDCs, labor-intensive logistics practices, and closed transport markets. Virtually all trade is transloaded at the border from trucks of the country of transit to trucks of the LLDCs.

Current priorities: Customs computerization now appears more advanced in Bhutan and Afghanistan, but still needs substantial completion in Nepal, to have all the requisite ASYCUDA modules installed and working—at border posts as well as headquarters—and to ensure power supplies and technician capacities are adequate to maintain service quality and reliable communication among the installations.

Regarding the transit countries' handling of movements to and from the LLDCs, progress in customs modernization in India and Pakistan has reduced bureaucratic obstacles to transit. Computerization of the resultant reduced requirements would need to be applied at all border posts dealing with intraregional trade and transit flows—and again supported with measures to ensure reliable operation.

Ultimately, the countries in the region may consider a regional transit framework under the South Asian Association for Regional Cooperation (SAARC). Meanwhile, some attention should be given to the revision of transit treaty protocols to include some of the practices described in this volume and to phase out transloading and repeated procedures. Revision of the very lengthy bilateral treaties should be an opportunity to limit the role of government agencies in favor of the promotion of compliant operators able to operate across borders, which is essentially not possible today.

India and Bangladesh are in early stages of discussing a treaty that would look at transit through their respective countries for their own trade, as well as for Nepal and Bhutan. It has the potential to develop new trade routes in the Bengal region, to reduce transloading, and to introduce transit under multicountry bonds.

Pakistan and Afghanistan have just revised their bilateral transit treaty. At this stage, the transit supply chain remains broken at the border, but as of the end of 2010, constraints other than the transit regime—such as security considerations—have more impact on this route.

Another step that would accelerate the long-delayed improvement in customs treatment of the LLDCs' trade, and one that would have valuable long-term effects, would be to expand the main inland clearance depots transformed into dry ports (that is, at Birganj in Nepal and Kabul in Afghanistan). Shipping agents would be appointed and the shipping lines persuaded to accept the move of their containers inland, using through-bills of lading. The dry ports should attract offices of relevant logistics service companies. And Nepal hopes to provide an attractive site for new manufacturing or service enterprises.

Truck operations sufficient to support the activities described could be provided under current arrangements, although it would be desirable to replace the standard transshipment at the border with open competition among truckers of both nations for the full journey from seaport to inland destination.

Reform Transport Market Regulation

Actions taken: Extensive efforts have been under way over the past 20 years, especially in India and Pakistan, to modernize management structures of state-owned major transport entities, including some separation of regulatory responsibility. Also, many services have been concessioned to the private sector, particularly in India. Road freight services are almost entirely provided by the private sector, with strong competition modified in some places by local associations. Technical regulation is weakly enforced, and the quality of standard services is low.

Current priorities: Badly needed throughout the region is more effective control of the overloading of road freight vehicles. Existing overloading enables the offering of almost uniquely low freight rates, but it has serious effects on safety and road infrastructure. Increasingly effective control would cause the vehicle fleet to shift toward vehicles larger than the two-axle trucks typically still used, offering in turn a more reliable, higher quality service—with vehicles like semi-trailers that are also useable for transit in the Islamic Republic of Iran or Turkey and are TIR-compatible.

A carrier registration system should be designed to set up agreed standards regarding transport company management, finances, and safety standards, and to verify compliance. This would help improve the quality of carrier service available and would be a step toward achieving the ability to designate some carriers as "accredited operators" whose goods could be given expedited treatment at border posts.

None of the three LLDCs now has significant freight railway lines, but there is no doubt that their transit trade, as well as trade with the transit countries themselves, could generally be carried out more reliably and less expensively by rail than by road. Thus, it could be stimulated by greater use of rail. The obstacle has been shortage of capacity—especially wagons and locomotives—resulting from underinvestment, which itself is due mainly to prolonged offering of most passenger services at below cost. Because of the shortage, railways have set tight limits on interline lending of wagons when a railway has excess demand, thus further limiting the potential of railways in total freight traffic.

Develop Trust and Cooperation

Actions taken: All the countries in the subregion have been moving, at varying speeds, from bureaucratic authoritarianism to a much greater scope for independent private-sector initiatives. Each LLDC has been almost totally dependent until now on a single transit country. In a regional context of exceptionally low cross-country cooperation in transport, transit countries have still permitted LLDC trucks to cross borders in some cases; in others, goods still have to be transloaded at the border. Transit country claims of LLDC imports leaking back to them have sometimes led to withdrawal or restriction of transit rights for some products.

Current priorities: Although creation of one-stop border posts is not considered realistic for any land frontiers in South Asia, the need for greater cross-border cooperation is widely recognized. SAARC has stimulated exchanges on the subject, and the 2005 Agreement on the South Asia Free Trade Area commits the countries to pursue transport and trade facilitation. Major existing inefficiencies in trade among the countries must be overcome, and bases must be laid for amicable, constructive outcomes to the opportunities now beginning to open for establishment of major new trade routes, several of which will convert LLDCs into potentially important transit countries, notably Afghanistan.

The revised Afghanistan–Pakistan Transit Agreement signed in October 2010 is intended in part to lay the foundation for extensive trade between Central Asia, rich in minerals, to Pakistan and beyond. Another Afghan route being developed, with assistance from India, would carry traffic from Central Asia to the port of Chabahar in the southeast of the Islamic Republic of Iran. Interest is also rising in the possible eventual expansion of Nepal's existing road link with Tibet, via Kodari, into a major trade route, linking with China's railway from Lhasa.

The prospects of such developments would clearly be significantly improved once South Asia catches up with areas more advanced in having smooth flows of freight across borders, as in Europe or southern parts of Africa and Latin America. The more ambitious, holistic approach to trade and transport facilitation that is being taken by Pakistan on its National Trade Corridor and that may be applied by India in implementation of its Dedicated Freight Corridors, would indicate good possibilities of surmounting past difficulties and raising cooperation to new levels.

Monitor Corridor Performance
Priority corridors:
    Kabul–Karachi (1,600 km)
    Kathmandu–Birganj–Kolkata (1,060 km)
    Thimphu–Kolkata (800 km)

Other LLDCS: Armenia, Lao PDR, FYR Macedonia, and Moldova

Improve the Transit Regime
Actions taken: Much attention has been given to facilitating border crossing in all four countries—Armenia, Lao PDR, FYR Macedonia, and Moldova—but especially in southeastern Europe, because of the many new borders that sliced across main corridors after Yugoslavia's disintegration. Customs reform has been stressed, and truck transit licenses increased. Although FYR Macedonia still scores notably low on the Customs dimension of the Logistics Performance Index, customs improvement, computerization, and application of risk management are thought to be the main factors in reducing trucks' border-crossing delays in that country, and in Moldova the delays were reduced from an average of eight hours in bad cases to two hours. The vehicles of these two countries have used permits provided under bilateral agreements and some under ECMT quotas. They have been major users of TIR carnets, FYR Macedonia normally using 20,000–30,000 per year and Moldova's use steadily rising from some 20,000 in 2001 to nearly 80,000 in 2008.

The border-crossing infrastructure of Lao PDR has been improved. Thai reforms have somewhat reduced customs delays and increased competition for freight carriage to and from Lao PDR.

In 2004, to speed up benefits from infrastructure investments, the Greater Mekong Subregion (GMS) countries (Cambodia, China, Lao PDR, Myanmar, Thailand, and Vietnam) adopted a Cross Border Transit

Agreement to simplify crossing and make available regional transit licenses and guarantees.

Surface routes open to Armenian traders and exporters are limited to ones across Georgia and the Islamic Republic of Iran, with the former being more familiar but traditionally subject to large informal payments. Opinion surveys and interviews indicate far greater concern about the allegedly limited simplification or acceleration that have resulted from modernization and computerization of Armenia's own customs services.

Current priorities: The GMS Cross Border Transit Agreement should be brought into operation as soon as possible. Main immediate needs are completion of ratification of the component annexes, especially by Thailand, and reinforcement of Lao PDR's implementation abilities. Test runs have been carried out, all the documents prepared since 2004 have been fully ratified by Lao PDR and two other countries, issuance of guarantees has been negotiated, and the system would be the first major application of regional transit arrangements in Asia. A common problem that has now arisen in Lao PDR is difficulty in adapting supply and pricing of road freight services to fluctuating import and export balances: an inland container depot (for example, at Vientiane) would probably be worthwhile, partly to offer better information about backhaul opportunities.

Border-crossing problems continue to be of highest interest in all four countries and are recognized to need further efforts as well as sustained attention to prevent renewed deterioration. Computerization, modern risk management, and full, up-to-date publication of procedures are recognized to have made important contributions, with continued shortfalls in border-crossing efficiency often attributable mainly to application that is as yet incomplete.

Issues that appear to have received insufficient attention so far in these countries' efforts to improve border-crossing performance often relate to coordination with other government agencies that have particular responsibilities (for example, health and agriculture) but remain delinked from customs or immigration agencies' electronic information systems. Questions also arise about the functions handled by customs beyond collection of import or export duties: for instance, the need for import or export licensing, the extent of documentation and data demanded from traders, and controls to verify and raise export quality standards. More attention must be given to integrated border management, and reduction of corruption should not be connected with collection of import duties but with peripheral functions.

Reform Transport Market Regulation

Actions taken: With few exceptions—such as Armenia's main airport at Yerevan, concessioned in 2002, and the executive public agency set up to manage Armenian roads—the four countries' large transport agencies remain state administrations (for example, national highway departments) or public companies with limited independence (for example, railways). Road freight is now largely in the hands of private suppliers, with some large companies as well as many owner-operators. Modern logistics and freight forwarding capacities are not yet strongly developed, especially in Lao PDR or Moldova.

Fearing major inefficiencies (from fractionalization) in transport's institutional structure in a region contiguous with the EU—and expected to become part of it—the European Commission has strongly promoted regulatory reform, and on a consistent regional basis, which would therefore apply now to FYR Macedonia (and other southeastern European countries) and potentially later to Moldova.

A 2004 agreement set up a South-East Europe Transport Observatory (SEETO) (signed by governments of Albania, Bosnia and Herzegovina, Croatia, FYR Macedonia, Montenegro, and Serbia and by the United Nations Mission in Kosovo and the European Commission) to monitor performance and coordinate plans. Among the most important results to date have been agreements on air and rail transport. The whole area was to have been included by 2010 in the EU's single market for air transport, involving major restructuring to lay the base for more competitive services and faster traffic growth. The aim agreed for railways is to implement the EU *acquis communautaire* by 2012, with particular emphasis on consistency across the region in management structure, access for independent operators, access pricing, and efficient border crossing.

Current priorities: The SEETO efforts have been setting a large and helpful agenda for southeastern Europe, which needs much country-level follow-up, decision making, and implementation of planned actions. FYR Macedonia, already an important transit country, has been among the leaders in applying EU railway structuring policies. It is also applying an intelligent scheme to upgrade railway data transmission services to meet the needs of both railways and customs for advance information on freight train content—with significant resultant reduction in train waiting.

The road issue that has come to the fore in the facilitation work to date in all four countries is financing of road maintenance, in particular, the need for a larger contribution from freight vehicles. It is likely that road freight vehicles are at present paying less than marginal costs in all of these countries. Serious overloading requires attention in Moldova. In the field of road user charging too, FYR Macedonia is developing solutions, at least on its busiest trunk road, the EU north–south Corridor X, which may turn out to be of wider use. It is moving from an old-fashioned, cash-only, toll-booth system to an electronic system, much facilitating payment and expected to eliminate leakage, now estimated at 30–40 percent.

Of particular importance for Armenia is adjustment of the regulatory approach to air transport. Despite large growth of overall exports since the late 1990s, air freight shipped from Yerevan fell by more than half, and indications are that this was due to a reduction in the competitiveness of air transport services resulting from a restrictive aviation policy. Consequently, the state monopoly on aviation was eliminated when two private operators entered the Armenian aviation market in 2001 and 2002. Furthermore, in 2008 Armenia signed a horizontal agreement on specific aspects of air services with EU member countries, as well as an "Open Skies" agreement with the United States.

Develop Trust and Cooperation

Inherited situation: Armenia, Lao PDR, FYR Macedonia, and Moldova emerged in the 1990s from long incorporation within, or strong dependence upon, other countries. Emergence was generally unexpected, sometimes violent, and often took place in a regional environment marked by inherited tensions. The governments first faced the task of building national strategies that would bring economic success despite the constraints of their landlocked situation—which were peculiar to them in their respective subregions. The international community has tried to encourage and promote the development of substantive cooperation with neighbor countries, as in the GMS program led by the ADB and EU programs for Southeastern Europe. Armenia is still in a particularly difficult situation because of closed borders and lack of diplomatic relations with two of its four contiguous neighbors.

Current priorities: Building trust, which is most important at this time for the development of these countries' trade and economies, requires

Table A2.1   Impact and Ease of Implementation of the Proposed Measures

Measure proposed	Impact on trade costs			Ease of implementation/Acceptability		
	Costs	Delays	Reliability	Technical	Domestic	International
A. Make transportation and logistics services work for trade.						
Promote quality and competition in services.	A	B	B	F	F	F
Provide cross-border transport legal instrument.	B	C	C	D	E	F
Optimize multimodal and railroad potential.	A	C	C	F	E	E
Supply prospects for air cargo exports.	0	A	B	E	F	D
B. Focus on improving transit systems.						
Focus on regional transit systems.	C	B	B	E	E	E
Reengineer the customs transit regime.	B	A	A	F	F	E
Provide transit soft infrastructure.	C	C	B	F	E	D
Streamline border processing and control.	C	B	C	E	F	F
Initiate transit in ports.	B	A	B	E	F	E
C. Build trust.						
Focus on corridor performance.	C	B	C	E	E	D
Foster public– private synergies.	0	B	C	F	E	E

Source: Authors.
Notes: A = greatest impact, B = significant impact, C = little impact, D = very easy/consensual, E = require sustained effort and consensus building, F = difficult potentially face resistance, 0 = no or negative impact.

improvement of outsiders' confidence in the seriousness of the commitment to implementation and delivery—on the part of both government and private-sector participants.

As small countries located on the margin of some of the world's most productive areas, these four are well placed to participate in modern production networks. Key to acceptance for such a role is the foreign partners' assessment of how reliable a potential new participant will be in fulfilling the supply commitments it undertakes; that partner, in turn, must embrace the reliability of the customs, logistics, and other services of its own country and, as needed, the transit neighbor. Thus, a main current need is to fulfill in timely manner commitments already made—governmental or private—and to insist on realistic time schedules in devising new ones.

Success of trade facilitation efforts in bringing about actual improvements depends on high-level attention, which needs to be sustained. Success can be greatly helped too by high-quality and objective monitoring against concrete targets, with timely publication of results in a location (such as a Web site) readily accessible to all interested parties.

Monitor Corridor Performance

SEETO will be continuing to monitor major corridors, including EU Corridor X.

Priority corridors:

Yerevan–Gyumri–Batumi–Poti (800 km)

Yerevan–Tabriz–Esfehan–Bandar Abbas (2,600 km)

Vientiane–Nongkhai–Bangkok/Laem Chabang (700 km)

Dansavanh–Danang (300 km)

Part of EU Corridor X: Skopje–Thessaloniki (250 km)

Chisinau–Leuceni–Birlad–Bucharest (450 km)

Overview of the Policy Recommendations: Impact and Ease of Implementation

Chapter 9 concludes this volume by proposing a series of 13 recommendations to move forward the agenda to improve corridor performance and transit systems. The impact and ease of implementation of those measures are likely to vary considerably according to topic and region. This is especially true for the first three categories of eleven measures (building trust; making transport and logistics services work for trade, and redefining or improving transit systems). The last category about global standards and indicators includes suggestions for the working program of international organization.

The first matrix (table A2.1) gives a qualitative picture not only of how the individual recommended measures (the first eleven, to be implemented locally) should impact logistics costs in terms of (direct) costs, delays, and reliability, but also of how difficult they

Table A2.2 Main Recommendations for Consideration and Action at Country and Regional Levels: Priorities by Region

	Eastern Africa	Southern Africa	Central Africa	Western Africa	South America	Central Asia	Southeast Asia	Southeastern Asia	Southeastern Europe
A. Making transportation and logistics services work for trade									
Promote quality and competition in services.	B	A	A	A	A	A	A	B	C
Optimize multimodal and railroad potential.	B	C	A	A	B	A	A	C	C
Run regular shuttle trains to and from ocean port.	A	B	B	A	C	B	B	—	C
Supply prospects for air cargo exports.	A	C	A	A	B	A	B	C	C
B. Focusing on improving transit systems									
Focus on regional transit systems.	A	B	A	A	A	A	A	C	C
Reengineer the customs transit regime.									
Build accredited or authorized operator system.	A	C	A	A	A	A	A	A	C
Transit soft infrastructure: optimize usage of ICT systems to support transit.	A	B	A	A	B	A	A	B	B
Streamline border processing and control.	A	A	A	A	A	A	A	A	A
Initiate transit in ports. Expedite release of imports at transit port.	A	A	A	A	C	—	B	C	C
C. Building trust									
Focus on corridor performance.	A	A	A	A	A	A	A	B	A
Foster public-private synergy.	A	C	A	A	A	A	A	A	A

Source: Authors.

Notes: A = Very important in immediately coming years; B = Further progress needed, but not so urgent; C = Already largely resolved; — = not available.

may be to implement given their complexity, palatability to domestic stakeholders, or international discussions. Not surprisingly, there is a trade-off between potential impact and ease of implementation. The measure with the greatest potential effects—reengineering of the transit regime—may also be the most difficult to implement in many subregions.

The second matrix (table A2.2) depicts the degree of urgency that is believed to attach to pursuit of each of these recommendations in each of the nine regions of the developing world that contain one or more LLDC (including, for this purpose, Afghanistan and Mongolia with the Central Asian and Caucasus countries with which they are contiguous). As is already clear, the current baseline varies very much from region to region.

These ratings are subjective, based on the authors' personal experience and knowledge of different regions of the world.

Trade Growth and Logistics Performance: LLDCs and Transit Neighbors

Table A3.1 Eastern and Southern Africa: LLDCs and Transit Neighbors

Country	Per capita income, 2006 (PPP US$)	GDP growth, 1990–2006 (% per year)	GDP, 2006 (current US$, billions)	Exports of goods and services (% of GDP) 1990	Exports of goods and services (% of GDP) 2006	Increase in volume of goods exports, 1995–2006 (%)	Sectoral source of increase in goods exports, 2000–06 (%) Energy and agriculture	Minerals	Manufactured goods	No. of 3-digit SITC coded items exported, 2006	Export concentration index (%) 1995–96	Export concentration index (%) 2005–06	Trade with neighbors as share of all trade, 2006 exports and imports (%) Exports	Imports
Ethiopia	630	4.6	13.3	10	16	148	90	7	3	62	64	42	14	6
Uganda	880	6.5	9.4	12	15	177	51	17	32	133	60	25	30	17
Rwanda	730	1.6	2.5	5	12	51	45	47	8	31	46	54	28	47
Burundi	320	-0.7	0.9	13	11	94	-2	49	53	24	63	61	21	13
Malawi	690	3.2	3.2	30	17	43	77	—	23	89	63	56	30	56
Zambia	1,140	2.2	10.7	36	38	161	7	87	6	139	78	61	15	55
Zimbabwe	170	-0.7	3.4	38	57	1	15	64	21	155	28	23	55	71
Botswana	11,730	5.7	10.6	51	55	69	2	92	6	139	n.a.	73	13	89
Lesotho	1,810	3.6	1.5	21	51	590	-9	53	56	n.a.	n.a.	42	18	78
Swaziland	4,700	3.0	2.6	75	81	166	-353	93	160	162	n.a.	40	81	89
Kenya	1,470	2.8	22.8	33	26	64	3	2	95	216	23	20	33	1
Tanzania	980	4.2	12.8	24	24	124	22	59	19	135	28	35	14	5
Mozambique	660	6.6	6.8	16	41	1,491	12	83	5	107	42	57	19	40
Angola	3,890	5.2	45.2	82	74	126	—	100	—	70	90	95	1	8
Namibia	4,770	4.3	6.6	49	54	44	24	54	22	187	n.a.	30	32	84
South Africa	8,900	2.8	255.2	23	30	64	6	51	43	253	20	15	8	3
Madagascar	870	2.2	5.5	24	30	215	n.a.	n.a.	n.a.	120	27	20	—	—

Sources: Per capita income, 2006: World Bank 2008a, table 1.1.
GDP growth, 1990–2006: Calculated from World Bank 2008a, table 4.1.
GDP, 2006: World Bank 2008a, table 4.2
Exports of goods and services (percentage of GDP): World Bank 2008a, table 4.8.
Increase in volume of goods exports: World Bank 2008a, table 6.2.
Sectoral source of increase in goods exports, 2000–06: Authors, drawing on Comtrade database.
Number of 3-digit Standard International Trade Classification, Rev.3 (SITC) items exported, 2006: UNCTAD 2008, table 4.1.1.
Export Concentration Index: World Bank 2008b.
Trade with neighbors as share of all trade, 2006: Authors, drawing on Comtrade database.

Note: GDP = gross domestic product, n.a. = not available, — = not applicable, PPP = purchasing power parity, SITC = Standard International Trade Classification.

Table A3.2 Western and Central Africa: LDCs and Transit Neighbors

Country	Per capita income, 2006 (PPP US$)	GDP growth, 1990–2006 (% per year)	GDP, 2006 (current US$, billions)	Exports of goods and services (% of GDP) 1990	2006	Increase in volume of goods exports, 1995–2006 (%)	Sectoral source of increase in goods exports, 2000–06 (%) Energy and agriculture	Minerals	Manufac- tured goods	No. of 3-digit SITC coded items exported, 2006	Export concentration index (%) 1995–96	2005–06	Trade with neigh- bors as share of all trade, 2006 exports and imports (%) Exports	Imports
Mali	1,000	4.7	5.9	21	32	200	16	84	10	74	59	77	7	41
Burkina Faso	1,130	5.8	6.2	14	11	185	115	–3	–12	62	59	59	9	59
Niger	630	2.9	3.7	17	15	–6	–100	100	–100	53	48	47	27	24
Chad	1,170	6.5	6.5	22	59	n.a.	—	100	—	n.a.	n.a.	n.a.	n.a.	8
Central African Republic	690	0.9	1.5	20	14	69	145	–55	10	15	45	46	1	10
Mauritania	1,970	3.8	2.7	37	55	–8	26	68	6	n.a.	50	75	7	3
Senegal	1,560	3.5	9.2	31	26	108	14	49	37	168	30	23	34	24
Guinea	1,130	3.8	3.3	21	32	–28	14	96	–10	57	66	66	10	4
Côte d'Ivoire	1,580	2.0	17.6	42	51	33	23	53	24	147	36	32	23	31
Ghana	1,240	4.6	12.9	24	39	48	53	13	34	117	44	34	16	14
Togo	770	3.1	2.2	32	35	64	n.a.	n.a.	n.a.	74	32	29	53	11
Benin	1,250	4.4	4.8	20	13	51	17	74	9	53	53	60	4	45
Nigeria	1,410	3.8	115.3	44	56	–20	1	97	2	174	95	87	3	5
Cameroon	2,060	2.4	18.3	24	26	–5	30	67	3	92	35	46	4	31

Sources: See table A3.1.
Note: GDP = gross domestic product, n.a. = not applicable, — = not available, PPP = purchasing power parity, SITC = Standard International Trade Classification.

Table A3.3 Central and South Asia and the Caucasus: LLDCs and Transit Neighbors

Country	Per capita income, 2006 (PPP US$)	GDP growth, 1990–2006 (% per year)	GDP, 2006 (current US$, billions)	Exports of goods and services (% of GDP) 1990	2006	Increase in volume of goods exports, 1995–2006 (%)	Sectoral source of increase in goods exports, 2000–06 (%) Energy and agriculture	Minerals	Manufactured goods	No. of 3-digit SITC coded items exported, 2006	Export concentration index (%) 1995–96	2005–06	Trade with neighbors as share of all trade, 2006 exports and imports (%) Exports	Imports
Kazakhstan	8,700	1.0	81.0	39	51	n.a.	2	89	9	199	22	60	20	44
Uzbekistan	2,190	n.a.	17.2	28	38	n.a.	35	38	27	131	52	27	43	43
Turkmenistan	3,990	n.a.	10.5	75	72	n.a.	-6	92	14	59	45	61	19	41
Tajikistan	1,560	-3.0	2.8	66	23	n.a.	71	47	-18	52	47	61	31	60
Kyrgyz Republic	1,790	-1.0	2.8	29	39	n.a.	20	22	58	139	16	30	61	57
Afghanistan	n.a.	n.a.	8.4	n.a.	12	n.a.	50	50	—	n.a.	n.a.	n.a.	38	52
Azerbaijan	5,430	1.4	19.9	28	70	n.a.	6	89	5	129	61	59	35	42
Armenia	4,950	3.3	6.4	24	22	n.a.	16	47	37	118	24	33	20	43
Nepal	1,010	4.3	8.9	25	14	-23	55	57	-12	109	45	15	52	80
Bhutan	4,000	n.a.	0.9	n.a.	37	n.a.	14	34	52	n.a.	33	34	67	61
Russian Federation	12,740	-0.6	986.9	29	34	n.a.	5	82	13	248	26	35	10	7
China	4,660	10.3	2,644.7	23	40	610	2	4	94	254	7	11	2	12
Iran, Islamic Rep.	9,800	4.0	217.9	22	42	28	6	82	12	220	83	78	4	1
Georgia	3,880	-1.2	7.7	26	33	n.a.	23	25	52	136	17	17	47	44
Pakistan	2,410	4.4	126.8	17	15	122	13	12	75	204	24	23	9	4
India	2,460	6.4	911.8	11	23	n.a.	8	39	53	254	13	14	9	10
Turkey	8,410	4.5	402.7	20	28	269	14	4	82	213	11	13	8	19
Bangladesh	1,230	5.1	61.9	11	19	40	3	2	95	149	36	40	3	36

Sources: See table A3.1.

Note: GDP = gross domestic product, n.a. = not applicable, — = not available, PPP = purchasing power parity, SITC = Standard International Trade Classification.

Table A3.4 Other LLDCs and Their Surrounding Regions

Country	Per capita income, 2006 (PPP US$)	GDP growth, 1990–2006 (% per year)	GDP, 2006 (current US$, billions)	Exports of goods and services (% of GDP) 1990	2006	Increase in volume of goods exports, 1995–2006 (%)	Sectoral source of increase in goods exports, 2000–06 (%) Energy and agriculture	Minerals	Manufactured goods	No. of 3-digit SITC coded items exported, 2006	Export concentration index (%) 1995–96	2005–06	Trade with neighbors as share of all trade, 2006 exports and imports (%) Exports	Imports
East Asia														
Lao PDR	1,740	6.4	3.4	23	36	158	14	82	4	n.a.	26	32	66	87
Mongolia	2,810	3.4	3.1	48	65	56	4	93	3	82	50	43	71	64
Thailand	7,440	4.7	206.3	42	74	113	5	10	75	244	10	10	13	13
Vietnam	2,310	7.8	61.0	33	73	291	20	24	56	237	21	23	13	24
China	4,660	10.3	2,644.7	23	40	610	2	4	94	255	7	11	2	12
Russian Federation	12,740	-0.6	986.9	29	34	n.a.	5	82	13	248	26	35	10	7
Latin America														
Bolivia	3,810	3.7	11.2	23	42	136	6	95	–1	145	22	38	55	66
Paraguay	4,040	2.5	9.3	59	49	104	87	1	12	123	34	34	36	34
Chile	11,300	5.7	145.8	29	45	126	14	77	9	228	30	39	12	27
Brazil	8,700	2.8	1,067.5	7	15	180	30	25	45	248	9	9	16	16
Uruguay	9,940	3.0	19.3	19	30	64	n.a.	n.a.	n.a.	185	17	23	n.a.	n.a.
Peru	6,490	4.8	92.4	13	29	200	11	80	9	216	24	26	9	16
Argentina	11,670	4.0	214.2	10	25	78	46	22	32	243	14	13	41	29

(continued)

Table A3.4 *(continued)*

Country	Per capita income, 2006 (PPP US$)	GDP growth, 1990–2006 (% per year)	GDP, 2006 (current US$, billions)	Exports of goods and services (% of GDP) 1990	2006	Increase in volume of goods exports, 1995–2006 (%)	Sectoral source of increase in goods exports, 2000–06 (%) Energy and agriculture	Minerals	Manufactured goods	No. of 3-digit SITC coded items exported, 2006	Export concentration index (%) 1995–96	2005–06	Trade with neighbors as share of all trade, 2006 exports and imports (%) Exports	Imports
Eastern Europe														
Macedonia, FYR	7,850	0.3	6.2	33	50	n.a.	17	14	69	180	14	18	46	28
Moldova	2,660	-2.5	3.4	49	46	n.a.	32	5	63	155	25	23	29	34
Serbia	9,320	n.a.	32.0	17	27	n.a.	n.a.	n.a.	n.a.	241	9	11	15	12
Albania	6,000	4.1	9.1	12	25	n.a.	8	21	71	119	24	27	17	27
Bulgaria	10,270	0.9	31.5	45	64	n.a.	9	38	53	230	9	15	21	14
Romania	10,150	1.8	121.6	28	34	n.a.	4	16	80	242	13	12	9	4
Ukraine	6,110	-2.1	106.5	47	47	n.a.	15	10	75	247	11	15	6	2
Greece	30,870	3.0	308.4	15	19	n.a.	21	25	54	240	11	12	16	4

Sources: See table A3.1.

Note: GDP = gross domestic product, n.a. = not applicable, PPP = purchasing power parity, SITC = Standard International Trade Classification.

References

UNCTAD (United Nations Conference on Trade and Development). 2008. *UNCTAD Handbook of Statistics 2008*. Geneva: UNCTAD.

World Bank. 2008a. *World Development Indicators 2008*. Washington, DC: World Bank.

————. 2008b. *World Trade Indicators 2008*. Washington, DC: World Bank.

APPENDIX 4

Survey Findings on LLDC Logistics Performance

In recent years, a wide range of surveys has been developed, covering both opinions and factual data, to shed more light on ways in which LLDCs are affected by their landlocked state. Such surveys aim to help policy makers identify the main obstacles to overcome and issues to pursue. They relate to trade and growth and cover large numbers of both LLDCs and others.

Global Enabling Trade Report 2010

The Global Enabling Trade Report 2010 (WEF 2010) is the largest relevant work to date, prepared by the World Economic Forum (WEF) and published in June 2010. It scored the performance of 118 countries on a range of indicators related to "enabling trade." Coverage included 21 LLDCs, all of which had aggregate scores in the lower half of the entire sample of countries in the study. Most useful for this volume are the scores given for the various factors, or "pillars," that comprise the general "enabling trade" index score.

To help identify how LLDCs' performance compares with other relatively poor countries on a number of trade-related areas (such as the restrictiveness of tariffs and non-tariff barriers, border management, corruption, quality and availability of transport and trade infrastructure, and

Table A4.1 Trade-Related Survey Scores of LLDCs Compared with Other Poor Countries

WEF Global Enabling Trade Report 2010				World Bank Logistics Performance Index (LPI) 2010	
	Average scores		LLDC shortfall (%)*	Indicator*	LLDC shortfall (%)*
Pillar	LLDCs	Others			
1. Tariff and Non-Tariff Barriers	4.75	4.70	+1		
2. Breadth of Foreign Markets and Acceptance of International Rules	4.01	3.12	+29	International Shipments	–8
3. Efficiency of Customs Administration	3.46	4.28	–19	Customs	–15
4. Efficiency of Import Procedures	2.72	4.84	–44	Timeliness	–10
5. Corruption at Border	2.90	4.08	–29		
6. Transport Infrastructure Availability and Quality	3.18	4.49	–29	Infrastructure	–20
7. Transport Service Availability and Quality	3.27	4.04	–19	Logistics Competence	–17
8. Availability and Use of ICT	2.22	3.72	–40	Tracking and Tracing	–14
9. Treatment of Foreign-Owned Businesses	3.35	4.10	–18		
10. Physical Security	4.39	4.97	–11		
				Domestic 2010 LPI performance**	
				Physical inspection rate	+79
				Export lead time (median)	+211
				Import lead time (median)	+84
				Export container charge	+92
				Import container charge	+78

Source: Authors.

Note: ICT = information communications and technology.

* Performance of the LLDC relative to the coastal country. Negative values mean LLDCs performed worse than the LLDC.

** Excess physical inspection rate, time, and cost in LLDCs compared to coastal countries. Positive values indicate that moving LLDCs trade takes longer and is more costly.

so on), the authors calculated average scores on each component pillar for the 22 LLDCs and the 38 other countries falling in the lower half of the overall sample of countries. A country's score on each factor is a composite of its scores on two to five particular trade-related issues, some factual and some judgmental, based on studies by various international bodies and associations, as well as the views of WEF's regular multinational business contacts.[1] WEF assesses each indicator on a scale of 0 to 7, with 7 indicating the best performance. The results of the comparison are summarized in table A4.1 and are interpreted below.

Connecting to Compete: The Logistics Performance Index (LPI) 2010

World Bank Logistics Performance Index (LPI) 2010 is another survey the authors similarly analyzed, which was conducted by the World Bank among practicing logistics and trade professionals around the world in some 150 countries. The survey posed factual questions about the performance experience in the country where the respondent was based and also requested judgmental assessments on a wider range of issues in up to eight other countries with which the respondent had regular dealings. Of the 26 LLDCs covered, all but five—Kazakhstan, Uganda, Uzbekistan, the former Yugoslav Republic of Macedonia, and Paraguay—also fell in the lower half of the entire sample, when considering the general score obtained by all countries considered in the LPI. The Enabling Trade and LPI studies showed that the opinion of business executives and freight forwarders attaches overriding importance to three key factors explaining trade logistics performance. In declining order, they are as follows:

1. Reduction of long and unpredictable times for organizing and carrying through freight shipments (especially imports) and for bringing down the costs
2. Application of information and communication technologies
3. Improved transport infrastructure.

Especially notable in table A4.1 is the big difference between the LLDCs and the other poorer countries in the WEF assessment of "Efficiency of Import Procedures," which is based mainly on time, cost, and documentation information. The differences between the scores on related issues covered in the LPI survey illustrates the same pattern between LLDCs and low-income coastal countries.

Doing Business in Landlocked Economies 2009

In 2008, the World Bank/International Finance Corporation Doing Business group published *Doing Business in Landlocked Economies 2009*, distinguishing for the first time between landlocked and other countries. This survey's results highlight the same differences between countries as the previous studies, for exports as well as imports, and in a somewhat broader context than that provided by the WEF trade report.

Their database, reflecting assessments by many associated lawyers, accountants, and businesspeople, mostly in developing countries, covers a broad range of issues relating to the environment for small enterprise growth. Among the ten areas covered, however, by far the largest difference between landlocked and coastal economies arises on the "Trading across Borders" indicator, which reflects lead time, documentation, and overland transport costs for exports and imports. For example, time required to organize and implement an export shipment averages twice as long for landlocked as for other countries.

Comparing the Experience of Countries by Region

These worldwide surveys document that cost and time penalties borne by LLDCs' international trade are indeed high and problematic. More detailed insights can be found in the Logistics Performance Index (LPI), especially for the key case of Africa. Table A4.2 provides some of the

Table A4.2   Regions with Poorly Performing LLDCs by LPI Score*

Background data	Sub-Saharan Africa		South Asia	
	LLDC	Coastal country	LLDC	Coastal country
Overall LPI	2.37	2.43	2.27	2.61
Selected LPI components				
Logistics competence	2.16	2.32	2.13	2.45
Infrastructure	1.98	2.07	1.83	2.30
Customs and trade processes	2.16	2.18	2.14	2.26
LPI input data				
Customs clearance (days)	8.5	3.6	3.85	1.6
Physical inspection (percent)				
(higher is worse)	53	28	43	13
Lead time to (days)				
Export (median) shipper? →port	14.5	5	1.9	1.8
Import (median) port? →consignee	8.4	6.7	5.2	2.6

Source: Authors, based on the World Bank Logistics Performance Index (LPI) 2010.
* LPI Score on a scale of 1 to 5.

background data that go into the LPI calculations for two regions, and a comparison of landlocked and coastal countries for them.

These data lead to the conclusion that the transport infrastructure of LLDCs in Sub-Saharan Africa still imposes a penalty, which is 5 percent worse than for coastal countries. The competence of services exert a larger penalty on LLDCs: on average, about 7 percent worse than coastal countries. However, the data for time to export or import in Africa suggest that being landlocked adds nine days to exports and two to imports, the period to move trade from the producer's factory to the purchaser's premises, including clearance at destination.

For LLDCs in South Asia (with average values heavily affected by the very low scores of Afghanistan), *transport infrastructure* is a serious constraint: 20 percent worse for landlocked than coastal countries. This is a significantly greater problem than the customs and logistics services quality component of the LPI (which are about 5 and 12 percent worse for landlocked than for coastal countries, respectively). Transit time for imports and clearance is also disproportionately high for these countries.

Despite the difficulties that the African LLDCs face, they have sometimes been able to outperform the coastal countries on important dimensions of the LPI. For instance, Uganda is among the top-performing countries in the region based on its overall LPI score, outranking some of the coastal countries, such as Tanzania in East Africa, and Côte d'Ivoire, Ghana, and Togo in West Africa.

The Penalties by Region of Being Landlocked

The LLDCs differ greatly in the level of development they have attained and the use they have made of international trade. A major theme of almost all the recent country assessments of trade prospects, such as the Diagnostic Trade Integration Studies,[2] is the need to reduce transport transit times and delays and procedural obstacles. However, it is useful to examine the recent trade development experience of all the LLDCs concerned and their coastal and transit neighbors on a common basis to the extent possible. In appendix 3, tables A3.1–A3.4 present the statistics for all 31 countries and their transit neighbors in regional groups.

The evidence in field and operational experience, trade facilitation assessments, and other research on trade and competitiveness points out the difficulties LLDCs face, except for those unusually rich in natural resources, in trying to expand international trade and increase incomes. Their goods face high competition in foreign markets. Their diversification from traditional natural-resource exports has been more limited. Their overall foreign exchange earnings have been at much lower levels than in economies of similar size with direct access to the sea.

Eastern and Southern Africa

One striking feature of the picture in Eastern and Southern Africa, clearly evidenced in table A3.1, is the still low role of exports (less than 20 percent of gross domestic product [GDP]) in all five of the East African LLDCs, which together have some 140 million inhabitants. Another is the very limited scale of exports from the region's LLDCs into the larger, richer coastal economies of Kenya, South Africa, and Tanzania. Growth of international trade in East Africa has suffered from periodic major problems in overland infrastructure maintenance and port congestion, just as it has benefited in southern Africa from the strong transport infrastructure and competitive organization of road freight services in the countries of SACU (Southern African Customs Union) and their neighbors.

Relatively strong development records over the past 10 to15 years have been established by Lesotho and Uganda. Trade has been a major factor in their success, with the particularly noteworthy recent success of Uganda in increasing manufactured exports to inland Democratic Republic of Congo, Rwanda, and Sudan (Selassie 2008). In Ethiopia, too, trade growth has benefited from the policy attention given to it.

The relatively good trade performance of Ethiopia, Lesotho, and Uganda is reflected in their comparatively high LPI scores, due especially to good scores for timeliness and competitive local logistics costs. Compared to other resource-poor African countries, all three also score high on the Trading across Borders dimension of the Doing Business surveys. The latest round of the latter implies that a main requirement to achieving much-needed further expansion of exports in these countries may be to address some broader common legal obstacles to business development.

Western and Central Africa

The five LLDCs of Western and Central Africa (table A3.2) have a combined population of some 55 million. Apart from the Central African Republic, they have generally achieved somewhat stronger growth over the past 15 years than their counterparts in Eastern Africa. However, with the notable exception of Mali, their role in international trade has tended to decrease. Exports as a share of GDP have dropped in three of the countries, to well below 20 percent. The LLDCs have made little or no progress in diversification of export commodities or in exploitation of market opportunities in the coastal countries, despite efforts of ECOWAS (Economic Community of West African States) and UEMOA (West African Economic and Monetary Union) to bring about stronger integration.

Among both landlocked and coastal countries in this part of Africa, there has been little development of exports outside the energy and minerals sectors. The main exceptions are Ghana and, on a smaller scale, Burkina Faso and Senegal. Among all the LLDCs, those from Western and Central Africa score lowest on both LPI and Doing Business indicators.

Central and South Asia

Aided by the minerals boom of the years up to 2008, the Central Asian economies grew rapidly from the turn of the century, recovering from the substantial drops in GDP in the 1990s connected with the breakup of the Soviet Union and their shift to direct participation in the world economy. According to the recent PPP (purchasing power parity) estimates, per capita income levels are comparable to those of the richer African countries. On the UNDP (United Nations Development Programme) Human Development Index, the Central Asian economies generally score higher, reflecting, in particular, better health and education.

Central Asian exports have grown rapidly and now account for a much higher proportion of GDP than is the case for the African countries. However, involvement in trade beyond neighbors and fellow members of the former Soviet Union appears still very limited outside the energy field (table A3.3). Substantial growth in agricultural and manufactured exports has occurred only in Uzbekistan, and to some extent in the relatively small economies of Tajikistan and the Kyrgyz Republic. From 20 to 60 percent of each country's exports still go to regional neighbors, including the Russian Federation—five or more times as high a proportion of their exports as the coastal neighbors sell in that limited market.

Among all the ex-Soviet LLDCs, only Armenia seems to make substantial sales of agricultural and manufactured goods outside the region. On the Trading across Borders element of Doing Business, it also achieves scores as good as most, but not all, of the five LLDCs in Africa and Europe where manufactured goods figured large in the growth of exports from 2000 to 2006. Kyrgyz and Uzbek non-mineral exports may well be mainly to neighbors and Russia at present, perhaps not yet requiring standards of quality or timeliness demanded by the larger world market. But their fairly high LPI scores may indicate that they are preparing also for a larger direct role on the world market.

Since the figures assembled in these tables relate mainly to the past five or ten years, Nepal shows up with a relatively weak performance, reflecting the political and social tensions that it has suffered. With progress in the reforms being introduced to resolve those problems, the country may be able to resume the strong development of manufactured exports that it achieved in earlier periods. The new development could gradually take the form of major growth of intra-industry trade of parts and subassemblies with Indian companies, jointly serving world markets for selected product lines.

Southeastern Europe

The two small European developing LLDCs, FYR Macedonia and Moldova, have been finding new paths of development following the major changes that led to their creation as independent states in the 1990s. Benefiting from the infrastructure inherited from the past and relatively educated work forces, they have given high priority to exports as a source of much needed job creation. They have achieved substantial growth, mostly with manufactured goods. This is the same pattern as in these countries' coastal neighbors, as shown in table A3.4, but the latter are at present still reaching wider world markets.

FYR Macedonia is one of the LLDCs most highly rated on both the Doing Business and the LPI indicators, and Moldova is not far behind. Export trade for both might also increasingly emphasize intra-industry exchanges with countries near at hand, benefiting from economies of scale in production and other constructed comparative advantages.

South America

Exports from Bolivia and Paraguay have grown substantially and now account for 45–50 percent of GDP, higher than in most of their Latin American neighbors with their larger domestic economies. The LLDCs appear however to have greater difficulties in reaching markets outside the region. That said, the concentration of trade on neighbors sometimes reflects special factors such as the above-world-market prices that Brazil will pay for some of its neighbors' soy bean production because of their complementarity to its own output.

Paraguay was rated appreciably higher than Bolivia on the LPI, as well as on non-trade dimensions of the Doing Business assessment. The LPI points to problems in both countries with customs procedures and performance, and Doing Business stresses shared problems in excessively rigid employment regulations and restrictions.

East Asia

The two small East Asian landlocked economies—isolated and sparsely inhabited Mongolia, contrasting with the Lao People's Democratic Republic, readily accessible from both Thailand and Vietnam—have each made significant progress over the past 15 years. They have strongly expanded exports, but in both cases so far mostly by exploiting their energy and mineral resources to serve neighboring countries' markets. Trade and transport service improvements that have already been started have a major contribution to make to the growth of much more diverse export activities for the next phase of each country's development.

Notes

1. In table A4.1 the authors slightly modified the titles given for some of the WEF pillars to capture more precisely the scope of the aspects covered. This adjustment was made because of the focus here on the pillars rather than the overall summary scores.

2. The studies are prepared by joint teams from the international agencies under the Integrated Framework for Trade-Related Technical Assistance for the Least Developed Countries, an initiative led by the World Trade Organization. http://www.integratedframework .org/doctype/dtis.htm.

References

Selassie, A. A. 2008. "Beyond Macroeconomic Stability: The Quest for Industrialization in Uganda." Working Paper 08/23, International Monetary Fund, Washington, DC.

WEF (World Economic Forum). 2010. *The Global Enabling Trade Report 2010*. Geneva: WEF.

World Bank. 2008. *Doing Business in Landlocked Economies 2009*. Washington, DC: World Bank.

World Bank Logistics Performance Index (LPI) 2010 (database). World Bank, Washington, DC. http://info.worldbank.org/etools/tradesurvey/model b.asp.

Measuring Transit Corridor Performance Parameters

The two basic measures of transit corridor performance are cost and time, preferably measured separately for exports and imports.

The definition of cost is in two parts, formal costs (such as those that would appear on an invoice or for which a receipt would be given) and informal costs (such as those incurred at informal transit barriers and bribes). The costs are those that would be incurred if no unforeseen and unexpected costs were incurred. Bribes and other incentives for activities to be completed more quickly are difficult to deal with. We propose that the basic cost estimate includes the "expected minimum" payment for bribes and other informal expenses.

The calculation separates formal costs and informal costs. Similarly, it distinguishes formal lengths of time (such as for the movement of a truck in transit or the waiting period for approval of documents) and informal lengths of time (such as imposed delays because one does not pay a bribe or because a facility that should be open for business is closed). The calculation also uses minimum feasible costs and times for the formal measures and estimated average costs and times for the informal measures (since the minima are assumed to be zero).

The unit of cost is per TEU (20-foot equivalent unit) or per truck load, whichever is the most relevant to the corridor. Since a single TEU can usually be legally carried on a three-axle truck and a 40-foot container on a five-axle truck, these are used as the truck/TEU equivalents. An alternative would be to accept overloading reality and use a 12-ton GVW (gross vehicle weight) two-axle truck and a 20-ton GVW four-axle truck as the equivalents.

The calculation does not use a value of time, so that time costs can be added to transit costs to derive a total generalized cost. There is too much controversy concerning, and too much variation in, time values to make this worthwhile. Its inclusion would divert attention from the real issue of what the time and cost indicators are intended to show.

Locations at Which Measurements Will be Made

Measurements should be made at several locations to cover the entire transportation phase. For LLDC exports, measurements should start when the goods leave the exporter's premises, off to the unloading from the ship in the destination port. For imports to the LLDC, these should be measured from the origin port, up until the delivery of the goods in the premises of the importing company. These are broken out into seven principal locations, which are specified as follows:

1. Pre-transport activities
   a. loading and inspections in origin country
2. Transport in origin country
   b. waiting for transport from origin city
   c. transport in origin country
3. Border
   a. transfers at border in origin country
   b. transfers at border in transit country
4. Transit country
   a. waiting time for transport at border
   b. transport in transit country
5. Transit country port
   a. unloading and storage at port,
   b. charges and inspections at port
   c. loading at port

6. Maritime transport
   a. waiting at port for maritime transport
   b. maritime transport
7. Destination port
   a. unloading at destination port
   b. inspections at destination port.

The measure of variability is the extra time and cost above the minimum to be certain that a shipment arrived at its destination in the required time without incurring cost penalties. There is a conceptual problem, in that on a probability basis, not all cost and time penalties at each stage of transport will be incurred, and freight forwarders take account of these probabilities when scheduling shipments. Hence, total cost and time variation is not equal to the sum of the variations at each stage of transport. The calculation therefore includes an estimate of the delay at each stage and the overall delay, and is later adjusted by a coefficient.[1]

In addition to the data for each stage of the corridor, the calculation includes some indicators of the corridor as a whole, such as the number of national and provincial border crossings and the frequency of sailings from the port to each of the three main markets, and whether TIR or other transit regimes apply in the corridor. It might also be useful to include an indication of the fixed costs associated with freight movements in the corridor (as suggested in Arvis, Raballand, and Marteau 2010).

The Products and Their Transport Unit and Transport Route

Given that most export and import products to LLDCs are containerized, the standard product for which costs and times are measured is a 20-foot container with products having a market value between US$50,000 and US$250,000. This will cover most LLDC exports, including some high-value agricultural products (such as processed foods and spun cotton), some semiprocessed mineral products (such as copper ingots), and most semimanufactured goods (textiles and electronic components). It will also include most final consumer products that are imported to LLDCs, including processed foods, household electrical products, and basic clothes. Where applicable, other product categories can be used, such as refrigerated containers (for perishable food exports such as fruit), bulk solids (for basic agricultural products such as soya and wheat), and basic minerals (such as washed coal and unprocessed raw minerals).

To ensure that the estimates made for different corridors, and for a given corridor at different times, are consistent, we propose that costs be measured for the following specifications of consignment size:

- Containerized transport, the regular shipment of 5 containers each month
- Bulk transport, the regular shipment of 1,000 tons per month
- Loose transport, the regular shipment of 50 tons per month.

The transport route for which costs and times are estimated will be that most used for trade between the LLDC and third countries. Many LLDCs (such as Mongolia and some Central Asian republics) have only one feasible route, but others have more than one (for example, some LLDCs of Eastern Africa can use ports in Kenya, Mozambique, South Africa, or Tanzania). Where more than one route is feasible, we propose that costs be estimated for those most used for exports and imports—which might not be the same; therefore, sometimes two different routes will need to be analyzed. There might be special circumstances where other routes are of interest, particularly where a reduction in their transit costs and times could make them competitive with the current most-used route.

The Cost and Replicability of Making the Measurements

Since the measurement of costs and times are to be replicated for each corridor at intervals, the method of their measurement must be relatively simple and at low cost. But it also needs to provide reliable and consistent results. Experience from gathering data for the LPI indicates that a combination of international and local freight forwarding companies can provide consistent and reliable information. These considerations led us to propose a method than can be implemented without the use of international consultants, but does not rely on the self-completion of questionnaires by freight forwarders or others active in international trade. We propose that a relatively simple form be devised that can be completed by local consultants during the course of a face-to-face interview of less than one hour, conducted with a minimum of three freight forwarding companies, two of which should be based in the LLDC and one be a representative of a large international forwarding company.

The World Bank is working with the developers of FastPath to create a new version—FastPath Lite—that is more directly aimed at the desirable characteristics listed earlier. The result is expected to be highly compatible with the United Nations Economic and Social Commission for

Asia and the Pacific (UNESCAP) method of computing corridor performance, although some definitions will remain different between the two methods. The data produced will be compatible with the corridor graphics based on the UNESCAP approach. So it will be possible to reproduce these graphs from the data from our proposal, perhaps superimposing the cost and time graph from one corridor on that from another to get a simple picture of how the corridors compare.

Note

1. The coefficient is the ratio of the overall delay to the sum of the partial delays.

Reference

Arvis, J. F., G. Raballand, and J. F. Marteau. 2010. *The Cost of Being Landlocked*. Washington, DC: World Bank.

Maps of LLDCs and Transit Corridors, by Region

Map A6.1 Africa Region

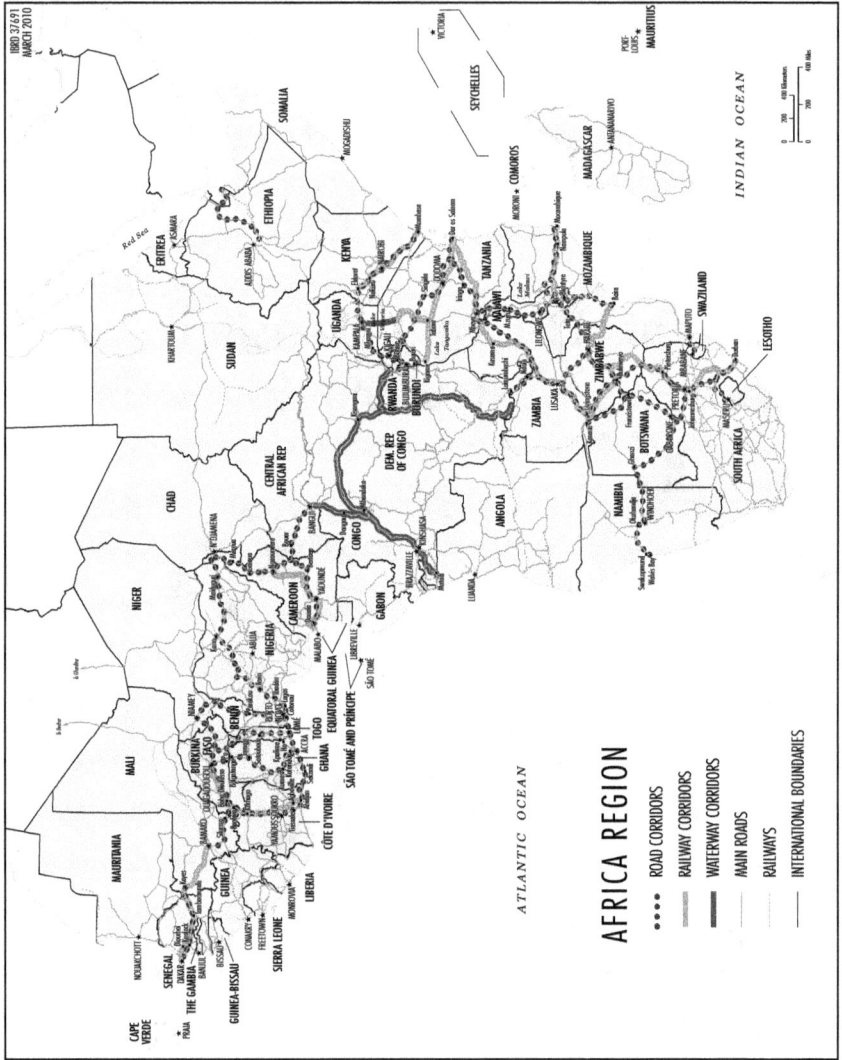

Map A6.2   Latin America Region

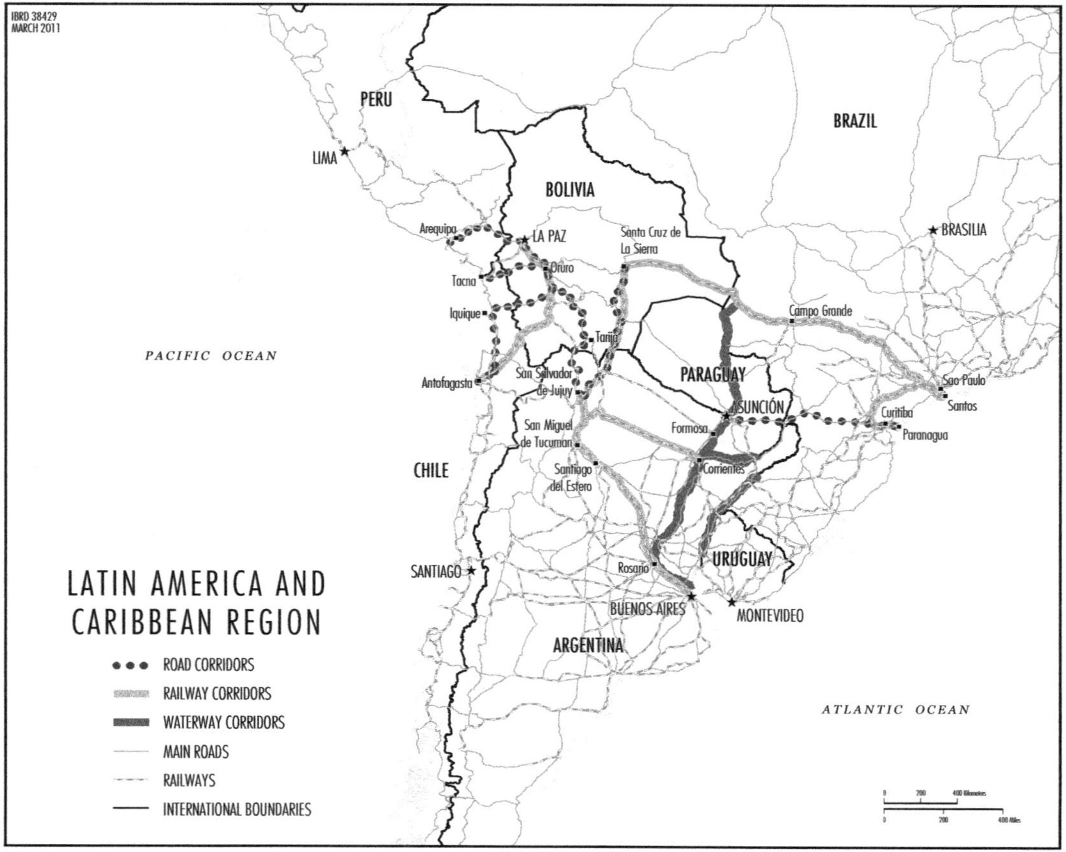

LATIN AMERICA AND
CARIBBEAN REGION

ROAD CORRIDORS
RAILWAY CORRIDORS
WATERWAY CORRIDORS
MAIN ROADS
RAILWAYS
INTERNATIONAL BOUNDARIES

IBRD 38429
MARCH 2011

255

Map A6.3   Europe and Central Asia Region

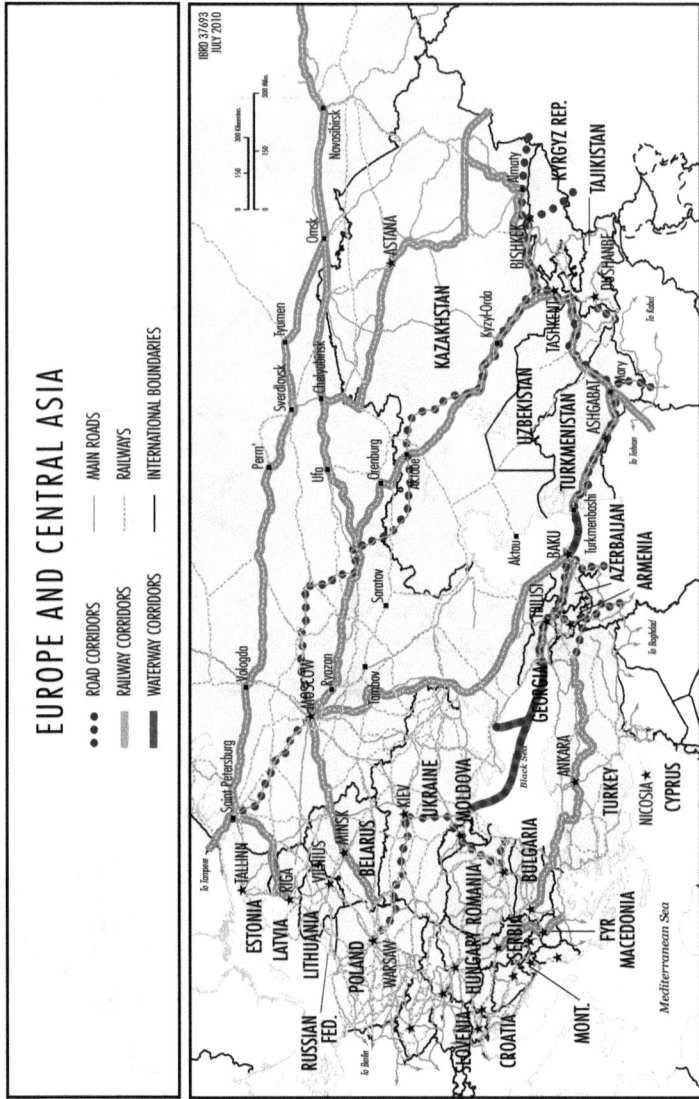

EUROPE AND CENTRAL ASIA

- ••• ROAD CORRIDORS
- RAILWAY CORRIDORS
- WATERWAY CORRIDORS
- MAIN ROADS
- RAILWAYS
- INTERNATIONAL BOUNDARIES

Map A6.4   South Asia Region

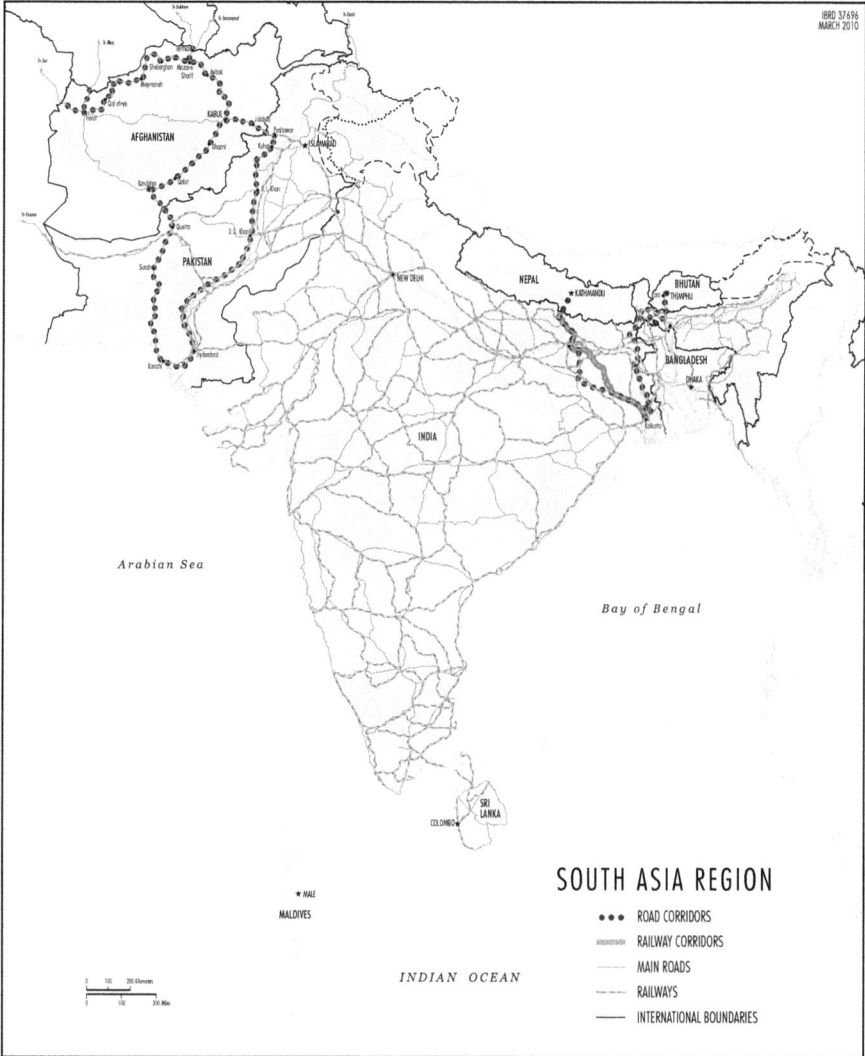

Map A6.5   East Asia Region

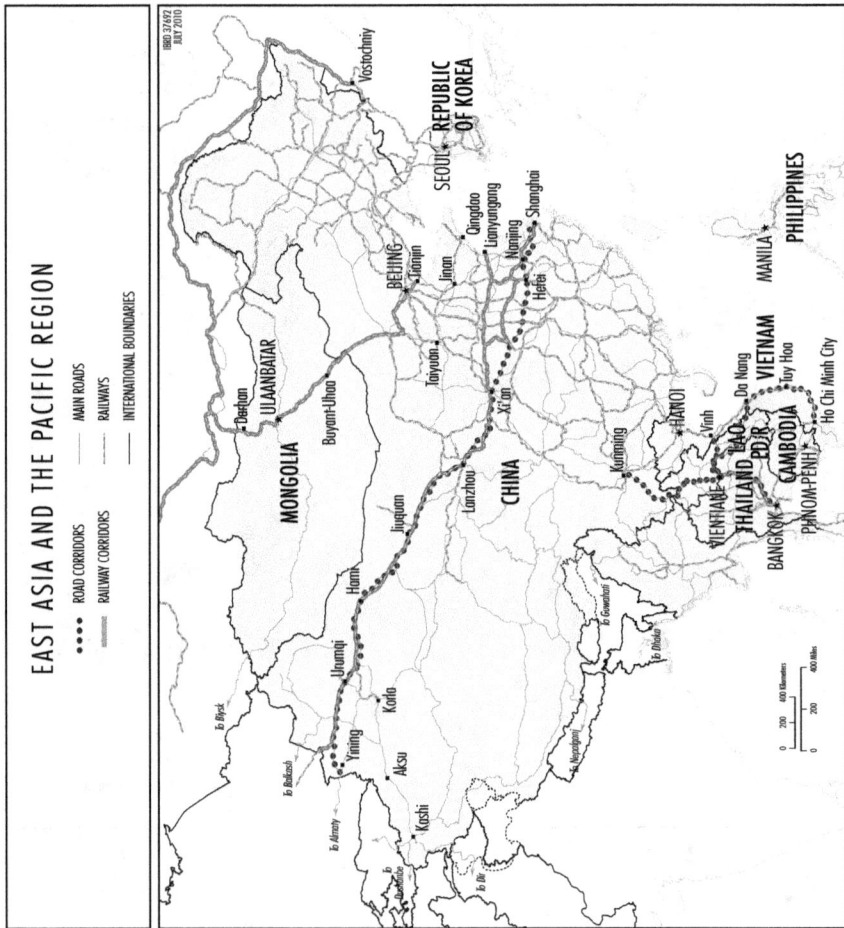

EAST ASIA AND THE PACIFIC REGION

•••• ROAD CORRIDORS
▬▬▬ RAILWAY CORRIDORS
— MAIN ROADS
··· RAILWAYS
— INTERNATIONAL BOUNDARIES

IBRD 37692
JULY 2010

Map A6.6   Middle East and North Africa Region

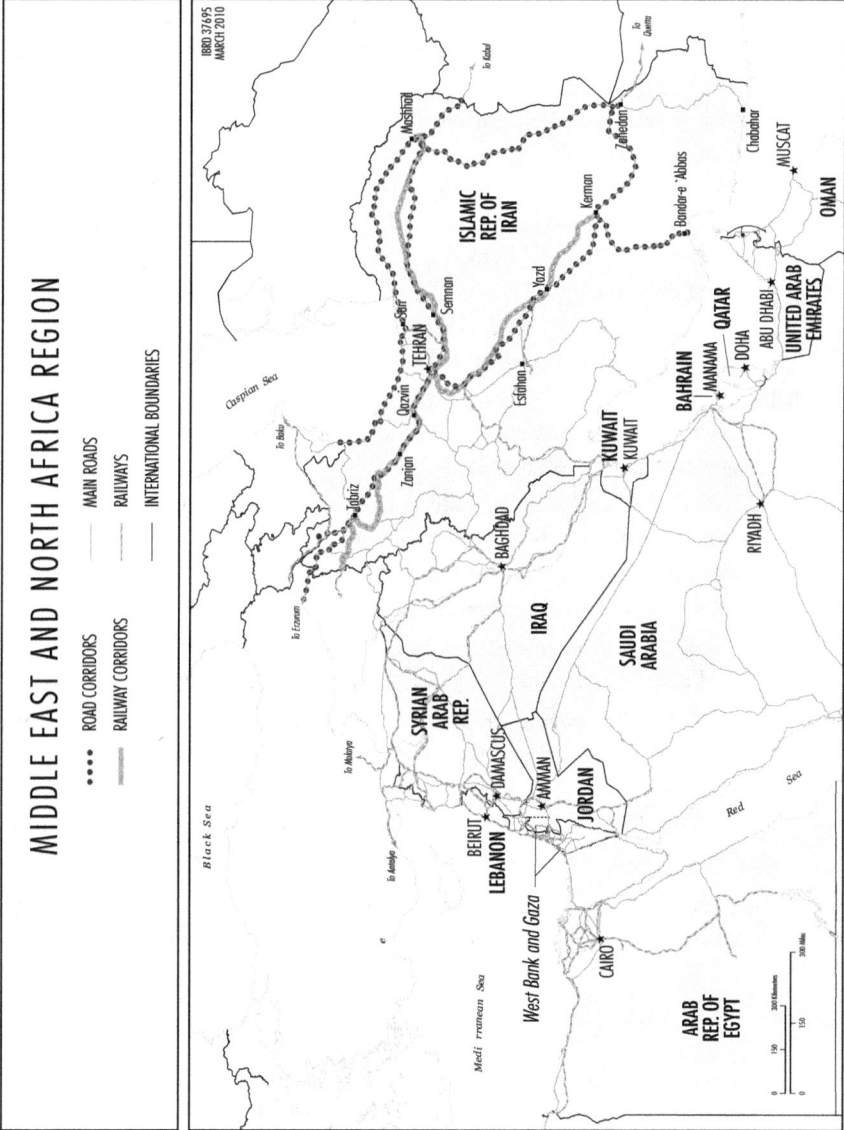

MIDDLE EAST AND NORTH AFRICA REGION

•••• ROAD CORRIDORS   —— MAIN ROADS
▬▬ RAILWAY CORRIDORS   ---- RAILWAYS
                              —— INTERNATIONAL BOUNDARIES

IBRD 37695
MARCH 2010

259

Appendix References

Arvis, Jean-François, Gaël Raballand, and Jean-François Marteau. 2010. *The Cost of Being Landlocked: Logistics Costs and Supply Chain Reliability.* WB Directions in Development. Washington, DC: World Bank.

Delft, C. E. 2008. *Handbook on Estimation of External Costs in the Transport Sector.* http://ec.europa.eu/transport/costs/handbook/doc/2008_01_15_handbook_external_cost_en.pdf.

FIAS (Foreign Investment Advisory Service). 2008. *Special Economic Zones: Performance, Lessons Learned, and Implications for Zone Development.* Washington, DC: World Bank.

Kitain, A. 2008. "Benefits of a Landlocked Country's Transit Traffic for the Transit Country: The Case of Kazakhstan (Central Asia)." Unpublished working paper, World Bank, Washington, DC.

Selassie, A. A. 2008. "Beyond Macroeconomic Stability: The Quest for Industrialization in Uganda." Working Paper WP/08/231. International Monetary Fund, Washington, DC.

UNCTAD (UN Conference on Trade and Development). *UNCTAD Handbook of Statistics 2008.* New York: United Nations.

WEF (World Economic Forum). 2008. "Global Enabling Trade Report 2008." Geneva: World Economic Forum.

World Bank. 2009. *Doing Business in Landlocked Countries 2009.* Washington DC: World Bank. http://www.doingbusiness.org/documents/DB09_landlocked.pdf

———. 2008a. "Improving Trade and Transport for Landlocked Developing Countries: World Bank Contributions to Implementing the Almaty Programme of Action."

———. 2008b. *World Development Indicators 2008.* Washington, DC: World Bank.

———. 2008c. *World Trade Indicators 2008.* Washington, DC: World Bank.

———. 2007. Logistics Performance Index: Connecting to Compete: Trade Logistics in the Global Economy. Washington, DC: World Bank.

Index

Boxes, figures, notes, and tables are indicated by *b*, *f*, *n*, and *t* following page numbers.

A

Abidjan
   container terminal operated by
      consortium, 151
   mango exports, 129
   as port of choice, 36, 37, 156
Abidjan–Lagos Corridor Organisation
      (ALCO), 179, 180–81*n*2
Abidjan–Ouagadougou rail corridor, 131,
      132, 133–34*b*, 156
Accord for River Navigation on the
      Paraguay and Paraná Rivers (1996),
      147*b*
AEOs. *See* authorized economic operators
Afghanistan
   Pakistan trade corridor agreement, 162
   smuggling, 52
   as trade corridor, 50, 51, 55*n*1
Africa. *See also specific countries and regions*
   cross-continental trade of landlocked
      countries, 14
   infrastructure investment, 27, 28*b*
   monitoring observatories, 178–79
   queuing systems, 26

road freight costs, 24
streamlining passage of transit data,
      95, 95*b*
sustainability of trade of landlocked
      countries, 29
transit regimes and landlocked
      countries, 85
African Development Bank, 181*n*2
African Growth and Opportunity Act
      (2000), 31
AfricaRail, 28*b*
agent fees, 18
Agreement on International Land
      Transportation (ATIT), 86
agricultural trade, 43
air freight, 139–43
   market development of, 141–43, 142*b*
   recommendations, 157, 186
   traffic volume, 140–41
   unit value of products, 139–40
ALCO (Abidjan–Lagos Corridor
      Organisation), 179, 180–81*n*2
Almaty Programme of Action, xi,
      4–5, 5*b*, 9

ALTID (Asian Land Transport Infrastructure Development) project, 28*b*
América Latina Logística (ALL), 135, 151, 158*n*5
Andean Manifest, 86
Aqaba and queuing system, 107
Arab League, 86, 109, 114
Arab Maghreb Union (AMU), 28*b*
Arab Manifest, 86
Argentina
    railway corridors, 135
    truck companies, 102
Arica, Chile, 134
Arnold, John, 162
Arvis, Jean-François, 13, 26, 41, 174, 175
ASEAN (Association of Southeast Asian Nations) region corridors, 173*b*
Asia. *See also specific countries and regions*
    highway network, 28–29*b*
    infrastructure investment, 27, 28*b*
    road transport as major transport method, 100
Asian Development Bank, 164
Asian Land Transport Infrastructure Development (ALTID) project, 28*b*
ASYCUDA documentation system, 93, 94, 152, 159*n*13
ATIT (*Acuerdo sobre Transporte International Terrestre*, or Agreement on International Land Transportation), 86
authorized economic operators (AEOs), 53, 82, 90–91*b*, 91–92, 106
automation and interconnection across borders, 94–95
axle load limits and road damage, 114, 115–17

B

backhaul capacity, 50, 129, 154
Barcelona Convention on Freedom of Transit (1921), 47
barges. *See* waterway transport
Baumol, W.J., 174
Beira, Mozambique
    as port of choice, 36
    transit initiation and clearance times, 81
Belgrano Railway, 135
Benin

competition among trade corridors, 37–38
inland container depots (ICDs), 155
railway, 28*b*
bilateral agreements, 6, 109–14, 162. *See also* quota systems; *specific countries*
    ad hoc nature of, 47
    negatives of, 88
    reform needed, 54
Bolivia
    bottlenecks in transit, 23
    Chile–Bolivia agreement on trade corridor, 162
    inland container depots (ICDs), 155
    railways and access to ports, 127, 134–35
    roads and freight costs, 101
    smuggling, 52
    surcharges and demurrages, 23
    as trade corridor, 50
    transit time, 100
    waterway transport, 144
bonds. *See* guarantees
border crossings
    costs of, 52, 100, 101*t*
    delay at, 21
    misconceptions about transit facilitation, 83–84, 87
    procedures, 107–9, 113–14
    quotas. *See* quota systems
    rail transit, 128, 128*b*
    recommendations, 119, 185, 187
    trucks, 107–9
Botswana, charges for border crossings, 115*b*
bribes, 27, 52
Burkina Faso
    competition among trade corridors, 37–38, 39*f*
    cut off from transit state access, 36
    informal checkpoints for trucks, 117
    mango exports, 43, 129
    railways, 28*b*, 131
    trade comparison with Mali, 131–32, 132*t*
Burundi trade corridor management agreements, 163, 165

C

Cameroon
    inland container depots (ICDs), 156
    transit routes, 20–21, 55*n*1, 93

caravan trade, 45–46, 47
CAREC (Central Asia Regional Economic
    Cooperation) Program, 164, 172
carnet systems, 65–73. *See also* TIR
    definition of carnet, 65, 188*n*1
    European common transit system,
        70–73, 82
    nonreporting problems, 80
    recommendations, 186
    types and functions of, 68–70,
        69*f*, 109
CCTTFA (Central Corridor Trade and
    Transport Facilitation Agency),
    165, 181*n*2
CEMAC (Economic and Monetary
    Community of Central Africa), 85
Central Africa
    import time, 17
    integration goals, 85, 86
    road freight costs, 24, 25
Central African Republic. *See also* Douala
        corridor in Central Africa
    all-weather access, need of, 31*n*3
    river corridor, inaccessibility of, 55*n*1
Central Africa Transport and Transit
    Facilitation Project, 21,
    92–93
Central Asia
    border crossing standards, 108
    CAREC committee, 164, 172
    fraud, risk of, 83
    gateways to, 51
    landlocked countries, 1, 3, 14
    railways, 61, 131, 135–39, 137*b*, 157
Central Asia Regional Economic
    Cooperation (CAREC) Program,
    164, 172
Central Corridor Trade and Transport
    Facilitation Agency (CCTTFA),
    165, 181*n*2
CGNet (Ghana), 95, 97*n*3
Chad. *See* Douala corridor in Central
    Africa
Chile–Bolivia agreement on trade
    corridor, 162
China
    border crossing standards, 108
    border policies with Mongolia, costs of,
        52, 139
    financing railways in Argentina, 135
    long-distance transit in ancient China,
        45–46

CIC (Comite Intergubermental
    Coordinator de los paises de la
    cunca de la Plata), 148*b*
CIH. *See* Intergovernmental Committee for
    the Waterway
clearance. *See* customs clearance
climate change, 36
Colbert (French finance minister), 46
Colombian flower exports, 141–42
colonial expansion of trade corridors, 47
Columbus Programme (WCO), 91*b*,
    159*n*14
Comite Intergubermental Coordinator de
    los paises de la cunca de la Plata
    (CIC), 148*b*
Common Market for Eastern and Southern
    Africa (COMESA), 28*b*, 82, 85
competitiveness
    logistics services, 24–27
    promotion of, 185
    rail transit, 126–29
    between transit countries and LLDCs,
        42–43
concession comparison between Côte
    d'Ivoire and Senegal railways, 132,
    133–34*b*
conflicts, effect on LLDC transit corridors,
    35–36, 131
Congo, Democratic Republic of
    charges for border crossings, 115*b*
    customs brokers' role, 81
    Dar es Salaam Corridor management,
        164
    landlocked portions of, 2
    trade corridor management agreements,
        163, 165
Congo River, 144
consensus-building institution model of
    trade corridor management, 165
consortia for rail operation, 132, 133–34*b*,
    134, 136, 137*b*, 151
constitution for management of Dar es
    Salaam Corridor, 164
container leasing contracts, 23–24
contracts between clients and trucking
    companies, 26, 106–7. *See also*
    queuing regime
convoys, use of, 82–83
cooperation among countries, 39, 53–55,
    167. *See also* bilateral agreements;
    international legal agreements;
    regional systems

corridors. *See* trade corridors
corruption, 27, 52, 183
The Cost of Being Landlocked (Arvis,
    Raballand, & Marteau), xiii, 7
costs
    annual vehicle license fees, 49*b*
    comparison of time penalties and costs,
        101, 101*t*, 108
    convoys, use of, 82–83
    freight costs, 100–102, 101*t*
    guarantees, 80
    indirect costs incurred by transit
        countries, 48
    logistics costs. *See* logistics services
    of performance monitoring, 177–78
    railways, 126–27
    road freight costs, 24–27, 25*t*
    transit fees, 18, 49*b*, 50
Côte d'Ivoire
    competition among trade corridors,
        37–38
    investors in mango exports from Mali
        and Burkina Faso, 43
    political crisis in, cutting off LLDC
        gateway, 36, 156
    railway, 28*b*
    trade comparison with Senegal, 131–32,
        132*t*, 133–34*b*
cross-border procedures. *See* border
        crossings
customs, role of, 41, 52, 59, 64–65, 185
customs brokers, 43, 81, 85, 149, 150,
        152–53
customs clearance, 17, 64–65, 81
    preclearance, 83, 84, 187

D

Dakar–Bamako railway corridor, 131, 132,
        133–34*b*
Dakar–N'djamena–Djibouti Highway
        Corridor (Trans-Sahelian
        Highway), 28*b*
Dar es Salaam
    agreements governing Dar es Salaam
        Corridor, 162, 165
    Corridor Committee, 164
    as port of choice, 36, 144
    transit initiation and clearance times, 81
delay. *See* transit times
Democratic Republic of Congo. *See* Congo,
        Democratic Republic of

demurrage charges, 23, 130
dependence of LLDCs on transit countries,
        34–45. *See also* political economy
        of trade corridors
deposits, 64
deregulated market transit,
        54–55, 102
"destination principle" of taxation, 58
developing countries
    landlocked countries. *See* landlocked
        developing countries (LLDCs)
    transit regimes for, 79–98. *See also*
        transit regimes
direct economic benefits to transit
        countries, 48–50
Djibouti
    clearance, 97*n*1
    customs, role of, 41
    documentation flow, 63
Doha Round, 3
Doing Business Indicators, 170
*Doing Business in Landlocked Economies
        2009* (World Bank), 16
Douala corridor in Central Africa, 6, 24,
        85, 92–93
dry ports. *See* inland container depots
        (ICDs)
Dubai Ports World, 134*b*
due diligence, 65
Durban
    customs brokers, role of, 82
    as port of choice, 37, 38*b*

E

EAC. *See* East African Community
East Africa
    border crossing standards, 108
    Central Corridor, 162
    coffee or tea trade from, 43
    convoys, use of, 83
    customs brokers' role, 81
    import time, 17
    integration goals, 85
    Northern Corridor, 6, 162, 163, 170,
        178, 179, 181*n*2
    railway concession, 151
    trade agreements, 162
East African Community (EAC), 28*b*,
        82, 85
econometric studies comparing landlocked
        and coastal countries, 14

Economic and Monetary Community of
    Central Africa (CEMAC), 85
Economic Community of West African
    States (ECOWAS), 28b, 85, 179
Economic Cooperation Organization
    (ECO) Transit Framework
    Agreement, 86
economic potential of LLDCs, 14–17
economies of scale, 48
Egypt
    fruit and vegetable exports, 142b
    truck companies, 102
e-seals, use of, 96
Ethiopia, flower exports from, 142
e-TIR, 94–95
Europe
    history of trade, 45–46
    landlocked countries, 1
    NCTS (New Computerized Transit
        System), 71, 94
European Free Trade Association, 70
European Union (EU). See also TIR
    collection of extraunion duty, 84
    common transit system, 70–73, 82
    truck quotas, 111–12
exports
    air freight, value of items as
        consideration for, 140
    bulk commodities, 42, 129
    choice of transit route, 37
    importance of, 30–31
    inland container depots (ICDs),
        role of, 154
    of raw materials, 30
    time in Africa, 17
extra- vs. intra-regional trade, 30–31

F

Fahrer, Chuck, 34
FastPath software, 172, 173b, 178
fast-track authorized operators. See author-
    ized economic operators (AEOs)
fees. See costs
Ferrocarril Antofagasta Bolivia
    railway, 135
FIATA (International Federation of Freight
    Forwarders Associations),
    151, 157
flower exports, 139–43, 176
formal checks for truck transport,
    114–15

former Soviet republics
    as landlocked countries, 3
    LLDC-transit state relationships, 35
    railway corridors, 137–38
    waterway transport, 145
Framework of Standards to Secure and
    Facilitate Global Trade, 90b
fraud, risk of, 83
freedom of navigation, 146
freedom of transit, 4, 6, 47–48, 109–11
freight forwarders, 59, 65, 149,
    150–52, 158
French ancien regime, 46
fruit and vegetable exports, 43, 129,
    142b, 176
fuel shortages, 23
fuel tax, 49b, 116–17

G

Gallup, John Luke, 35
garment trade. See textile and garment
    trade
General Agreement on Tariffs and Trade
    (GATT)
    Article V, 4, 35, 48, 50, 73, 110, 188
    transformation into WTO, 3
General Agreement on Trade in Services
    (GATS), 110–11
Geneva Convention (International
    Convention on the Harmonization
    of Frontier Controls of Goods), 73,
    76
Geneva Convention on the High Seas
    (1958), 48
Ghana
    CGNet, 95, 97n3
    competition among trade corridors,
        37–38
    integration goals, 85
Glassner, Martin Ira, 34
The Global Enabling Trade Report 2008
    (World Economic Forum), 16
global financial crisis and economic
    recovery, 15
global standards, 73–78, 96–98, 184, 188
GPS tracking of truckers, 96
Great Asian Highway, 28–29b
Greater Mekong Subregion Agreement for
    Facilitation of Cross-Border
    Transport of Goods and People in
    Asia, 70, 120n4

Grosdidier de Matons, Jean, 88
guarantees
    ceiling limits on trucks, 82
    described, 59, 63–64
    developing countries' poor management
        of, 80–81
    EU common transit system, 71, 72f
    global standards, 97
    integration goals and, 85
    rail exemption, 61
    TIR Convention, 67, 72f
    unified transit guarantee, 43

H

Heidelberg Resolution of 1887, 146
high risk cargo, 59

I

ICDs. See inland container depots
ICT. See information and communication
        technologies
imports
    categories of country-specific markets
        for, 42
    importance of, 30–31
    of manufactured goods, 30, 129
    preferred transport mode for, 50
    time in Africa, 17
improvements. See infrastructure; quality
        improvements
India
    access to ports, 51
    bilateral agreement with Nepal, 89b
    border policies with Nepal, costs of, 52
    long-distance transit in ancient India,
        45–46
    Northeastern States of, 2
inflation, 15
informal checks for truck transport,
        117–18
informal payments, 27, 52
information and communication technolo-
        gies (ICT), 94–96, 95b, 187
    limitations in developing countries,
        80–81
infrastructure
    economies of scale from increased
        volumes, 48
    investment, 27–30, 28–29b, 41, 163
    roads and freight costs, 101–2

inland container depots (ICDs), 154–56,
        158, 186
inland waterways. See waterway transport
institutional arrangements for waterway
        transport, 146, 147b
integration goals, 84–87, 97
intercontinental shipments, 23
Intergovernmental Committee for the
        Waterway (Comite
        Intergubernamental de la
        Hidrovia—CIH), 147b, 148b
International Convention on the
        Harmonization of Frontier
        Controls of Goods (Geneva
        Convention), 73, 76
"International Convention on the
        Simplification and Harmonisation
        of Customs Procedures"
        (WCO), 62
International Federation of Freight
        Forwarders Associations (FIATA),
        151, 157
international legal agreements, 6, 73–78,
        74–75b, 76t, 87–88, 87t, 162. See
        also bilateral agreements
International Railway Union, 47
International Road Transport Union (IRU)
    carnet system and, 67, 70
    certificate of professional competence
        (CPC), 104
    electronic procedure for submitting
        "predeclarations," 152
    guarantees and, 68
    need for standards and guidelines, 92,
        188
    on TIR-related claims, 80
    training courses, 104b
International Trade and Customs Broker
        Association, 153
International Union of Railways (UIC),
        136, 137
international vs. national transit, 58–59, 60f
International Warehouse Logistics
        Association, 154
international waterway commissions, 148b
International Weight Certificates
        (UNECE), 116
Internet, carnet system on, 68, 70
Iran as transit country to Central Asia, 51,
        55n1
IRU. See International Road Transport
        Union

Isaka–Kigali–Bujumbura Railway, 28*b*
Italian trade, historical, 46

K

Kazakh Railways, 51, 136, 137*b*
Kazakhstan
    canal systems, 144
    informal payments, 27
    railway corridors, 135–38
    as trade corridor, 50, 51
Kenya
    coffee or tea exports, 43
    flower exports by air freight, 140,
        141–42
    fruit and vegetable exports, 142*b*
    integration goals, 85
    trade corridor management
        agreement, 163
    unrest in, cutting off LLDC
        gateway, 36
Korea Transport Institute, 171
Kyoto Convention (1999), 73,
    88, 97

L

landlocked developing countries (LLDCs).
    *See also specific regions, countries,
    and transport types*
    comparison with resource-rich
        LLDCs, 15
    dependence on transit countries, 34–45.
        See also political economy of trade
        corridors
    development priority of access, 2–3
    economic challenges of, 13
    economic potential of, 14–17
    list of, 1, 2*t*, 11*n*1
    logistics services. *See* logistics services
    market structure, 24–27
    measuring of economic disadvantages, 5,
        14–16
    modest trade volumes of, 37
    transit role, potential from, 50–51
land transport. *See* road freight transport
Lao PDR
    inland container depots (ICDs), 155
    Thai exporters from, 43
    as trade corridor, 50
League of Arab States. *See* Arab League
League of Nations, 47
"leakage," 58, 61, 82, 97

legal instruments, excess of, 6, 87–88, 87*t*.
    See also international legal
        agreements
legislative model of corridor management,
    163
Lesotho, charges for border crossings, 115*b*
leverage of multiple corridors, 36–38
licensing
    annual vehicle license fees, 49*b*
    quality licensing, 103–4, 106
LLDCs. *See* landlocked developing
    countries
Logistics Performance Index (LPI), 16–17,
    16*t*, 170
logistics services
    competition in, 24–27
    costs, xiii, 18, 23, 174–75
    customs brokers. *See* customs brokers
    development of, 149–56
    freight forwarders. *See* freight forwarders
    inland container depots. *See* inland
        container depots (ICDs)
    performance, 16–17, 34
    recommendations, 157–58, 185–86
    third-party logistics providers. *See* third-
        party logistics providers (3PLs)
Lomé, 41
Lomé–Ouagadougou Corridor, 27
LPI. *See* Logistics Performance Index

M

Maghreb Highway Project, 28*b*
Malawi
    charges for border crossings, 115*b*
    cut off from transit state access, 36
    Dar es Salaam Corridor management,
        164
    road funding, 29
    transit routes, 3, 18–19, 38*b*
Mali
    competition among trade corridors,
        37–38
    cut off from transit state access, 36
    informal checkpoints for trucks, 117
    mango exports, 43
    rail corridors, 131
    trade comparison with Burkina Faso,
        131–32, 132*t*
mango exports, 43, 129
manufactured goods, 30, 129, 139, 177
Maputo Corridor, 173*b*

market structure, 24–27
Marteau, Jean-François, 174, 175
measuring of economic disadvantages,
    14–16
Mekong greater subregion (GMS), 113,
    120n4, 144
Mellinger, Andrew D., 35
Mercosur, 86
Middle Ages transit rules, 46
Middle East
    convoys, use of, 83
    queuing systems, 26
Millennium Development Goals, 4
misconceptions about transit facilitation,
    83–84, 87
Moldova's waterway transport, 143–44
Mombasa, 41
Mombasa–Nairobi–Addis Ababa Corridor
    Development Project, 28b
Mongolia
    border policies with China, 52
    Columbus Programme and, 91b
    inland container depots (ICDs), 155
    railway corridors, 138–39
    roads and freight costs, 102
    surcharges and demurrages, 23
    transit time, 100
    truck companies, 102
monitoring of performance, 170–73
    cost and replicability, 177–78
    design of, 175–78, 176t
    development of common tool for, 180,
        184, 185, 188
    FastPath, 172, 173b
    observatories in Africa, 178–79
    products, transport unit, and route,
        176–77
most favored nation clauses, 111
Mozambique
    charges for border crossings, 115b
    civil war in, cutting off LLDC
        gateway, 36
    toll roads, 115b
multilateralism, 45. See also international
    legal agreements
multimodal carnet, 68

N

Nacala as port of choice, 36, 38b
Namibia
    charges for border crossings, 115b

Walvis Bay Corridor Group, 165
national associations and TIR requirements,
    67, 68
nationality of truck drivers, border
    crossings and, 113
national trade facilitation committees
    (NTTFCs), 167, 168–69b
national vs. international transit,
    58–59, 60f
natural resources
    of LLDCs, 14
    oil prices, 15
    transport of coal and mineral ores, 135,
        138, 145
    transport of oil and gas, 135, 138,
        143–44
NCTS (New Computerized Transit
    System), 71, 94
NEPAD. See New Partnership for Africa's
    Development
Nepal
    border policies with India, costs of, 52
    inland container depots (ICDs), 155
    as trade corridor, 50, 51
    trade corridor through India, 55n1
New Computerized Transit System
    (NCTS), 71, 94
New Partnership for Africa's Development
    (NEPAD), 6, 27, 28b
New York Convention on Transit Trade of
    Landlocked Countries (1965), 48
Niger
    competition among trade corridors,
        37–38
    exports to Côte d'Ivoire or Ghana
        from, 31
    inland container depots (ICDs), 155,
        159n15
    railway, 28b
Niger River, 158–59n6
Northern Corridor Transit Transport
    Coordination Authority
    (NCTTCA), 163, 179
NTTFCs (national trade facilitation com-
    mittees), 167, 168–69b

O

OECD countries and deregulated market
    transit, 54–55
oil. See natural resources
overhead, 27

overloading of trucks, 116
ownership of rail containers, 130

P

Pakistan
  Afghanistan–Pakistan trade corridor
    agreement, 162
  as transit country to Central Asia, 51
Paraguay, railways and access to ports in,
    134, 135
Paraguay–Buenos Aires Rail Corridor, 156
Paraguay–Paraná river system, 144, 145,
    146, 147b, 148, 157, 159n9
Paranagua, Brazil, 134
passports for truck drivers, 113–14
performance monitoring. See monitoring of
    performance
perishable goods. See flower exports; fruit
    and vegetable exports
Pliny the Elder, 46
political economy of trade corridors, xiv,
    9–10, 33–55
  benefits to transit countries, 48–50
    direct economic benefits, 48–50
    empty backhaul capacity, 50, 129
    transit fees, 50
  LLDC relationship with transit country,
    34–45
    leverage of multiple corridors, 36–38
    private sector and service delivery,
      39–40
    private services and commercial
      activities, 41–43
    public sector functions, 40–41
    quality improvements, limits on,
      44–45
  public-private partnerships, 45–48
    freedom of transit, evolution of,
      47–48
    history of, 45–46
  transit role of landlocked countries,
    50–51
  vicious to virtuous cycles, 52–55
    incentives for cooperation and mutual
      benefit, 53–55
Polzug (German–Polish railway
    consortium), 137b
ports. See inland container depots (ICDs);
    waterway transport; specific ports by
    name
preclearance, 83, 84, 187

principal and guarantor, 63
prisoner's dilemma, 53
private sector and service delivery,
    39–40. See also public-private
    partnerships
private services and commercial activities,
    41–43
PRO committees, 167, 168–69b
project coordination model of trade
    corridor management, 163–64
public-private partnerships, 45–48
  freedom of transit, evolution of,
    47–48
  history of, 45–46
  model for corridor management, 61,
    164–65, 166, 167–70
  recommendations, 186
  reliance on, 61
  in transit regimes, 58
public sector and service delivery, 39–41,
    40t. See also public-private
    partnerships

Q

quality improvements
  limits on, 44–45. See also vicious cycles
  promotion of, 103–4, 185
queuing regime, 106–7
  bilateral agreements and, 88
  elimination of, 54, 107
  queuing systems, 26, 82, 118–19
  recommendations, 118–19
quota systems, 109–14
  bilateral agreements and, 88
  cross-border, 101, 109–11, 113–14
  effect of, 50
  EU truck quotas, 112
  freedom of transit, 109–11. See also
    freedom of transit
  LLDC truck quotas, 26, 111–13
  recommendations, 119
  UNECE Resolution R.E.4, 110, 110b

R

Raballand, Gaël, 26, 174, 175
rail transit, 61, 125–39
  border performance indicators, 128, 128b
  Central Asian railways, 135–39, 137b
  commodities transport, 129
  competitiveness, 126–29

rail transit (*continued*)
  concession comparison between
      Côte d'Ivoire and Senegal, 132,
      133–34*b*
  containers
      compatibility with bulk products, 129
      ownership of, 130
      unitized container trains, 42, 130
  economic comparison of rail services,
      132*t*
  empty backhaul capacity, 50, 129
  logistics companies and, 151
  as preferred transport for bulk
      products, 50
  recommendations, 156–57, 186
  regional perspective, 130–39
  South American railways, 134–35
  Sub-Saharan African railways, 131–33
  traffic volume, 42, 126, 129
  transport distance, 126–29, 127*t*
  underused potential, 125–30
  water transport and rail connections,
      123, 124*t*, 186
reengineering, 88–92, 184, 186–87
reform. *See also* reengineering
  champions of change and, 183
  incentives, 53–55
  policies of improvement, 184
refrigeration units for rail transport, 129
regional leadership role of transit
      countries, 48
regional systems
  integration goals, 84–86
  of rail transit, 130–39
  of trade, 29
  in transit regimes, 58, 86–87
regulation. *See also* transit regimes
  balancing regulation and protection,
      34, 104–6
  framework of, 102–3
  lax regulation, effects of, 81–82
  overregulation, effects of, 52
  quality regulation, 103–4
relationship of LLDCs with transit coun-
      tries, 34–45. *See also* political
      economy of trade corridors
rent-seeking behaviors, 34, 44, 44*f*, 81, 89
Rhine–Danube system, 143, 145
River Plate Basin Permanent Transport
      Commission (Comision
      Permanente de Transporte de la
      Cuenca del Plata), 147*b*

road freight transport, 10, 99–121
  agency regulation of, 41
  backhaul capacity, 50
  bilateral agreements, 109–14. *See also*
      bilateral agreements
  contracts between clients and trucking
      companies, 26, 106–7
  costs and time penalties, 24, 101,
      101*t*, 108
  cross-border procedures, 107–9, 113–14
      recommendations, 119
      trucks, 108–9
  facilitating truck movement, 114–18
      axle load limits and road damage,
      115–17
      formal checks, 114–15
      ICT usage, 96
      informal checks, 117–18
      recommendations, 119–20
  harmonization of customs procedures,
      185
  high freight costs, reasons for, 101–2
  importance of, 100–102
  imports using, 50
  international vs. domestic companies,
      105
  IRU training courses, 104*b*
  logistics services, 24
  queuing regime, 106–7
      elimination, benefits of, 107
      queuing systems, 118–19
      recommendations, 118–19
  quota systems, 109–14. *See also* quota
      systems
  recommendations, 118–21
  regulation, 43
  road tolls, 49*b*, 50
  SADC cost recovery mechanism, 115*b*
  southern Africa vs. West Africa
      industry, 43
  structure of industries, 102–6
      balancing regulation and protection,
      104–6
      quality regulation, 103–4, 106
      recommendations, 118
      regulatory framework, 102–3
  in transit countries, 100–102
  transit times, 100*t*
Roman customs and transit systems, 45–46
Russia
  transit policies with Mongolia, 138–39
  water and canal systems, 144, 145

Rwanda
    clearance of transit cargo, 22*b*
    coffee or tea trade from, 43
    cut off from transit state access, 36
    flower exports, 142
    inland container depots (ICDs), 155
    paying informal payments to Tanzania at
        weigh stations, 117
    trade corridor management agreements,
        163, 165

S

Sachs, Jeffrey D., 35
SACU (Southern African Customs
    Union), 84
SADC. *See* Southern African Development
    Community
Safe-TIR number, 94–95
sales taxes, 84
seals, 62–63, 62*b*
security concerns, 59, 67, 82–83
Senegal, in trade comparison with
    Côte d'Ivoire, 131–32,
    132*t*, 133–34*b*
shipping lines, 24
shocks, effect of, 15
Shoprite supermarkets, 42
Silk Road trade, 46
Sitarail, 133*b*, 156
smuggling, 52, 83
South Africa
    alternative transit state access for
        LLDCs, 36
    no compulsory access charges at border,
        115*b*
    toll roads, 115*b*
    transit data transfer to other countries,
        95, 95*b*
South America. *See also specific countries*
    integration goals, 86
    landlocked countries, 1
    railways, 130–31, 134–35, 156
South Asia
    convoys, use of, 83
    integration goals, 86
    landlocked countries, 1
    queuing systems, 26
    transport infrastructure, 17
    truck quotas, eliminated in Greater
        Mekong subregion (GMS), 113,
        120*n*4

Southern Africa
    import time, 17
    integration goals, 85
    long-distance transport, 24
    North–South Corridor, 179
    road freight costs, 25
    road freight industry, 43
Southern African Customs Union
    (SACU), 84
Southern African Development
    Community (SADC)
    border clearance documents, 82
    cost recovery mechanism, 114, 115*b*
    integration goals, 85
    NEPAD First Short Term Action Plan,
        28*b*
South–South trade, 14
special economic zones, 48
stakeholders' role in reform, 53
streamlining and common transit data,
    70–73, 82, 95, 95*b*
Sub-Saharan Africa
    landlocked countries, 1, 15
    railways, 130, 131–33, 156
    transport infrastructure, 16
Sub-Saharan Africa Transport Policy
    Program, 179
Switzerland's use of vignette, 49*b*

T

Tanzania
    air freight, 140
    alternative transit state access for
        LLDCs, 36
    annual vehicle license fees, 49*b*
    charging informal payments to Rwandan
        trucks, 117
    customs brokers' role, 81
    Dar es Salaam Corridor management,
        164
    flower exports by air freight, 140, 141
    integration goals, 85
    trade corridor management agreements,
        165
tariffs, 3, 25, 113, 140
taxes
    in ancient transit, 45–46
    "destination principle" and, 58
    fuel tax, 49*b*, 116–17
    global standards to prevent multiple
        taxation, 97

taxes (*continued*)
  as transit country revenue stream,
    48, 50
  value-added taxes (VATs) or sales
    taxes, 84
tea exporters, 37
technical assistance, 92
technology. *See* information and communi-
    cation technologies (ICT)
Teravaninthorn, Supee, 26
textile and garment trade, 15, 31, 37, 140
Thailand
  annual vehicle license fees, 49*b*
  trade routes, 43
third-party logistics providers (3PLs), 149,
    150, 153–54, 158, 159*n*11
"through bill of lading," 151
TIA (Transportation Intermediaries
    Association), 153–54
TIR (Transports Internationaux Routiers).
    See also carnet systems
  Asian and Middle East use of, 86
  certificate of professional competence
    (CPC) and, 104
  e-TIR, 94–95, 152
  history of, 47
  knowledge of, as personnel
    requirement, 61
  as model for other regions, xiv, 84,
    87, 88, 89, 187
  principles, 66–68
  savings and benefits of, 64, 80
tobacco and alcohol carnet, 68
Togo
  competition among trade corridors,
    37–38
  delays at informal checkpoints, 117
  railway, 28*b*
toll roads, 49*b*, 50, 115*b*
tour de role systems, 50, 82, 106, 107
TRACECA (Transport Corridor
    Europe–Caucasus–Asia), 128,
    136, 158*n*4
tracing goods, 95–96
Trade and Transport Facilitation in
    Southeast Europe Program, 6
trade corridors, 4–6, 10, 13–32, 161–82
  agreements among corridor
    bodies, 152
  conceptual framework for, 7–9
  efficient management, 165–70
  geographic locations of, 2

infrastructure investment, 27–30,
    28–29*b*, 167
  leverage of multiple corridors, 36–38
  logistics. *See* logistics services
  management models, 162–65
    consensus-building institution
      model, 165
    legislative model, 163
    project coordination model, 163–64
    public-private partnership model, 61,
      164–65, 166, 167–70
  national trade and transport facilitation
    committees, 168–69*b*
  overhead and informal payments, 27
  performance monitoring, 170–73
    cost and replicability, 177–78
    design of, 175–78, 176*t*
    development of common tool for,
      180, 184, 185, 188
    FastPath, 173*b*
    observatories in Africa, 178–79
    products, transport unit, and route,
      176–77
  political economy of, 33–55. *See also*
    political economy of trade corridors
  PRO committees, 167, 168–69*b*
  products, transport unit, and route,
    176–77
  public-private partnerships. *See*
    public-private partnerships
  recommendations, 186
  supply chain
    bottlenecks and, 17–21, 18*f*, 19*t*
    linkages, 30–31
    types of, 161, 162–65
    unreliability, cost of, 21–24
    Vientiane-Laem Chabang, 176*t*
trade facilitation, 3–4
Trade Facilitation Program for the
    North–South Corridor, 28*b*
transit countries, 4–6
  benefits to, 48–50
  relationship with LLDCs, 34–45.
    See also political economy of
    trade corridors
transit declaration, 65. *See also* TIR
transit fees. *See* costs
transit initiation, 81
transit procedure and clearance, 64–65
transit regimes, 10, 57–98
  authorized economic operators (AEOs),
    90–91*b*

bilateral agreements, 88, 89b
carnet systems, 65–73. *See also* carnet
    systems
conceptual framework, 7–9
control mentality and convoys, 82–83
defined, 58
described, 59, 60f
in developing regions, 79–98
documentation flow, 63
Douala Corridor, pilot improvement
    program, 92–93
fraud, risk of, 83
global standards, 73–78, 96–98
guarantees, 63–64, 80–81
improvements for, 79–98
information systems, limitations of,
    80–81
integration goals, 84–87
international legal agreements, 6, 73–78,
    74–75b, 76t, 87–88, 87t
lax entry regulation, 81–82
misconceptions about transit facilitation,
    83–84, 87
overview, 59–61
principal and guarantor, 63
public-private partnerships, 58, 61
rail transit, 61
reengineering, 88–92, 184, 186–87
regional systems, 86–87
role of, 58–59
seals, 62–63, 62b
technology and, 94–96, 95b
    automation and interconnection
        across borders, 94–95
    tracing goods, 95–96
transit initiation, 81
transit procedure and clearance,
    64–65
Transit Routier Inter-États (TRIE), 70,
    85, 87
transit system. *See also* transit regimes
components of, 7–8, 8f
framework and assumptions for, 8–9
redefining and improving, 186–87
transit times, 17, 30, 42, 59
guarantees and, 81
land transport, 100–101, 100t
rail transport, 130
Trans-Kalahari Corridor, 162
transport agencies, role of, 41
Transportation Intermediaries Association
    (TIA), 153–54

Transport Coordination Committee of
    the Regional Economic
    Communities, 179
Transports Internationaux Routiers
    Convention. *See* TIR
Transrail, 134b
TRIE, 70, 85, 87
trucking. *See* road freight transport
trust building, 9, 61, 167–70, 183, 185
Turkey, history of trade in, 46

U

UEMOA (West African Economic and
    Monetary Union), 85, 179
Uganda
    clearance of transit cargo, 22b
    coffee or tea exports, 43
    cut off from transit state access, 36
    flower exports, 141, 142
    railways, 126
    trade corridor management agreements,
        163, 165
UIC (International Union of Railways),
    136
United Nations
    Centre for Trade Facilitation and
        Electronic Business, 180
    Conference on the Law of the Sea
        (1958), 48
    Conference on Trade and Development
        (UNCTAD), 49b, 85, 93, 167, 170,
        184, 188. *See also* ASYCUDA
        documentation system
    development of performance-monitoring
        tools, 180, 184
    Economic and Social Commission for
        Asia and the Pacific (UNESCAP),
        28b, 73, 136, 171, 172f, 178, 184
    Economic Commission for Europe
        (UNECE), 70, 110
        International Weight Certificates, 116
        need for standards and guidelines, 92
        Resolution R.E.4, 110, 110b
        TIR evaluation, 188
    global conference on LLDCs (2003), 4
    review of Almaty Programme of Action
        (2008), 5
United States and rail transit with
    Mexico, 61
unitized container trains, 23–24, 42, 130
unreliability, cost of, 21–24

U.S. Agency for International Development
    (USAID), 171, 173*b*, 179
Uzbekistan
    railway corridors, 136
    trade routes, 55*n*1

V

value-added taxes (VATs), 84
vicious cycles, 44–45, 44*f*, 52–55
Vienna Treaty of 1815, 146
Vientiane–Bangkok Corridor, 24, 173*b*
Vientiane-Laem Chabang Corridor, 176*t*
vignettes, 49*b*
Vinod, H.D., 174
virtuous cycles, 45, 52–55
visas for truck drivers, 113–14
Volga–Don Canal system, 144

W

Walvis Bay Corridor Group, 165
warehousing, 155. *See also* inland container
    depots (ICDs)
"Washington Consensus," 3
waterway transport, 143–49
    deadweight tonnage, 159*n*8
    institutional arrangements for, 48,
        146, 147*b*
    international waterway commissions,
        148*b*
    overview, 145–46
    products, costs and demand for, 146–49
    recommendations, 157, 186, 187
    traffic volume, 42
WATH (West Africa Trade Hub), 179
WCO. *See* World Customs Organization
West Africa
    bilateral agreements, 88
    competition among trade corridors,
        37–38, 39*f*
    fraud, risk of, 83
    import time, 17
    integration goals, 85
    joint project of manufacturers and
        World Bank for corridor
        improvement, 42
    rail transit, 61
    road freight industry
        convoys, use of, 83
        costs, 24, 25, 26
        fragmentation of, 43
        informal checks, 117

tour de role systems, 50, 82, 106
traditional trading networks, 44, 156
TRIE, 85
West African Economic and Monetary
    Union (UEMOA), 85, 179
West Africa Trade Hub (WATH), 179
World Bank
    on air freight, 139
    Central Africa Transport and Transit
        Facilitation project, 21
    development of performance-monitoring
        tools, 180, 184
    *Doing Business in Landlocked Economies
        2009*, 16
    exports to Côte d'Ivoire or Ghana from
        Niger, project on, 31
    on informal payments, 27, 117
    LLDC initiatives of, xi, 6, 185
    on road damages from overloaded
        trucks, 116
    on tariffs, 25
    Trade and Transport Facilitation
        Assessment, 29
    West African joint project with
        manufacturers for corridor
        improvement, 42
World Customs Organization (WCO)
    authorized operators, 53, 90–91*b*
    Columbus Programme, 91*b*, 159*n*14
    Framework of Standards to Secure and
        Facilitate Global Trade (SAFE), 90*b*
    "International Convention on the
        Simplification and Harmonisation
        of Customs Procedures," 62
    need for standards and guidelines, 92,
        188
World Economic Forum's *The Global
    Enabling Trade Report 2008*, 16
World Trade Organization (WTO), 3, 50,
    110, 188

Z

Zambia
    charges for border crossings, 115*b*
    clearance of transit cargo, 22*b*
    rail backhaul capacity, 129
    trade corridor management, 164, 166
    transit routes, 3
Zimbabwe
    charges for border crossings, 115*b*
    streamlining passage of transit data, 95*b*